Fragile Dreams

Fragile Dreams

Tales of Liberalism and Power in Central Europe

JOHN A. GOULD

University of Michigan Press
Ann Arbor

For questions or permissions, please contact um.press.perms@umich.edu

Published in the United States of America by the
University of Michigan Press
Manufactured in the United States of America
Printed on acid-free paper
First published October 2021

A CIP catalog record for this book is available from the British Library.

Library of Congress Cataloging-in-Publication Data

Names: Gould, John A., author.
Title: Fragile dreams : tales of liberalism and power in Central Europe / John A. Gould.
Description: Ann Arbor : University of Michigan Press, [2021] | Includes
    bibliographical references and index. |
Identifiers: LCCN 2021028018 (print) | LCCN 2021028019 (ebook) |
    ISBN 9780472075041 (hardcover) | ISBN 9780472055043 (paperback) |
    ISBN 9780472129461 (ebook)
Subjects: LCSH: Liberalism—Europe, Central—20th century. | Liberalism—
    Europe, Central—21st century. | Europe, Central—Politics and
    government—1989- | Europe, Central—Social conditions—1989- | Europe,
    Central—History—1989-
Classification: LCC JC574.2.E8515 G68   2021 (print) | LCC JC574.2.E8515
    (ebook) | DDC 320.510943—dc23
LC record available at https://lccn.loc.gov/2021028018
LC ebook record available at https://lccn.loc.gov/2021028019

Cover illustration: *After the demonstration—Hlavné námestie, Nové Zámky,
Czechoslovakia, Nov. 1989.* Photograph © Ondrej Berta, used with
permission of the artist.

Contents

Digital materials related to this title can be found on the Fulcrum platform via the following citable URL: https://doi.org/10.3998/mpub.11955636

Preface and Acknowledgments

METHOD, MEET MADNESS! If you are a middle-aged teacher like me, you have probably noticed a recent trend in your new students. Most are unfamiliar with the touchstone events of our generation. A recent school trip a colleague and I took to Sarajevo made this perfectly clear. Our students had heard of World War II and the Holocaust, and they knew that there was once a Soviet Union, but they were shocked to learn that there had been a genocidal Bosnian war in 1992-95, and they were devastated by an exhibit on the Srebrenica massacre of July 1995. When pressed, only a couple could identify other major events of the post-Cold War period, like the demise of the Berlin Wall; the fragmentations of the Soviet Union, Yugoslavia, and Czechoslovakia; the expansion of the European Union (UN) and the North Atlantic Treaty Organization (NATO); or even the relatively recent Russian occupation of Crimea. Wherever I focused, momentous events since 1989 remained a mystery.

This book will bring students up to speed as well as jog the memories of those of us who lived through the events. Yet, it is by no means a detailed or complete history. Rather, it is also in part an intellectual guidebook to what "we" were thinking at the time and how these thoughts and related choices shaped the lived experiences of my generation. It is immersed in a merger of (mostly) comparative politics theory, policy choices, and the personal experiences of friends, family, and me.

This personal angle is admittedly invasive. As a white, male, US passport holder with a hefty dissertation research grant and a couple of New York-based consulting gigs, I experienced the 1990s with a privileged degree of security that set me apart from Central Europeans more than the languages I was struggling to learn. So, no, I could not begin personally to experience how Central Europeans felt about the revolutions of 1989, the communist era that preceded it, or the nationalism, neoliberalism, war, EU expansion, corruption, and populism that followed. My positionality wasn't quite located in the downtown hotels to which a famed journalist once summoned locals for interviews, but it wasn't too far down the street.

Yet somewhere in the middle of this story, I met a woman in Bratislava, Slovakia, named Simona. We dated, negotiated three years of long distance, married, finished grad school, and had two incredible kids. Along the way, my wanderings along Central Europe's unique postcommunist lane grew from an academic project to a very personal commitment. So, I'm no longer the outsider that I was. Still, I am not an insider either, and never will be.

I've nevertheless taken the liberty to gently dip into the lived experiences available to me—particularly those of my Slovak family and my network of friends. I hope that this dip will be generic—typical rather than revealing. I really don't want to share too much of what is not mine. And, yes, I've received permission to share from my "informants." I've also anonymized names and identifying details of many of the participants in this story.

WHICH STORIES? This is a book of tales blended with history and theory. I include the stories like sugar—a sweet taste to help make the theory and history more memorable and palatable. Yet the stories are not just for flavor; they serve a theoretical purpose. Many of the tales offer what I call "trendline illustrations." They portray what we would expect to happen given our beliefs and expectations about prior similar events or given simple logic. A trendline illustration is sort of like following the path of a single snowflake in a storm. It has unique characteristics, but its path charts the general pattern of flakes around it.

Yet, there are also deviant cases that fail to fit the pattern. Why would a small group of flakes appear to be swirling upward? Well, that's a mystery that needs to be solved. It might even tell us something more broadly about the storm. As a political scientist, I often find these stories to be the most exciting. They beg us to think with greater nuance about how the world works.

This is also a work in the field of comparative politics. I cover a number of topics that are important to the construction of power within and across states in Central Europe after communism. I structure each chapter around a part of the literature that has been relevant to the experience. I have unfortunately had to leave out many important topics. Nor have I attempted to be comprehensive in the literature that I do cite. My goal is to give the careful reader the vocabulary to become conversant on some of the foundational literature in a range of subfields. Ideally, by the end of this book, readers will have a pretty good insight into how one might craft answers to the classic questions of political science, "Who received what, when, and how?" and as importantly, "Who lost in this process, and how did their exclusion and marginalization play a role in others' gains?"

To assist readers in this task, I bold key concepts, events, and persons and provide a brief definition of each. Many of these bolded terms make up the basic academic jargon of my field. Others are events or people of importance to the region. It would help student readers to keep a record of these bolded terms and be able to identify them. This, plus a little review later, should help make some of the classic works in my field more accessible and less boring.

My definitions are not the final word on any topic. They are not even uncontroversial. I simplify at a cost, and there are few discussions here that will not be met by a "Yeah, but . . ." reaction from the regionally experienced or academically trained reader. I welcome that discussion because that is where the classic works that I just called boring become anything but. So think of this as both an introduction and an invitation. If I have really done my job, readers who start here will be in a better place to master and critique the literature that I reference and move on to others.

In sequential order, the chapters of this book focus on revolutions and social movements; the political economy of communism; early postcommunist political and economic change; ethno-national history, conflict, and identity; something we'll call "transitology"; institutional transfer; the enlargement of the EU and NATO; international relations theory; homophobia; populism; and contemporary illiberalism. As we scroll down this long, perhaps intimidating list of topics, we will also move around geographically and through time.

I am trying to "write what I know," following my personal, professional, and academic career choices, with references to many of the frameworks that others and I used to make sense of the world. As an academic, I usually tended to travel to where something interesting was happening or had just happened, so this narrative focuses on events that were telling in some way about the postcommunist European experience. Countries visited here include Czechoslovakia and its Czech and Slovak offspring; Yugoslavia and the successor spawn that today make up the Western Balkans; and, finally, Russia, Ukraine, and Hungary. At the risk of receiving a few stern lectures, I include the Western Balkans in Central Europe.

I make an effort throughout the book to include the experience of women, the elderly, sexual and gender minorities, and the Roma—a marginalized Central European ethnic group. Their positions are often what I would call liminal, meaning that they often occupy vulnerable positions in society and are thus more likely to suffer when policy choices expose their vulnerability. It is also important to consider how their marginalization made the successes of others possible. To ignore these experiences is to miss much of the story. I therefore center them here when I can.

Due to my position as a white, heterosexual male raised in the liberal,

Anglo-American tradition, this book cannot help but address "oriental-ism." Orientalism is a term used by Columbia professor Edward Said to describe the Western practice of writing about the lives of others with an unseen bias that reinforces "the West's" conceptions about itself.[1] Orientalism is used pejoratively for a reason; it tends to justify and re-create systems of domination and hierarchy. So, it's not a good thing to be an orientalist.

Still, I think my experiences are telling. Some help capture the story of how the European Union and the United States attempted to promote liberalism in Central and Eastern Europe, which to an extent *has* been an orientalist project. This work, in no small part, is about how many of these actors see themselves and how they have tried to perfect that idealized image elsewhere: It has been an arrogant endeavor whose proponents often fall prone to assumptions of their own superiority and occasionally a means-ends confusion about achieving outcomes.

Yet, other stories do not fit this pattern. There was nothing so exceptional about the European communist experience that it removed Central Europeans from European history. The majority of my liberal colleagues and friends in Central Europe and the Balkans draw from national liberal traditions that run from the French Revolution to their own contemporary struggles for human rights and liberal democracy. Liberalism in Central Europe is thus very much a local project. To suggest otherwise, to insinuate that somehow the struggle for liberalism in the region is *only* the expression of a "Western" bid for hegemony, is, well, orientalist. It is also a gift to populist authoritarians for whom "the West" is a convenient threat.

I use the term "liberal" in its classic 19th-century sense—a set of arguments for the superiority of individual agency in political and economic affairs. Classical liberals make the economic argument that economies perform best when individuals have the liberty to invest their land, labor, and financial assets free of undue government interference. Therefore, at its simplest, economic liberalism is a political plea for a set of economic institutions that we associate with freer markets; it is an ideology of political economy.

Liberal politics is similarly rooted in the sovereignty of the individual. The liberal tradition holds that humans are born with natural and inalienable rights to life, liberty, property, and the freedoms of speech and religion. These rights are best protected by the dispersion of power across political institutions, equality before the law, secular government, and free, fair, and regular elections for public office. The dream is to bind sovereign power to the will of the enfranchised but also to limit the ability of elected majorities to do what they want between elections. Still, sovereignty must always reside with the enfranchised. Some officials, like central bankers or judges, might be appointed, but the power of appointment must rest with the elected representatives of the sovereign people. In a liberal democracy, no centers of political power may be immune from popular sovereignty.

Both political and economic liberalism have a synergistic relationship with private property. Later we will talk about the "Lockean state," a regime that solves what I call the "paradox of state power." Following an insight I first heard from Barry Weingast, the paradox is that a sovereign who is powerful enough to protect private property from banditry is also powerful enough to take it away.[2] In 1689, English theorist John Locke published the *Second Treatise on Government* in which he proposed architecture that would force the state to listen to and respect the property-owning electorate. Locke's rough sketch proposed elections to representative parliaments that would be insulated from state tyranny through the dispersion of power broadly across institutions and the rule of law. Locke reasoned that a state under the indirect electoral control of property owners is least likely to do damage to their interests.[3]

These aspects of liberalism are not without tension. The first tension is between the liberal aspiration to give the people political power (called **popular sovereignty**) and the desire to organize these peoples by nation. While Central European liberals have been able to agree that power should reside with the people, the process of identifying who the sovereign people should be has been controversial and even violent.

The second tension resides between the electorate and liberal institutions and values. As Kevin Deegan-Krause has repeatedly observed, electorates are not above electing horrible people into office.[4] What is to prevent them from destroying the democratic institutions that brought them to power? The Lockean response is to limit and balance political power, to curtail the leader's power to do real damage while in office. Yet, how does one do this without rendering the voters' choice for change meaningless? In this respect, democracy is like a wobbly tray. The plates risk tumbling into dictatorship on one side or voter irrelevance on the other. Governments everywhere—and not just in Central Europe—have struggled to keep the tray from crashing.

The third related tension arises from conflict between the people's elected lawmakers and free market ideologues (often called "neoliberals") who value the free market destination over the voters' sovereign political choice. To many of these ideologues, even democratically derived limitations on economic liberty can feel like a form of serfdom. Frequently, they have sought to isolate economic policy decisions from the democratic process or relocate them to the transnational sphere. Both knock the tray to the side of voter irrelevance and democratic alienation.[5]

The (re)insertion of postcommunist countries into global markets for finance and production is a fourth source of tension. Market integration has served to remove economic control from the voters' reach. As the small countries of Central Europe have opened their economies to European markets, their elected policy makers have found their range of policy choice constrained by the choices of foreign consumers, foreign fiscal policies, and foreign investor confidence. Perhaps as importantly, Central Europe's relatively small economies have become accustomed to following the fiscal lead of Europe's most frugal governments, particularly Germany. The collective choice for frugality has had the significant distributional effect of fighting inflation in the European "core" at the expense of ongoing economic doldrums on the European "periphery." This, in turn, has helped fuel popular resentment and political alienation.

Finally, tension arises from the rich rewards that politicians can win anytime they control points where the state intersects the economy. Here, the Central European experience really has been unique. First, today's states inherited unprecedented amounts of property from their communist predecessors. For ideological and practical reasons, liberals committed early to privatization, the transfer of ownership over state property to private individuals. In the space of a few short years in the 1990s and 2000s, individual men and women became proprietors of the majority of the region's farms, factories, mines, trucking, housing, stores, offices, and much, much more.

Economically, privatization was not such a bad policy. As we will see in chapters 2 and 3, the state was not doing well as an owner. Privatization had problems, however. It was like a single roll of the dice that promised to make whoever won very wealthy. With such high stakes in play, many politicians and citizens preferred to load the dice. This was not good for the development of democracy. Yet, the property game did not end with the distribution of property. Once property was in private hands, the new property owners continued to win by controlling how the state interacted with economic activity.

The fight for economic control has helped poison democratic politics. If the stakes get high enough, politicians might choose to win by cheating rather than to lose by following the rules of the game. The cheaters are also good at claiming to speak for the people, identifying their enemies, and pointing to the significant threats that enemies pose should they take power. It's a pernicious story that can be a prelude to the harassment, silencing, or exile of rival politicians. And with greater control over politics, leaders can more easily shape state economic decisions in a way that benefits themselves or their associates. Like tart wine and a bag of Cheetos, illiberal politics pairs well with illiberal economics but gives everyone heartburn later on.

This book tells the story of how liberalism has both succeeded and stumbled in the postcommunist era. Yet, it also holds out hope. As battles over property, democratic institutions, and national identity unfold, the consistent enemies of illiberal politics have been people who seek to make democratic institutions work. The most readily available solution to liberalism's tensions has been more political liberalism. In this, the following work falls squarely in the tradition of Adam Smith, who in 1776 reminded us that the best remedy to any "conspiracy" of monopolistic insiders is to open the doors to the rooms where they conspire.[6] A meaningful, robust democracy can help open these doors. I hope that the citizens intermittently marching in the streets of Belgrade, Budapest, Bratislava, Warsaw, and Prague will find vindication in this lesson. They—and the voters they hope to win over—remain the biggest threat to Europe's newest generation of illiberal politicians.

In writing this text, I have incurred many debts. The first is to my students at Colorado College, who give me inspiration and hope. In this group there are a number who stand out for their insightful comments, corrections, or encouragement. This includes Jordan Biro, Laila Faruki, Jordan Fields, Emma Fowkes, Gina Jeong, Mary Kate Girard, Zach Glosser, Taylor Harris, Ben Hays-Lemmon, Annette Leyva, Izzy Lipacis, Maggie Mixer, Dan Mulco, Diellza Muriqi, Evyn Papworth, Antonio Sanchez, Madeline Sommer, Awais Ali Syed, Theodore Weiss, and Chandler Witt. A big thank-you goes to Kathryn Kenny, who provided indispensable help with the endnotes, and to Filip Čarnogursky and Samuel Schavoir, who provided additional research assistance. In particular, I would like to thank Abby Needell and her father, Allan, whose enthusiasm and encouragement after an early read through gave me courage to push through to complete the final several chapters. I also owe a beverage of choice to Ana Babović, Bill Gould Jr., David Hendrickson, Stephanie Linz-Gould, Mike McCune, Dan Miller, David Antonio Gonzalez Salgado, James Thompson, and two external reviewers from the University of Michigan for their deep reads and editorial suggestions. Colleagues who have generously helped along the way with insights, comments, and encouragement include Yogesh Chandrani, Joe Derdzinski, Douglas Edlin, Sofia Fenner, James Griffith, Vibha Kapuria-Foreman, Juan Lindau, Amanda Minervini, David Ost, and Shawn Womack. Throughout my career and this project, I have also benefited deeply from ongoing conversations with Samuel Abraham, Jozef Bátora, Mark Blyth, Kevin Deegan-Krause, Pavol Demeš, Slobodan Đinović, Sharon Fisher, Zsolt Gál, Tim Haughton, Darina Malová, Haris Mesinović, Edward Moe, Julie Newton, Srdja Popović, Christian Sorace, and Soňa Szomolányi. Finally, I thank Matthew Cooney of Colorado College for his work assembling the maps, Daniel Gundlach for compiling the index, Anne Taylor, Kevin Rennells, and Haley Winkle of the University of Michigan Press for editing and producing the final volume, and Elizabeth Demers of the University of Michigan Press for her enthusiastic embrace of a different sort of academic press book.

Parts of chapter 1 are adopted from an earlier article with Edward Moe, "Beyond Rational Choice: Ideational Assault and the Use of Delegitimation Frames in Nonviolent Revolutionary Movements," *Research in Social Movements, Conflict, and Change* 34 (2013). Similarly, chapter 9 draws from a work with Edward Moe, "Nationalism and the Struggle for LGBTQ Rights in Serbia, 1991-2014," *Problems of Post-Communism* 62, no. 5 (2015): 273-86. Chapter 10 draws inspiration and some prose from my published work with Darina Malová, "Toxic Neoliberalism on the EU's Periphery: Slovakia, the Euro and the Migrant Crisis," in Jozef Bátora and John Erik Fossum, eds., *Towards a Segmented European Political Order: The European Union's Post-Crisis Conundrum* (London: Routledge, 2020), 112-31. Chapters 2, 3, and 10 draw on short sections adapted from John A. Gould, *The Politics of Privatization: Wealth and Power in Postcommunist Europe* (Boulder: Lynne Rienner, 2011). Chapters 3 and 10 make some use of John Gould, "To Neoliberalism and Back? 20 Years of Economic Policy in Slovakia," in Mark Stolarik, ed., *The Czech and Slovak Republics: Twenty Years of Independence, 1993-2013* (Budapest: Central European University Press, 2016). All works are used with permission. Thank you to Lynne Rienner, Taylor & Francis, Routledge, and Central European University Press for allowing me to adapt these works for a different audience.

Those who know me know how much I owe to my wife, Simona. Without her nuanced insight into Central European politics and solid grounding in what it means to be a responsible citizen in a flawed democracy—wherever we find it—I'd never have been able to write this book. I have also learned immensely from Simona's parents and grandparents. Many liberals in my generation did not listen to their generations when Central Europe tried to regrow its liberal roots. All too often, we glossed over their objections, scoffed at their disappointment, and marginalized their voices. Had we been just a bit more concerned with their welfare, liberalism's roots might be more deeply rooted today. But we must also consider the possibility that the sort of liberalism practiced by some in the postcommunist period was simply incapable of such attention, that it only achieved the success it did via the marginalization of many of society's most vulnerable citizens. We will return to this possibility later.

To my sons, Lukaš and Marek, I dedicate this book to you. Our generation is handing you a hell of a mess. I hope your generation will appreciate the few things we did get right and learn from our mistakes.

CHAPTER 1

Revolutions

The Fall of Communism as Witnessed from a Beer Barrel and Beyond

*How Germans became activists . . . A brief theory of uprisings . . .
Šarka's little smuggling operation . . . Flat beer after prison . . . A
Sunday lunch that could get you arrested . . . 6,000 Germans go for
a train ride . . . Alan does some manual labor in Berlin . . . Czech
students get beaten up . . . Simona and Zuzka play hooky—and
become revolutionaries.*

PREFACE: This chapter relates events that heralded the collapse of communism in Central Europe. Chronologically, it should be the second chapter and there would be little harm done were you to read chapter 2 on communism first. Yet, the events of fall 1989 were the beginning of my personal experience in the region and thus receive pride of place here. This chapter on revolutions gets its catchy subtitle honestly. I really did spend a few cold nights in fall 1989 sleeping in a large, unheated beer barrel on the outskirts of Prague. In one short week, I also sat on a train with a brave graduate student as she smuggled illegal books into communist Czechoslovakia; I drank beer with a prisoner of conscience who had just been released from jail; I whispered my way through a "dangerous" conversation over beers about democracy with a Czech engineering student; and twice I watched stunned as citizens of the communist East Germany gave up everything for a chance to live in West Germany. These experiences were part of a remarkable set of events that changed history.

They certainly changed me. Already wary of the Reagan-era right's habit of suppressing critical thought with moral maxims and traditional texts, I saw firsthand the havoc the radical left could play with the human spirit. It seemed to me at the time, and I still believe it, that while the far right does not want us to think, the radical left wants to do all the thinking for us. In 1989, Poles, Hungarians, East Germans, Slovaks, Czechs, and many others made it plain that henceforth they would do the thinking for themselves.

ᔍ ᔌ

This book is my mother's fault. In fall 1989, I was a high school history teacher at the American School of Paris with a week of vacation looming. On a whim, I decided to go to Leipzig, Germany, to see "the Monday marches." Yet, before buying a ticket, I called my mom.

"Don't go to Leipzig!" she warned. "It's going to be another Tiananmen Square!" She recommended that I go to Prague instead—for the architecture and, of course, the legendary beer. It also had the advantage of being in Czechoslovakia, one of the few communist states not undergoing a political upheaval. I booked a ticket to Prague and headed down to the Czechoslovak embassy for a tourist visa.

This discussion will probably mean nothing to my students. Readers from my generation will most likely recall June 4, 1989, the day that Chinese authorities opened fire on the thousands of Chinese students who had occupied Tiananmen Square. The massacre, shown live on CNN, was a traumatic and depressing experience. The previous year had produced so much hope. The Soviet policies of *glasnost* and *perestroika* (promoting more open inquiry and economic reform, respectively) were morphing into *demokratizatsiya* (democratization); Soviet premier Mikhail Gorbachev was unilaterally ending the Cold War, and democratic opponents in the Soviet-allied country of Hungary had negotiated a full transition to free and fair elections, set for March 1990. With the Soviet cloud over Europe dispersing and students demanding basic rights in communist China, the Tiananmen Square repression came as a deep shock. My housemate in Boston at the time was a graduate student and the son of a high-ranking Chinese military official. As we watched the slaughter live on CNN, tears poured down his cheeks.

"They pushed too far! They pushed too far!" he repeated.

Less lodged in my generation's memory is that June 4, 1989, was also the day of the competitive parliamentary election in communist Poland.[1] By the time of the election, Poland's ruling Communist Party was in trouble. Inflation was out of control, and every time the party tried to do something about it, Polish workers would go on strike. To gain more worker cooperation and share the blame for the painful reforms that were coming, the ruling party struck a deal with an illegal, independent trade union called Solidarity. The party would allow Solidarity activists and allies to run for one-third of the lower house's seats and all the seats of the senate in exchange for worker cooperation in resolving the economic crisis.

Solidarity's main goal was to become a legally recognized, independent trade union. They distrusted the elections and were afraid that the communists would cheat. However, on June 4, the communists surprised them by actually holding a fair election. Then Solidarity leaders shocked themselves by sweeping every contested seat in the lower house and all but one seat in the senate. Finally, another shock: Solidarity's one-third minority became a two-thirds majority after Poland's formerly quiescent "loyal opposition parties" crossed lines to join them. The communists made a quick appeal to Moscow, but when Gorbachev offered no help, they allowed Solidarity to form a new government.

Just like that, the communist era in Poland came to an end.

The Polish experience was a quick reminder of an old lesson of politics: opportunity for civil disobedience abounds when a government *needs* its people to do something for them, like keep working while the state imposes painful inflation-fighting measures such as higher taxes, lower wages, longer hours, and worse working conditions. The people can simply refuse to obey, and the government may feel compelled to make major concessions.

In communist East Germany (formally known as the German Democratic Republic) the communist party was in a much stronger position in 1989. The economy was more stable, and the party monitored and disciplined the dissident opposition with a beefy, secret police force called the Stasi. Really, the government did not demand much of its citizens, except to show up for work and not share their critical thoughts publicly. East Germans thus had to create their own ways of expressing resistance. The most dramatic demonstration was to travel, by any means possible, across a heavily armed border to the democratic state of West Germany (the Federal Republic of Germany). There, East Germans would be granted citizenship under the West German state's Basic Law. In summer 1989, loosened border controls between Hungary and Austria allowed many thousands of East German "picnickers" to scamper across the border between the communist East and the democratic West. This forced the East German communist government to restrict travel to communist Hungary.

I was deeply moved by a march that took place each Monday night in Leipzig, a city in communist East Germany. Long before the Western press ever noticed them, citizens in Leipzig had been holding Monday prayer

Central and Eastern Europe - 1989

meetings at the 800-year-old Nikolaikirche. By meeting in a church, they achieved a limited degree of protection from the police. However hostile the communists were toward organized religion, it would look bad for the police to beat up and arrest people at prayer.

The churchgoers thus successfully created a dilemma action for the police—a term that we will come back to repeatedly in this book.[2] A dilemma action occurs when activists put their opponents in a "lose-lose" position. It helps explain why state use of violence will often backfire.[3] If police allow the march to go on unimpeded, they lose. Citizens have established the right to assemble freely and to express their displeasure for the regime! Yet if the police arrest or beat people at prayer, they may lose more! Onlookers might wonder what kind of inhumane people would do such a thing. Their moral shock might motivate them to overcome their own habits of obedience and fear, go out, and protest themselves.[4] Dilemma actions are part of the reason a state's oppression can often be self-defeating— transforming a small nonviolent movement into a large one overnight. Erica Chenoweth and Maria Stephan cover these dynamics in a remarkable book, *Why Civil Resistance Works*, which I highly recommend.[5]

Amazingly, the East German regime responded with textbook ineptitude to the prayer demonstrations, losing in both ways. However, before I explain this, I should discuss how the Germans overcame their collective action problem. A collective action problem exists when the sum total of each individual's best choice adds up to an undesirable outcome for the entire group. For protest movements, like that in Leipzig, solving the collective action problem has three components. First, some political economists emphasize that protest is personally costly. It usually involves a lot of inconvenience and varying degrees of risk for little personal gain. Think about it. It might rain, your boss might fire you, and, on a bad day, the police might arrest or beat you up. Yet, at the end of the day, you'll probably go home with very little accomplished. If one is calculating the costs and benefits and acting according to the models of some economists, your best choice is not to protest.[6]

Second, because protests are costly and even dangerous, many people sympathetic with the cause will look for some excuse *not* to help. This is called **free riding**. You are a free rider when you want to get something done but you prefer that others do it for you.

Finally, there is the **assurance problem**. This is the fear (or the lived experience) that others will free ride on your efforts. Would you volunteer to face down a line of possibly violent police if it were quite likely that nobody would join you? You might, but you would be a rare exception. By bearing all the costs and the risks alone, you get what political economists call "the sucker's payoff."[7]

In summer and fall 1989, East Germans in Leipzig solved all three of these problems. Duke University professor Timur Kuran has a theory that might help explain why. He argues that by 1989 a large number of Central Europeans disapproved of their governments but were quite naturally afraid to express it openly. It may be that the zone of comparative safety inside the Nikolai Church helped change this equation. At first, only motivated risk-takers attended—those rare activists ready to risk Stasi monitoring, harassment, unemployment, arrest, and violence—thus getting the sucker's payoff. As the meetings continued, however, the growing numbers of risk-takers may have helped reduce the perceived risks of attending. This might have created a space where cautious people also felt safe joining in. Greater numbers meant even more safety, permitting even more cautious people to participate, and so on.

We should be careful about reducing revolutions purely down to risks, costs, and benefits, however. While it is helpful to understand how we respond predictably to these sorts of incentives, a richer explanation will also consider how we filter them through social and psychological lenses. This is another way of saying that emotions and peer pressure, leveraged through family and community networks, explain many of the risks people take—including those that appear highly irrational in the rational cost-benefit framework just described. As Ed Moe and I have argued elsewhere, being part of a community legitimizes feelings of anger, frustration, and resentment that motivate people to take on possibly costly actions.[8] Communities are also laced with spiderwebs of communication that help reassure people that if they join a movement, others will too.[9] As noted, the relative solidarity and safety of numbers may in turn lead people to discount their fear and embarrassment about participating.

People are also likely to defend their status fiercely within their own social network. So, peer pressure, or what Tina Rosenberg calls the "social cure," becomes an important part of individual choice. If your friends are all joining the resistance, do you want to be the only one in your circle who stays home?[10] In short, uprisings occur when the costs seem manageable; when powerful emotions like anger help us to override legitimate concerns about risk; when social pressure and monitoring makes free riding an embarrassing choice; and when one's personal network dispels concerns about being stuck with the sucker's payoff. These and similar dynamics may also help explain why, in 1989, the Monday prayer meeting swelled into a weekly citizens' march to church to demand economic and political reform and basic human rights. The Monday demonstrations thus began what Kuran calls a "revolutionary bandwagon."[11]

My mom was right to worry, by the way. The East German leadership *did* seek a Tiananmen-style resolution to the Monday marches. On October 7-8, German police used limited violence against small groups of demonstrators who had protested elsewhere. Anger (moral shock) over this use of force probably drove many into joining the Leipzig march on Monday, October 9, but it also led some to stay home. Some families with small children even made sure one parent remained with the kids—in case something went drastically wrong at the march as it had at Tiananmen only four months earlier. This was smart, but as it turned out, a large-scale crackdown would have been difficult for the regime to carry out: The October 9 march was enormous (70,000-100,000), was strictly nonviolent (protestors carried candles, not rocks), and was framed using unifying and patriotic, if provocative, language ("We are the people") and peaceful gestures (prayers and songs). It was hard—if not impossible—for security officers to come up with a legitimate justification to undertake the considerable risk of beating tens of thousands of peaceful, pious, and patriotic citizens.

Social connections between the protestors and the security forces probably also helped. Before the Tiananmen Square repression, the Chinese People's Army allegedly had to rotate out locally sourced battalions before they launched their action. The generals purportedly feared that the young soldiers from the Beijing region would sympathize more with the protestors than with their officers. When the order came, troops from the distant interior of China carried out the crackdown.

In Leipzig, by contrast, it was entirely possible that the security officers had family and friends in the crowd. Reports are that an order to suppress the protests came from the aging chief of the Communist Party, Erich Honecker, but at the urging of the famed local orchestra director Kurt Masur and other local leaders, someone in the party hierarchy conveniently—and wisely—ignored it.[12]

℘ ℧

Developments in Germany were thrilling to watch from the safety of my apartment in Paris, but I am embarrassed to admit that on my mother's advice, on October 28, 1989, I left instead for a week's vacation in the "much safer" Czechoslovak capital, Prague. Travel from Paris to Prague at the time consisted of a 22-hour train ride. My compartment included

a French graduate student, Šarka, and an elderly Czech woman returning from a visit with a son who had immigrated to Paris in late summer
1968.[13] The trip was uneventful until, about an hour before the border,
Šarka informed me in casual conversation that her suitcase contained 30
books from Czech authors that the communist authorities had banned
for being subversive. To avoid drawing attention to herself at the border,
she then took a small bag to the restroom and convincingly transformed
herself from a hip Parisian graduate student to an unfashionable, older
woman in a tattered old cardigan.

Telling me about her illegal smuggling operation was probably a mistake. Neither am I particularly courageous nor do I have a good poker face,
but we lucked out. The border guard searched a large box owned by the
elderly Czech woman, found it to be full of laundry detergent, and left.

Perhaps to apologize for freaking me out at the border, Šarka offered to
use her fluent Czech—learned from her émigré parents—to help me locate
a hotel on my first night in Prague. Several calls from the main station,
however, established that all the affordable hotels were full of East Germans, which surprised her because it was not tourist season. Instead, we
caught a cab to her friends' apartment near the famous Charles Bridge.
Tanya and Alex were a young couple with a colicky, cloth-diapered infant
living in a studio apartment in the heart of Prague. Conversation switched
from French to Czech as we entered the apartment, but Šarka would now
and then translate: "You can sleep in the kitchen under the table, but first
we have to borrow a mattress from the next-door neighbor *who should be
released from jail* in the next hour or so."

Martin, the next-door neighbor, eventually arrived home from jail and
invited us over. He poured us stale beer from a pitcher that had been sitting in the fridge for at least two days and then brought me up to speed in
unpracticed English. Martin was a philosophy student studying by corre-
spondence at the University of Leuven in Belgium. His topic was Socra-
tes's impact on the youth. Perhaps, I thought, the government feared philosophers who would not consciously tell lies to their students, no matter
what the cost.

However, it wasn't Martin's philosophical interests that got him in
trouble. To understand this, we have to dip further into history to the
period of relaxed Cold War tensions in the early to mid-1970s known as
détente. The culminating event of détente in Europe was the Helsinki
Accords, signed in 1975 by the Americans, the Soviets, and the major
European countries. Among other things, the accords pleased the Soviets
by officially recognizing the borders between the Soviet-dominated com-

munist countries of Eastern Europe and Western Europe's democracies. In exchange, the Soviet Union and its allies in Central Europe cynically signed a pledge to uphold a detailed list of human rights and freedoms in their own countries. Many politicians in the West underappreciated the communist pledges on rights. They were not above supporting dictators abroad when it was convenient for their policies.

Yet, it soon became clear to human rights activists and religious dissidents in the communist East that their governments' signatures on the Helsinki documents gave them a powerful weapon. In Czechoslovakia, the main group to seize upon this opportunity was Charter '77, a group formed to pressure the government to uphold its pledge to guarantee the rights of its citizens. My unexpected philosopher-host in Prague that first night was Martin Palouš, an original member of the group and a friend of future Czech president Václav Havel. Martin had served as a Charter '77 spokesperson, and, accordingly, the authorities harassed him routinely. As an activist, Martin had been arrested two days earlier on what Šarka explained was the charge of "suspicion of having the potential to create a disturbance during the weekend," in other words, a 48-hour preventive detention. Hence, the stale beer. Within a year, Czechs would elect Martin to parliament, and thereafter he would balance a brilliant career that ranged from international diplomacy to academic life in international law and philosophy. We will meet him again in chapter 8.

While Charter '77 was the moral conscience of the Czechlands, its membership was in the low hundreds for most of the late communist era. In the parlance used above, Charter '77 members had difficulty overcoming the assurance problem and thus were used to receiving "the sucker's payoff." This was perhaps understandable, but again, we need more backstory to understand why. On August 22, 1968, an earlier effort to liberalize and democratize Czechoslovak communism known as the Prague Spring had ended with the Soviet-led Warsaw Pact invasion and occupation. Communist states then took a pledge to uphold their duty to protect other communist states from usurpation by "malign forces." As the policy emerged from the politburo of Soviet premier Leonid Brezhnev, it came to be known as the Brezhnev Doctrine.

After the invasion, the Soviets replaced the communist reformers with a government of communist hard-liners who would adhere more carefully to Moscow's expectations. To help ensure obedience, the unpopular new government asked party members and most workers to sign a document approving the invasion. Under threat of losing their jobs, most people signed. Charter '77 drew heavily from those who refused to sign these documents. Most were fired and had no choice but to work in difficult, boring, and low-paying jobs under constant state harassment and surveillance.

Their families also paid a price. My friend and the former department chair at Comenius University in Slovakia, the late Miroslav Kusý, was one of a handful of Slovak members of Charter '77 and accordingly received the focused attention of the state. His daughter, Dr. Dagmar Kusá, painfully recalls her father's arrest, his absence, and her subsequent ostracism at school and in the community. This was intentional. The government made sure that open acts of dissidence, like Professor Kusý's, would have a cost for his entire family. Given this, I personally don't know if I would have had the courage to follow Professor Kusý as he signed that document. In Slovakia, only a few brave civic and Catholic dissidents, artists, and environmentalists joined him in openly contesting the regime.[14]

Most people who signed the document disapproved of the 1968 invasion or were, at best, deeply ambivalent about it. In short, the ability to go to work each day depended on maintaining a public lie. The lies did not stop with the document. The state created all sorts of relatively meaningless rituals in the workplace, in schools, and even at home, designed to demonstrate one's loyalty to the state publicly. Failure to perform these rituals could have consequences. Citizens thus came to possess two personas— the first was one's public face, which obediently repeated the niceties of the loyal communist; the other was private, where one shared one's true feelings with family and only the closest of friends.

This tortured contradiction produced a great deal of interesting art and literature, some of which was undoubtedly in Šarka's suitcase when we crossed the border. While Šarka did not like Milan Kundera's works personally, I recommend *The Unbearable Lightness of Being*, if only for the story of Tomaš's refusal to disavow his preinvasion critiques of the government to keep his job.[15] It's a fair representation of the danger that high-level people faced for refusing to publicly lie about their convictions. Also well known are the plays of Václav Havel and particularly his essay "The Power of the Powerless," in which the author envisions the high cost to his career and family that a vegetable stand grocer would pay if he simply stopped repeating the party's empty Marxist slogans.[16]

My favorite work, however, is an obscure piece of performance art called *The Lunch II* by Slovak activist-artist Ján Budaj. Accomplished in 1978, *The Lunch II* was a live performance in which Mr. Budaj and three others moved a typical afternoon meal from the kitchen to a white square in a parking lot. Loudspeakers broadcast the normal lunch conversation to the neighborhood. The performance brilliantly demonstrated how just the

"The Lunch II" by Ján Budaj
Performance art, Bratislava, Slovakia, 1978. Under copyright, used with permission of the artist.

act of making a private conversation public was threatening to the regime. If everyone began saying what they really thought, the assurance and free-riding problems would be easier to solve, making resistance more likely!

That first night in Prague, I slept on Martin's borrowed mattress in Alex and Tanya's kitchen, and the next day I departed to find a hotel room. With the help of the state tourist agency, Čedok, I finally secured a bed in a large unheated beer barrel behind a pub. It was summer lodging, but even in late October, I was quite comfortable under a double-thick, goose-down duvet. Two nights later, I exchanged money on the black market and was instantly well off by Czech standards.

The source of this sudden wealth was the government's policy of currency inconvertibility. Officials did not allow average citizens to buy dollars freely; they had to have government permission, and then the official exchange rate was about 4 *koruny* to each dollar. Yet, this rate did not reflect the real demand for dollars. Many citizens were willing to pay much more in private exchanges.

I found this out when a café waiter offered to exchange money at the rate of 26 *koruny* to one dollar. Luckily, he was neither a police plant nor a swindler, and the exchange went as promised. Suddenly, my coffee cost a nickel and my next beer, 15 cents! I booked a room in a hotel so expensive that no East Germans had taken it. I then took the tram to my beer barrel lodging and checked out.

My week in Prague concluded with some of the most memorable events of my life. Before I left Paris, my school's librarian, a Czech immigrant, asked me to look up her sister while I was there. In 1968, the librarian had fled the country to escape the aftermath of the Warsaw Pact invasion. Sadly, the post-invasion government took revenge on her family in Prague. The librarian's sister was a promising glass artist in the city. The party banned her from the studio where she worked. Henceforth, her art career was limited to teaching kindergarten. She was also initially denied decent housing. I met her for tea at her apartment and then went out for drinks with her son, Jiří.

Jiří, an engineering student, was engaged politically. The previous week he had attended a demonstration of about 3,000 on the main square that police had broken up by force. In Leipzig, Germany, by contrast, over 300,000 had just protested. Jiří was frustrated but optimistic. In a loud and crowded bar, he expressed his anger in an almost comically quiet, head-to-head whisper. If stodgy Leipzig can do it, he said, so too can we. He promised me "the dam would break" in the very near future.

We followed our drinks with a stroll up to an overlook at Prague Castle. As we looked at the city lights below, we heard a large crowd let out an enormous roar from just down the hill. At first, Jiří was confused—the roar emanated from near the West German embassy. But he quickly figured it out. I did not know it at the time, but West German diplomats granted citizenship to any East Germans who could get into the embassy. Since the beginning of October, however, there had been no way to get from Prague to West Germany—the route through Hungary had been cut off. For the last several weeks, over 2,000 East Germans had been camping in the embassy gardens, hoping the Czechoslovak government would let them leave. With no room left at the embassy, an estimated additional 20,000 had occupied Prague's low-end hotels—hence my first nights of sleeping in a barrel. On this night, November 3, 1989, the Czechoslovak government had agreed to let the East Germans complete their journey to the West via the Czech-German border. That was what the celebration was about.

The scene in front of the embassy was chaotic and confused. We joined West German tourists and journalists as East Germans arrived from all over the city. CNN arrived, filmed a report that mistook celebratory fire-crackers on embassy grounds for gunshots, and disappeared into the night. Jiří and I had the pleasure of telling an intern they had left behind the real reason for the commotion. In an age before cell phones, all he could do was look at me in horror and ask:

"Can you help me find a cab?"

Inside the embassy foyer, I could see people jammed together, perched on anything that could be climbed or simply sitting on the floor. They were passing around coffee. A few young men with green canvas backpacks overburdened with beer tried to get in, but guards turned them away. Behind the building on the embassy grounds, there was a raucous party raging, and the young men wanted to keep it going.

In front, emotions were raw. Some West German tourists had tears in their eyes. One young man with a green backpack sat a few feet from the entrance, sobbing, and in the end retreated sadly down the hill. Then there were the arrivals: families, usually a young couple with one or two children, but also some individuals, and many young childless couples, walking up the hill to the embassy with no more than a couple of small bags. The pace of the arrivals accelerated as the evening went on. We watched as long as we could, but I reluctantly had to bid Jiři goodbye and catch the last tram to my hotel. The next morning, I returned to the main train station and took the train back to Paris.

So, that was it for Prague. Except for this:

When my train arrived the next day at the West German border, we were detained 45 minutes past our departure time. I began to doze. I awoke as a second train pulled into the station across the platform, its passengers roaring in celebration. Inside were many of the East Germans from the embassy, crying with joy, laughing, and shouting. I remember a man about my age holding his diapered infant to the window with joy and making eye contact. I couldn't help but smile back! The crowd hushed as the PA squawked, "Welcome to the Federal Republic of Germany!" and then burst into redoubled cheering. By now, most people on my train were cheering too. An older couple down the aisle were sobbing with joy.

We pulled out of the station, and I sank down into my seat. An elderly West German man settled in across from me, still flushed with joyous pride. "That was a *German* train!" he explained in English. "Inside are 1,000 *Germans*! There are *six* of these trains, and each arrives *on the hour!*" His wife tapped his arm gently as he emphasized the punctuality. This was a bit too much emotion.

In my compartment, too, were three Czech men about my age who had sat quietly through the entire show. They looked at each other with sullen expressions, saying nothing. I distinctly remembered Jiři's thoughts of the night before.

Now it was their turn.

It shocks me that the fall of the Berlin Wall is now deep enough in the past to require explanation. Along with big-hair metal bands and endless reruns of the sitcom *M*A*S*H*, it was one of the emblems of my generation, a clear demonstration to all that no matter how critical we could be of our own governments, at least they were not fencing us in.

After World War II, the Allies divided conquered Berlin into four sectors, American, British, French, and Soviet. In 1961, too many Germans in the Soviet-controlled sector were leaving permanently for other sectors, so the government walled it off, limiting all movement across a heavily armed and patrolled strip of land running through Berlin. I had a chance to visit the wall in 1987 with my brother and my friend Jeff. We visited the Brandenburg Gate on the West German side first, climbing an observation platform to peer at a similar platform on the other side. I recall feeling very sorry for the people on the other side looking back across.

Of course, when we went to the East German side the next day, the first thing we did was go to the gate and climb the platform facing West Berlin. There were no East Germans among us. Like the Eiffel Tour, the Roman Colosseum, or the Empire State Building, residents had little interest in going there. You know you have a problem when your chief tourist attraction is a well-armed no-man's-land, designed to keep the locals from emigrating.

With the opening of the border in Hungary in summer 1989 and then the opening of the Czech border that I witnessed on November 4, 1989, this wall could no longer contain East German citizens. I have not researched the numbers formally, but in my journal, I noted that by the time I returned from Prague to teach on Monday, November 6, 16,000 East Germans had entered West Germany through Czechoslovakia by train and another 12,000 by car. Pulling out my crystal ball in class that day, I told my students:

"The only way the East German government can stop this is by opening up the Berlin Wall . . . *but I can't see that happening!*" Oops! By Wednesday, my notes recall, the exodus had grown to 50,000 and by Thursday, 84,000—with tens of thousands more en route from East Germany to West Germany via Czechoslovakia.

That day was November 9, 1989. By most accounts, a confused order led East German border guards to open a checkpoint to the Western side. Others followed suit. Most of East Berlin subsequently made the trip across the once-deadly frontier. Occasionally they used some hard-earned Western deutsche marks to make a small purchase, but mostly they just looked around and enjoyed the privilege of visiting before returning home. Anecdotally, and I cannot remember the source, one of the final graffiti painted on the West German side of the wall commemorated the experience with a doctored quote from Shakespeare's *Julius Caesar*:

"They came, they saw, they did a little shopping."

That weekend, at least a quarter of my expatriate and Parisian friends hopped on trains to Berlin. I had to teach and couldn't travel until much later, but my close friend Alan took time off from work and spent several days drinking champagne on top of the wall.

"You could hear the wall before you could see it," he told me. "All along the wall, we were hammering away at it." Alan recalled that from time to time, the noises would stop way off in the distance as a joint East-West German border patrol would pass by in a bizarre bubble of silence. The hammering would start again as soon as they passed out of sight. Several of my students took the week off as their parents took them to Berlin to see the miracle. I still have two small fragments of the wall given to me by my student Nick upon his return—perhaps as an ironic apology for missing his "current events" quiz.

Meanwhile, in Bratislava, Slovakia, a friend who played a key role in that country's democratic resistance recalls how she felt fury that "even those obedient East Germans" could bring down their government. Meanwhile Czechs and Slovaks did nothing. Quietly, she and other opponents to the regime stepped up their preparations for the break they so desperately desired.

On November 17, 1989, a group of students in Prague applied for a permit to hold a "Student Day" celebration in memory of Jan Opletal and over 1,000 Czech students whom the Nazis had sent to concentration camps 50 years earlier. The Nazis had executed the heroic, young anti-fascist Opletal, making him a communist hero. The students' application was a classic dilemma action. Officials could deny the permit and look unpatriotic—too afraid to honor an official student icon. Or they could permit the "celebration" to go ahead and risk it turning political. They chose to take the risk.

The turnout was large, likely over 15,000. Leaders gave antigovernment, prodemocracy speeches and then began a march along a government-approved route toward the cemetery where Opletal was buried. Several thousand participants illegally broke off, however, marched down the hill, over the Vltava River, and up Národní (National) Street toward Václavské (Wenceslas) Square. As they did, students from nearby Charles University and others filled the ranks. Close to the square, police blocked and then enveloped the marchers, a practice known today as "kettling." The students sat down, held up their arms, and chanted to gesture their innocence:

"We have nothing in our hands!" Nevertheless, the police marched into the student ranks and beat them. A false rumor that one student had been clubbed to death quickly spread. It was broadcast on Voice of America, Radio Europe, and the BBC.[17]

The students' action set off a classic revolutionary bandwagon. First, the state's use of violence backfired. People like Jiři had become increasingly frustrated with the intransigence of the regime's pro-Soviet, conservative hard-liners. Now, however, they were both shocked and angered by the November 17 beatings. Villages and towns across Czechoslovakia annually sent their most talented sons and daughters to Prague's elite universities. These students had been nonviolent and seated when the police attacked. People were outraged! Anger, in turn, temporarily made thousands of citizens more acceptant of risk and motivated to bear the uncertain costs of protest.

Second, people knew from many hushed dinner table conversations and from the daily torrent of cynical jokes passed among trusted family and friends that their grievances were widely shared. As political scientist Joshua Tucker has pointed out, there are special times when people feel assured that they will not be alone if they speak out or act in opposition to oppression. This was one of them. The feeling of safety in numbers made action more likely.[18]

Finally, these same preexisting relationships, friendships, and networks made it socially important for many that they participate. Few wanted to miss what would become the most important event of their lives. For many, freeriding in late November 1989 was unthinkable.

My wife, Simona, was a high school student in the Slovak capital of Bratislava at the time. On Friday, November 17, teachers put her school on lockdown to prevent, as the principal announced, "unauthorized persons from entering [the school] to take advantage of your youthful impulsiveness, to the detriment of the whole society." She found this so hilarious that she wrote it down in her diary. On Monday, her PE teachers drilled the class for an upcoming Spartakiade, a party-organized, mass demonstration of youthful discipline and fitness. After school, she went to perform in *Carmen* at the National Opera with her youth choir, but the theater had gone on strike in support of Prague's students. She returned home to find her father glued to Voice of America on the radio, the volume turned up louder than usual.

Open demonstrations in Slovakia began the next day, November 21. Simona and her best friend, Zuzka, skipped their afternoon classes and started milling around downtown Bratislava with other kids—waiting for something to happen. Some university students soon organized them, and they marched to Gottwald Square, where the students began to make speeches. The numbers swelled into the thousands, and the entire group marched to the main Hviezdoslav Square for more speeches.

The demonstration unveiled a lot of prior planning. At day's end, Simona's diary reports, she and Zuzka were committed to three things that movements need if they are going to survive. First, they had a political vision—to abolish the constitutional provision giving the Communist Party a "leading role" in politics. Second, they had an understanding of the character of the movement—it would be cheerful, relentless, and, most important, nonviolent. Finally, they were assigned a set of individualized tasks that they personally could undertake—beginning with bringing their classmates to the next day's demonstrations.

With 16-year old choir girls mobilized, the regime really had no chance.

In what became known as the **Velvet Revolution**, networks of Charter '77 dissidents, religious and environmental activists, actors, academics, students, and professionals stepped up to provide leadership and organization to citizens fed up with the government. As documented in work by John Glenn, theaters became a prime coordinating point across Czechoslovakia.[19] By the evening of November 19, two loosely knit leadership organizations had formed nationally to give voice and coherent strategic planning to the movement. In Bratislava, Ján Budaj, Professor Kusý, and many others formed **Public Against Violence**, while Martin Palouš, Václav Havel, and others established the **Civic Forum** in Prague. Havel pressed Civic Forum's demands on the government, but by no means could he, Palouš, or anyone control the massive movement that assembled daily in the public squares of Czechoslovakia.

This was a good thing. It allowed for a "hands off the steering wheel" style of negotiations: a terrifying, unswerving acceleration of Czechoslovak society toward the frozen Communist Party leadership. Only the less-compromised communist functionaries had the agility to get out of the way. Many openly split from their hard-liner bosses to join the opposition. With a disciplined but loosely organized civic movement firmly in control of the nation's workplaces and squares, the regime was powerless. On November 29, the Communist Party agreed to stop monopolizing politics. On December 10, a cabinet of regime opponents and a few moderate communists formed a new government. And on December 29, 1989, the communist regime formally transferred the presidency to Havel. The first free and fair elections took place the following June.[20]

∽ ⌒

The dam had indeed broken. Across Central Europe, citizens fed up with being told what to do by self-serving government functionaries seized a brief opportunity to make government by the few momentarily impossible. Clearly bereft of public support and often skeptical of communism themselves, the authorities refrained from using force. Instead, in Poland, East Germany, Czechoslovakia, and Hungary, they turned power over to reform communists, resisters, and dissidents and began to consider how to preserve their interest under the uncertain future of democratic politics. We will return to this topic in chapters 3 and 4, but in the next chapter, we go back in time to consider the communist project in more detail.

CHAPTER 2

Communism

The Political Importance of Telling a Good Story

Ferko buys a car . . . On the political importance of a good story . . .
Marx and Lenin spin a tale . . . Looking for violence at Best Buy . . .
Peter explains why he might have to shoot my parents . . . John
Locke and global white supremacy . . . Why you should never trust a
lumberjack . . . Izidor privatizes a pig . . . Štefania milks more cows
than before . . . How not to make nails! . . . A flaw in the plan . . .
Learning to play make-believe . . . Ferko stocks up on
toilet paper.

PREFACE: Simona and her family enthusiastically participated in the Velvet Revolution of November-December 1989. Yet, they actually had it quite good under communism. Her father, František (Ferko), played trumpet for the National Opera, and her mother, Božena, taught middle school math and chemistry in a nearby school. With help from their parents in the countryside, they were even able to buy a new car and an apartment near the center of Bratislava. The new apartment gave Simona and her brother their own rooms—a big luxury among city kids—and it allowed her parents to walk to work rather than take the increasingly crowded trains, trams, and trolleybuses.

All through her childhood, Simona had access to adequate food, health care, housing, public transportation, education, ski vacations in Central Slovakia, state-protected parks for hiking and picking mushrooms, and a memorable week on the beach in Bulgaria. Her brother, Palko, benefited from a state-subsidized sporting complex that nurtured his talent for soccer, allowing him to play professionally after he turned 18. No one in the immediate family had faced any hunger since the war years—but that was *before* the communists took over. Nor, despite a traumatic experience of one side of the family in the 1950s, were Simona's grandparents unhappy with the material benefits of communism. The communists got many of the basic things right.

It is therefore a puzzle that, by 1989, virtually everyone in Simona's family was happy to see communism collapse. This chapter attempts to explain this thinking using the lens of political economy. We'll be looking, in particular, at the organizing and legitimizing principles of communism and comparing them with the liberalism that underpins capitalist market democracy. We will focus on how each system uses violence. We will then explore how communism played out in practice through the lived experience of Simona, her parents, and her grandparents. Chapter 3 will then explore the reintroduction of liberalism in the region.

Communism's mixed economic performance, its use of violence or the threat of it to stifle individual choice, and the lack of government accountability help to explain why so many Czechoslovak citizens poured into the squares in 1989. For Simona's family, it was not that they were suffering, particularly. It was that they—and millions like them—doubted the communists' story of why they, and no one else, had the right to be in charge. In 1989, the opportunity arose to hold the government accountable for its failures, violence, and arrogance. A majority of Czechs and Slovaks willingly embraced it.

℘ ෴

Simona's family remembers the fall of 1989 for the Velvet Revolution, of course. Yet equally emblazoned in family lore is her father's epic effort to buy a new car. After 17 years of service, their sturdy, red, Soviet-made Lada 1300 was tumbling to pieces. Ferko wanted to buy another Lada—and particularly the Italian-styled Lada Samara, which the Soviets had just started to export to their Eastern Block trade partners. Everyone said it was the best car on the market. However, the waiting list to buy a Samara was 2 to 3 years long. Ferko then tried to buy the reliable Czech-made Škoda 120. Again, there was a long, multiyear waiting list. Finally, against the advice of virtually everyone he knew, Simona's dad bought one of the few cars available right away—an Oltcit Club. This was a Romanian import produced from a joint venture between the Romanian government and Citroen. It combined modern styling with pitifully poor performance and notorious reliability problems.

"Why," Simona's mother asked her husband, "are there so many available for sale now? If it's available, it can't be any good!" Yet they needed a car, so Simona's dad bought it.

Božena was right to be suspicious. After a month, the transmission failed. The dealer promised to fix it for free. But, he added casually, it would take at least a year to get the parts delivered from the Romanian factory.

A good communist would have consoled Simona's parents by reminding them that inessential consumer items, like a quality car, could not become a state priority until other basic proletarian needs were met—such as decent infrastructure for Central and Eastern Slovakia's many poor villages, better health care for all, and a modernized Czechoslovak military able to compete with the capitalist enemies in the West. After all, the raison d'être of the Communist Party was to work for the good of the entire *proletariat* (working class) and not simply Simona's relatively well-off family in the capital city.

This raison d'être was vital to communist rule. Communism came to Czechoslovakia in a Soviet-sponsored coup d'état in February 1948. A convincing story for dispensing with democratic procedures was thus important to securing public cooperation with the dictatorship that followed. Many, like Simona's peasant grandmother, Štefania, embraced communism because it improved her life measurably. Others, like Štefania's husband, Alexander, were idealists. In World War II, he did costly things on behalf of the proletariat—at great personal sacrifice. Yet, many cooperated out of habit or because they feared what would happen if the authorities found out. Once the communists established new norms of expected behavior, people often complied with communist rules and norms simply because they were worried about what "the neighbors might think." As in the revolutions of 1989, peer groups were powerful arbiters of social behavior.

Whatever the reasons, the average citizen's "voluntary contributions to order" made up the regime's legitimacy. Without legitimacy, the government would have had to bribe or compel people to secure their day-to-day obedience. The communists, of course, did a lot of both, but they could not threaten or buy off everyone all the time. They needed people to obey even when no one was looking. Hence, in addition to idealism, fear, and greed, they nurtured a vital concoction of social expectations and feelings of what was appropriate so that citizens would voluntarily do what the party wanted them to do. The communists' legitimation story established a moral system that instructed people in what they were expected to value, that told them how to act to achieve it, and that justified punishments for deviation.[1]

This story was ordered around the stunningly ambitious thinking of Karl Marx and Vladimir Lenin. Thanks to Marx and his collaborator, Friedrich Engels, communists claimed a unique and privileged insight into the "laws of history," which they referred to as historical materialism. Historical materialism argued that history had to unfold in a certain, inevitable way that guaranteed the eventual collapse of the capitalist order followed by a final stage of communism.

Marx showed how capitalism is exploitative and unjust. Capitalists are the owners of the land, equipment, knowledge, and finance necessary to make wealth. They have property rights over these means of production and rely on the police and court system to prevent others from taking their property from them. The Marxist tradition emphasizes that this system is quite violent. It may not appear to you to be violent, but that is because in a legitimate capitalist system, few people violate the rules about property ownership. If you want to find the violence in the system, try walking out of a Best Buy with an unpurchased iPad. I don't recommend it. Indeed, all capitalist and democratic states rely on such violence to function, and the United States, with its racist system of policing and mass incarceration, relies on it more than many others. We will return to this below.

To get access to the benefits of capitalism, Marx argued, one had to exchange one's labor on the market for sustenance. However, one's labor alone did not bring much of a return. The fastest road to riches was therefore to accumulate the land, natural resources, knowledge, machines, and financial assets that go into building wealth. Marx's insight was that possessing capital allowed its owner to profit disproportionately from the labor of the many. This extracted profit was the "surplus value of labor."[2]

In his 1869 work *Capital*, Marx argued that the value produced by machines came from the laborers operating them, but ironically, as competition between firms drove production to become more mechanized, there would be fewer workers to exploit, and profits would fall. Capitalism was thus prone to periodic crises of overproduction in which many firms would fall into unprofitability and die. Marx predicted that these periodic crises would become more devastating as capital concentrated into the hands of fewer capitalists after each crisis. Eventually, the cycle would develop to such a level of dysfunction that workers, with some instruction from the communists, would revolt and displace the bourgeois ruling class at the head of the state.

Marx and his collaborator, Friedrich Engels, laid out many of these precepts in a pro-revolutionary 1848 pamphlet called *The Communist Manifesto*. This document became something of a sacred text among Marxists.[3]

The revolution would bring the industrialized world toward communism, the final stage of history. Marx praised the bourgeoisie for completing the historical task of creating a highly productive industrial and agricultural apparatus that could provide plenty for humanity—if only its products were distributed fairly and rationally. Once in control of the state, the workers' historical task was therefore to establish a dictatorship of the proletariat that would take control of the capitalists' property: their land, factories, mines, and shops. They would then operate the means of production on behalf of all, providing a fair share for everyone. When the progressive, egalitarian, and technocratic rule of the dictatorship eliminated material want, class conflict would cease. With no conflict, the need for a robust state to determine property relations simply would, to paraphrase Friedrich Engels, die out.[4]

People would change too. With people free from want, competition with others over property would dwindle, and humankind would no longer be obsessed with personal gain. Workers would no longer have reason to envy the rich (as the rich would no longer exist) while the former middle class would shed its "class consciousness" and selfish, "petit bourgeois" demands for things like . . . well, the functioning, privately owned automobile that Ferko tried to buy in 1989.

Marx got many things wrong. One of the most important was that in the advanced industrial nations, wages were going up. Marx had expected them to stay near subsistence level. Instead, factory managers found they had to compete with other managers to attract the most skilled laborers to meet industry's increasingly complex technology and organizational needs. They did this by offering higher wages. The combination of a scarcity of skilled labor and the ability of workers to combine into unions, which could collectively demand higher wages, helped improve the conditions of the working class.

This contributed to an important turn often referred to as Marxism-Leninism. In his classic work *What Is to Be Done?* (1902) and subsequent later essays, Russian Marxist thinker Vladimir Lenin observed that workers in the most developed industrial states were losing their revolutionary fervor as their wages improved. Instead of seeking to smash the system, trade unions were striking to gain a larger share of the profits, better working conditions, and more political participation. To Lenin, the rising prosperity of English workers was not an improvement. It divided the working class, softened the hard edges of capitalism where it was most advanced, and made revolution less likely.

Lenin grew particularly frustrated with those communist thinkers who, relying on a close interpretation of Marx, were content to wait for the inevitable crises of capitalism to produce a workers' revolution. *What Is to Be Done?* introduced the idea of the "Vanguard Party"—a disciplined group of revolutionaries whose historical task was to lead (and educate) the working class.[5] Later, in his work *State and Revolution*, Lenin made little mention of the Vanguard Party. Instead, he predicted that all people would eventually become administrators of the state apparatus.[6] In the Russian Revolution of 1917, however, Lenin's party of professional revolutionaries operated very much on the vanguard model.

Like capitalism, communism involved violence, but unlike capitalism, where violence was conservative, communist violence would be transformative—at least at first. I once had a student at Tufts University named Peter. He was a big, friendly guy who also happened to be a self-styled revolutionary. Anytime I criticized a 20th-century Marxist regime, he'd approach me after class to deliver a stern but respectful rebuke,

"But that wasn't Marxism!" he'd object. "Real Marxism has never been given a chance." We'd go back and forth on this quite frequently.

One day, however, Peter came in concerned. He'd found this new website on the internet run by the conservative, free market CATO Institute. Peter had taken a political personality test and took exception to the website's finding that he had an "authoritarian personality."

"But I want to help people, not hurt them," Peter told me after class.

"Pete," I asked, "do you believe that there needs to be a working-class revolution?"

Yes, Peter, agreed, we need to socialize wealth.

"Well, Pete," I responded, "my parents have two cars and a vacation home. Would they be able to keep those?"

No, Peter, admitted. They would not—there are many people with no home at all.

"And," I asked, "if they don't give it freely to the state through some democratic process . . . ?"

The revolution would have to take it by force, Peter continued.

"Armed force?" I asked.

Yes, by armed force, if necessary.

Give Peter dictatorial power and he might have to shoot my parents! But the point here is that a good communist might be unfazed by this. They would point out that while the revolution uses transformative violence to produce a more just society, capitalism uses violence to keep society unjust.

Marxist-Leninist thinking about violence and the state disrupted over three centuries of Anglo-American liberal thinking about justice, property, and state violence. The liberal tradition stresses the need to preserve the agency of the individual in relation to the state, defined by Max Weber as a "human community that (successfully) claims the monopoly of the legitimate use of physical force within a given territory."[7]

Individual liberty, liberals believe, is threatened by both too much and too little state power. Without a state, that is, *too little* state power, there is no one to protect individuals from being robbed, enslaved, or destroyed by better-armed bandits. As Thomas Hobbes pointed out in 1651, this threat suppresses one's willingness to invest capital and employ labor. Yet without individual investment in the future, poverty and human misery become normal.[8]

However, the tradition continues, states can also have *too much* power. In 1689, John Locke warned that when citizens allow a state to have "absolute arbitrary power," rulers may use it to rob individuals of the fruits of their labor. This threat also suppresses investments in capital and labor and can lead to poverty and misery.[9]

Liberalism thus envisions a paradox of state power. We need a state to protect us from banditry and chaos, but how do we keep the state from taking our property for its leaders? Is there a "Goldilocks zone" of state power? Locke tried to find it. He designed a constitutional structure intended to get the level of state power "just right." His solution was to make the right to be a lawmaker contingent upon the consent of the property owners and to separate the power to make laws from the power to execute and interpret them. Locke predicted that property holders would not elect tyrants who would vote to take away their property. He thus envisioned constrained, contractual forms of government in which the property-owning classes elect parliaments—separate from executives—that rule by the consent of the governed.

The accountability of lawmakers to the ruled and the separation of powers created a safer home for capital—allowing investments to flourish over time. I call this the "Lockean state," not because he invented it but because he described it best, first. Lockean states have property-holding electorates, representative parliaments, constrained executives, and laws that should apply equally to the enfranchised. By design, they tend to be self-restrained—at least toward those who have the vote.[10] Restraint, in turn, drastically decreases the risk of doing business. It creates what David Hume calls a "just society" in which capitalists are secure in their property, protected from coercion by both bandits and the state, and able to use the courts and police to uphold contracts they make with others.[11] As political economist Robert Bates points out, these reduce the risk of investing over time and promote economic development.[12]

It took Marx to point out that the Lockean state arguably has been the single most important innovation in the history of economic development. By harnessing state horsepower to an entrepreneurial cart, capitalists have created massive productive capacity that has the potential to permanently eliminate poverty. This is no small accomplishment, and in *The Communist Manifesto*, Marx seems almost effusive in his praise for the historically progressive accomplishments of the bourgeois state.

Yet, lest we get too comfy with Locke and the liberal tradition, we briefly need to explore the broader radical critiques in which Marx has played no small part. Radicals remind us that while the Lockean state helped harness the unprecedented productive power of capitalism, one cannot separate this accomplishment from the immiseration and impoverishment of millions. When Locke wrote his treatise, some of the worst atrocities of the Western era of humanity were already underway. Europeans had long established ownership over human beings from Africa and the Americas, and sovereigns across Europe embraced the Pope's 1494 doctrine of discovery that gave his Christian flock the sacred "right" to claim the communal and indigenous lands of peoples around the world.

The Lockean state did not create these systems of exploitation, but it did make them more efficient. In Locke's time and for well over 200 years afterward, parliaments were accountable to only a small slice of humanity. These *men* "legally" had unique access to power, which they used to direct the police, army, and courts to provide their domestic and foreign property with a greater degree of security than ever before. Locke's *Treatise* also implied that if indigenous peoples did not work the land in an agrarian manner familiar to Europeans, they lost the divine right to possess it. In short, Lockean states came to be authoritarian vehicles by which white, wealthy Europeans and European Americans used state power to carve out property rights at the direct and devastating expense of others. Building on earlier observations from Marx, contemporary scholar David Harvey calls processes like these capital accumulation by dispossession.[13]

Dispossession has undeniably been a racist and sexist process. Work by Barbara Fields, for example, shows how in the wake of the Enlightenment, racist ideology supplied liberals with ideas to explain why some men were "created equal" while others were enslaved.[14] Similarly scholars from the black radical tradition like W. E. B. DuBois, Cedric Robinson, Robin D. G. Kelly, Ibram X. Kendi, and many, many others show how the most egregious forms of dispossession have been justified by the racial and gendered differentiation of humanity—justifying serfdom, enslavement, enclosure, subsistence wage labor, colonization, incarcerated labor, and fewer legal privileges for women.[15]

The dispossessed have struggled both within and against the Lockean state. In 1944, socialist scholar Karl Polanyi wrote an important book called *The Great Transformation* in which he argued that the unbridled capitalist framework allows virtually anything to be turned into a commodity and sold. People in particular, he argued, are not a pure commodity. In addition to being workers in the market economy, we are also neighbors, fathers, mothers, and children. All of these relationships carry value that is diminished when we are treated as no more than an input into a production process. Polanyi expected rebellions against a system that prioritizes the market worth of land, labor, and capital more than their social value to communities. He saw Marxism as one such rebellion and fascism as another.[16]

A third option has been to become more democratic. Today, democratized Lockean states extend political and human rights to all adult citizens. Yet, this extension of the rights often fails to compensate for the past injustices of racism, and the legacy of dispossession remains a challenge for the Lockean state in the contemporary era. Unraveling racialized patterns of property ownership requires going *beyond* a simple commitment to equality. To the victims of past political disenfranchisement and economic exploitation, the mere extension of political and civil rights, often accompanied by an apology, is inadequate. It does not compensate for how the historically unequal application of "the rule of law" has expropriated the labor and land of past generations and placed their descendants in positions of deep structural disadvantage that, in turn, is reproduced generationally by a state that devotes its apparatus of violence to protect the *inherited* capital and property of the expropriators' descendants.[17]

Marx, Lenin, and the diverse radical tradition thus all have some critically devastating points to make about the historical functioning of capitalism. Yet, few contemporary radicals would advocate returning to Marxist-Leninist practice as a corrective. Lenin's concept of the Vanguard Party, in particular, is deeply problematic, particularly in his response to the paradox of state power.

Unlike liberals, Lenin did not see state power per se as a problem. He envied state power as a lumberjack would a chainsaw—it gave him power to decide which trees lived or died. Locke, by contrast, took the perspective of the forest's biggest trees. "Sure," the big trees might reason, "a chainsaw is nice to help keep our forest healthy and pruned of undergrowth that might compete with us for water and nutrients, but to make this happen, we need to control it." Lenin did not care about the trees' perspective. He handed the chainsaw to a party revolutionary and said, "Cut as you see fit!"

This deliberately unraveled Locke's resolution to the paradox of state power. It allowed the state to transform society but in the process created a number of new problems. The first, as my conversation with Peter revealed, is that the revolutionary Marxist state begins with the confiscation of wealth. This is quite likely to be a violent project.

Yet equally problematic is the means-ends issue that emerges whenever a social engineer like Lenin puts his utopian goals above the preferences of the people he is trying to help. Nobel Prize-winning economist Amartya Sen stresses that one of the great virtues of democracy is the safeguard it provides against the radical efforts of politicians to transform society. No democracy with a free press, he famously asserts, has ever suffered a famine.[18] This is because, returning to our metaphor, representative democracy provides the trees with an institutional channel to fire the lumberjack when he has terrible ideas about forestry. Lenin removed this safeguard.

The third problem with Marxist-Leninism is that it is prone to corruption. To see why, let's give it "the cookie jar test." What will happen if I leave a four-year-old unwatched in the kitchen with a tempting but forbidden jarful of chocolate chip cookies? At some point, the child is bound to think, "No one would ever notice if there was one missing." Will the kid be able to resist taking one?

The Anglo-American tradition is to be skeptical. "If angels were to govern men," James Madison famously wrote in *Federalist 51*, "neither external nor internal controls on government would be necessary." In suggesting constitutional principles, Madison thus echoed Locke and others in advocating representative parliaments and the broad distribution of power across institutions that watch each other suspiciously. Individuals simply cannot be trusted! Lenin, by contrast, had confidence in the ability of his Vanguard Party to police *its own* behavior and eventually cede power to the people, who would then become administrators of the state. This faith in the ability of communists to restrain themselves turned out to be naive.[19]

We now turn briefly to how these problems unfolded in 20th-century communist Europe—with a focus on Czechoslovakia. We will see how, in practice, European communism accomplished a lot but also how it turned out to be violent, personally invasive, and, over time, self-serving for Communist Party bureaucrats. We will explore the performance of some of the Lockean postcommunist states that followed in subsequent chapters.

෨ ෨

Marxist-Leninist violence turned out to be heavily frontloaded because the party's major impositions on citizens usually took place near the start of its rule. Most obviously, seizing the "means of production" meant separating many rich (and not so rich) people from their possessions. This entailed physical coercion or the threat of it. Once property was under centralized party control, moreover, Communist Party bureaucrats often could not help but "rig" its distributional formulas in their own favor.

The violence that accompanied the birth of the Soviet Union had an important wrinkle not envisioned in Marxist thought. At the time of the Russian Revolution in 1917, the "means of production" were too underdeveloped to provide plenty for the proletarian class. In a deep irony of history, communists took power in the one major country where capitalism had yet to create a full-fledged industrial economy. Historically, most countries in the 19th and 20th centuries developed by moving agricultural workers from low-productivity jobs in the countryside to higher-productivity jobs in the industrial sector. By World War I, Russia had a basic industry, but it still had many more peasants farming the land with comparatively low-tech equipment and methods. The communists knew that at some point they would have to complete the Russian bourgeoisie's unfinished task of transforming the countryside and creating an industrial society.

After a period of stabilization and recovery in the 1920s called the New Economic Policy, Soviet leader Joseph Stalin took on this project of making industrial workers out of surplus peasants. Beginning in 1929, the party imposed the dual policies of compulsory agricultural collectivization and rapid industrialization. The basic logic of collectivization was simple: by forcibly organizing peasants around large collective farms, the party could introduce technology, improve economies of scale, and raise the productivity of the countryside. An increase in productivity occurs when a factory or a farm can make its products with a lower proportion of inputs. Collectivization aspired to improve the ratio of inputs to outputs in the countryside and to release the resulting surplus of rural workers, grain, and livestock to pay for and staff a crash industrialization program. On paper, at least, it was a win-win vision. But ideological training and physical coercion were added into the mix to ensure that the peasants did not offer too much resistance.[20]

The Soviet state orchestrated this policy with military force. When farmers held back the requisitioned labor, grain, and livestock, Stalin ordered the party to be ruthless. The subsequent rural pacification campaign effectively murdered, starved, and terrorized *millions* of rural workers, especially in Ukraine, where the resulting famine of 1932-33 is remembered as the Holodomor. Millions more were herded into vast slave labor camps, known as gulags, where they were forced to work under inhumane conditions that no voluntary labor force would ever accept. The new state farms never achieved the productivity gains that the communist social engineers had envisioned, but they did extract enough grain and labor to drive Soviet industrialization in the 1930s.[21]

In the Czechoslovakia of Simona's grandparents, the era of front-loaded costs began with a Communist Party coup in 1948.[22] Czechoslovakia was relatively developed compared to the Soviet Union—especially in the western Czech lands that had developed as the industrial heartland of Austria-Hungary. This preexisting accumulation of industrial capital took some pressure off the collectivization program. Early nationalization and collectivization policies in Czechoslovakia were thus limited initially to breaking the power of elites by seizing their industries and their large, landed estates. Medium and small farmers and shop owners kept their properties for a while but had to pay high taxes. This temporarily spared Simona's grandparents from the attention of the state.

Early Czechoslovak communism was harder on industrial laborers and large owners. With the outbreak of the Korean War in 1950, Stalin put pressure on Central Europe's communist states to produce more by working longer hours under poor conditions while undergoing endless party indoctrination. Seizing large businesses and farms required a lot of coercion. The communist state arrested those who resisted and forced them into a gulag-style, conscripted labor force for jobs—like uranium mining—that were too dangerous to attract workers voluntarily.

Stalin died in 1953. While the Czechoslovak regime continued to repress its dissidents harshly, a lighter grip from Moscow, rural resistance, and industrial unrest led the government to moderate its policies. Communism thus came to Simona's family's small village in Slovakia with a lighter touch. Before the communist coup, Simona's paternal grandfather, Izidor, was a relatively prosperous farmer in a small farming village near Piešťany, Slovakia. His children like to joke that he had the "biggest manure pile in the village"—meaning that he had more livestock than most. With 10 hectares (25 acres) of land, he did qualify as relatively wealthy by rural Slovak standards.

Joining the collective farm was "voluntary" for small and medium-sized farmers like Izidor. Yet, party officials soon put extreme pressure on farmers to sign over their assets and labor on the state farm. According to family lore, near the start of the campaign, party officials detained Izidor and other farmers overnight in Pieš'tany, where they were told about the advantages of joining the collective farm and the dangers of not cooperating. One young farmer took his life the next day, leaving his wife and two toddlers alone to cope.

Over the next year, Izidor's neighbors gave up their farms and joined the state farm. Finally, he was the only private landholder left, and the costs of resistance increased. The party tried to keep a detailed list of his livestock and ensured that he paid very high taxes on his sales. Party officials repeatedly visited Izidor in his kitchen to intimidate and reason with him, but he would simply turn to the window and pray. On occasion, his family would gather to slaughter a pig that should have gone to the state. To hide it from party officials, they'd do it in the barn rather than in the yard. Their immediate neighbors knew but kept quiet.

This and other forms of what James C. Scott calls "everyday resistance" were small-scale efforts, but they demonstrate the importance of legitimacy to the state. Repeated hundreds of times across the Czech and Slovak countryside, private rebellions exacted a cost.[23] Izidor's extracurricular husbandry deprived the state of an important resource—in this case a whole pig—for state canneries, cafeterias, and butcher shops. Yet, to stop farmers from privately consuming pigs, the government would have had to step up its surveillance—a costly proposition when you consider the many hundreds of small villages in Czechoslovakia.

Nevertheless, resistance proved stressful on everyone in Izidor's family—especially when they needed the state to do something *for them*, like purchase their surplus produce or employ their children. His two oldest sons paid the highest price. Classmates belonging to the local communist youth organization bullied Simona's father, Ferko, and her uncle Bernard almost daily. When it came time for Simona's father—a talented musician—to graduate from his music conservatory in 1955, he was left standing on the stage after all the awards and diplomas had been given out. This traumatic humiliation grieves him to this day. Similarly, Bernard, a promising science student, was denied entry into medical school despite his clearly qualifying grades. In the end it was too much. At the urging of his six children, Izidor gave up and signed over his livestock, horses, and fields to the collective farm. He was allowed to keep some chickens and a cow, raise one pig for slaughter each year, and maintain a family garden.

Yet, this story has a happier ending. Henceforth, Izidor and his wife, Františka, would work for the state on the collective farm. Despite their earlier resistance and observant Catholicism, they eventually became enthusiastic and respected members. They were known for their hard work and given increasing responsibilities. Izidor even gained control over the farm's wine and spirits stores—a testimony to his sobriety and honesty. The farm paid them a comparatively high salary, and each year they received a substantial bonus that was somewhat proportional to the original assets they had "given" the farm in 1956. In the 1970s, they had savings to loan to their children—enough to help Simona's parents buy a larger apartment in Bratislava's nicest neighborhood. When he retired in the late 1970s, Izidor had a good pension and free health care.

Joining the collective farm made life easier for Izidor's children as well. His oldest son, Bernard, was admitted to medical school and became a dentist. Simona's dad quietly received his diploma and went on to do his compulsory military service playing trumpet in Czechoslovakia's Artistic Army Ensemble. This was followed by a successful career with the National Opera. His remaining brothers and sisters all also went on to have successful careers.

Simona's other grandfather, Alexander, had a rougher life—despite starting out as an ardent communist. He joined the Slovak Communist Party after being conscripted into the Slovak army during World War II and was wounded fighting against the Nazi-backed state in the Slovak National Uprising of 1944. But his career fell apart due to his short temper, alcoholism, and an altercation in which he killed a man in self-defense at a dance party in his fiancée's home village.

The burden of raising five children fell to Simona's grandmother, Štefania. She was born poor, but under communism her work operating a mechanized milking facility on the collective farm gave her a much higher standard of living than her day-laboring parents obtained in the market economy before communism. She, too, eventually earned enough to loan her children money and was the principal source of the loan behind Božena and Ferko's apartment purchase in the late 1970s. Her children did quite well in school, and Simona's mother, Božena, became the first in her family to attend university.

Simona's grandparents lived in adjoining villages. As a child in the late 1970s and early 1980s, Simona spent her summers living with Štefania and Alexander, bicycling between the two villages, playing with her many cousins, and feasting on the products of the small, summer gardens that surrounded their homes. On weekends in the late fall, she would return from the city with her parents to help one or the other side of her extended family slaughter and process their pig. This was a daylong process—

lubricated by plenty of home-distilled plum brandy (known as *slivovica*). In the winter, they supplemented the sparse state markets with smoked sausages from the "pig killing" and fruit and vegetable preserves from the summer gardens.

As Simona's childhood makes clear, once her family fully joined the system—or, to put it differently, once the state achieved legitimacy in the form of the family's voluntary compliance with state expectations—they did not do too badly. It is therefore important that we do not overly demonize communism. To do so is to fail to understand how many perceived the liberal era that followed communism with all its contradictions: its opportunities and opportunism, its liberties and personal burdens, its new tolerances and old hatreds, its deep recessions and high growth, and its new generational and regional inequalities.

That said, by 1989, the main problems of communism's basic economic model were becoming irrefutable—especially when contrasted with the West.[24] The communist command economy had produced growth by mixing basic 20th-century industrial technologies with a growing labor force, drawn from the household and the countryside. In politically important sectors—those given many resources—the growth was rapid.

However, the sources of rapid growth turned out to be limited. By the early 1970s, for example, Simona's mother, her grandmothers, and her aunts were *all* in the official workforce. The state expected them to be there. Party officials knew that, by requiring them to work in the official economy, women would provide more labor for the state and boost growth. Yet at some point, there would be no additional women available. Overall, *unless each worker could produce more with the same inputs, limitations on their numbers would eventually constrain growth.*

Indeed, in the long run, labor and resources were finite. The communists thus needed to learn to grow by substituting better organization, machines, and technology for labor. Contemporary work by economists William Easterly and Stanley Fischer demonstrates how command economies could not really make this a sustained feature of the system.[25]

The communists' obsession with mobilizing labor was also "differentially gendered," meaning that women experienced communism differently than men. Francine du Plessix Gray has demonstrated how in the Soviet Union most women had two jobs, known as the "double burden." The first burden was their job in the official economy, and the second was their unofficial job maintaining a household. This second job was essentially unpaid production—and it was only partially recognized and enabled by the state. Nor did communism do much to change the patriarchal divisions of labor that saddled women with most of this unpaid domestic labor.[26]

The opportunity to work and the respect offered women's official labor were appreciated and even celebrated by many, if not most, women. This included Simona's mother and grandmother, who enjoyed rewarding and productive careers. They appreciated the independence and freedom that an independent career gave them in their relationships with the men and others in their families.[27] Nevertheless, patriarchal expectations about the role of women in the household remained unchanged and complicated their lives enormously. Božena spent a great deal of her "free time" after work shopping for essentials, often waiting in long lines for the most basic items. She reserved Saturdays for additional shopping, laundry, baking, and a thorough cleaning of their apartment. On most Sundays, Božena would get up early to prepare an elaborate Sunday afternoon supper—their one formal family meal each week. On Monday morning, she would return to work in her official job, never really having had any time to rest.

Women, in general, were stressed. There were improvements, of course. By 1989, Simona's relatively well-off family had a washing machine, a telephone, a car, a vacuum, and other basic household items that her grandparents had never possessed. These time-saving devices at home helped free women for more work in their official jobs—and made the double burden more tolerable.

Yet even this could not change the fact that once most women and former rural workers were mobilized into the industrial economy, growth began to slow. Worse, the economy often proved unresponsive to new additions of capital and even technology. Why was this? One influential explanation emerged from Austrian economist Friedrich Hayek. In a 1945 article, he argued that command economies lost a vital source of information when they eliminated the price mechanism. In a market economy, the price mechanism did all the work of allocating goods and services. In a command economy, prices were controlled by law, so allocation decisions had to be made by a central planning agency.[28] Recall that when Simona's dad tried to buy a Soviet-made Lada, he had to get on a two- to three-year waitlist. In a market economy, the long line of people queuing up would have signaled to the dealer that he should raise the price of that car. As the price went up, people of comparatively modest means, like Ferko, would have dropped out of line, and the Soviet Lada factory would have had an incentive to produce more of that particular export model. Eventually, a market equilibrium price would have been reached where the number of cars people wanted at that higher price matched the number of cars produced.

Hayek's insight was that *prices carry information that central planners do not readily have.* In a command economy, by contrast, the planners chose both prices and production targets through a long, often negotiated bureaucratic process that had little to do with end users' needs. The producer of Lada automobiles, Avtovaz, thus had to gain Soviet bureaucrats' permission to raise prices and produce additional Samara cars for export to Czechoslovakia. In short, no one could act autonomously on the information conveyed by the lines of people outside their doors (or, conversely, the suspiciously large stock of unsold Romanian Oltcits available down the street). To "get the prices right" the planners had to be either lucky in their pricing guesses or actively interested in gathering up-to-date information about inventory and the lines of people waiting to buy it.

Some readers may be thinking that this was a simple technical management problem, long ago solved by firms like Home Depot and Target with bar codes, scanners, and real-time inventory management. Yet even had the planners had access to today's point-of-sale information systems, there is no guarantee that they would have acted upon the information they gained. Indeed, planners might be perfectly content allowing a long line for cars to persist permanently—especially if the sort of auto that Simona's family wanted competed for the material needed to produce items of "greater importance" to the interests of the "proletarian class," like petrochemicals or heavy industrial machinery.

It also bears repeating that economic control mattered deeply to the communists. The entire *justification for a communist monopoly over politics* was that the struggle for communism required a period of dictatorship in which the party developed and operated the means of production *on behalf* of the proletariat. Relying on the price mechanism to determine what to produce, or even some elaborate consumer-driven, information technology workaround, might have implied that the preferences of citizens—through their individual consumer choices—were superior to the insights of the Vanguard Party. This would have undermined the communists' legitimation story and eliminated a justification for one-party rule. Market-driven pricing was a potential threat to the commanders in the command economy.

Yet the alternative—centrally controlled prices and centrally directed economic activity—was inherently flawed. This is not to say it didn't work. It did, but only to a point. After that, a number of problems plagued systems of central planning. The most legendary problem was the producers' imperative to respond to the output demands of the central planners rather than to the practical quality needs of their customers. This is a phenomenon that Hungarian economist János Kornai calls "the expansion drive."[29] There are countless examples of this, but my favorite comes from one of my teachers at Columbia University, David Stark, who spent months in the 1980s observing command economies from the industrial shop floor.[30]

Stark's story—loosely recreated here—begins with central planners in Moscow commanding a regional nail factory to produce nails. The planners order all the resources necessary to make nails—the requisite metal, skilled and manual labor, electricity, transportation, and so on. It also determines where the nail factory's product will go and what price the customers will pay.

Let's assume the nail manufacturer effectively meets the planners' target in the first year. Records indicate growth in the production of nails and a rise in the number of buildings constructed with those nails. The plan appears to work so far.

In the second year, however, the central planners want more efficient production—that is, they would like to see some productivity growth. They thus order the nail manufacturer to produce *more* nails with the *same* inputs. It is up to the factory manager to accomplish this goal. Under pressure to meet the order to increase *quantity*, however, the nail factory manager simply skimps on *quality*. There are many ways to do this. For example, he may retool the machinery to produce more but shorter nails. He meets his production "target," yet when the shorter nails are delivered to the carpenters they find they cannot secure important joints. A shortage of quality long nails and a problem with poorly constructed buildings immediately develop. There is no indication of either in the official statistics.

The story continues. The director of the state-run construction enterprise might then explain to the central planners that his carpenters need longer nails. The planners then include length and quantity in their directive to the nail factory. The factory manager compensates by making long nails but skimping on their width—making them brittle and equally useless to the carpenters.

As the system develops, a number of things occur. First, the plan gets increasingly complex—with huge information requirements challenging the central planning agency. To make the system work, for example, the planners may choose to specify and monitor nail length and strength as well as output.

Second, in the face of shortages of items people really need, enterprises (and families) seek self-sufficiency—losing many of the benefits of specialization. Indeed, the construction enterprise might choose to go into the nail production business and, ironically, given the inability of the construction enterprise to build units to house nail factory workers, nail factory managers may decide to produce their own housing units. Some shortages were deliberate. In Romania, rather than reward families for raising more children, planners suppressed birth control and outlawed abortions. The goal was to induce women to produce more children who would grow up to provide additional labor "inputs" for the economy.[31]

Third, as shortages ripple through the system, factories (and families) have an incentive to hoard resources—even those resources not directly linked to production needs. As a result, enterprises build large underutilized inventories, idle for the long term. This is a loss to the economy that is not reflected in growth figures.

Enterprises hoard labor too. Professor Stark observed a Hungarian state enterprise that went idle for a significant part of the year while the managers struggled to obtain the requisite material inputs. When the inputs did arrive, the factory had to "fulfill the plan" in a shortened period of time. This required 24-7 production runs and three shifts of labor. Factories thus had an incentive to staff what he calls a "labor reserve."[32] Ironically, this overloaded workforce produced little for months at a time—at least officially—another important loss to the economy.

The oddities of the command economy were omnipresent in family life. By the time Simona became a teenager, she found clothing choices and availability so poor that she—like many of the large state enterprises surrounding her—chose to forgo the advantages of specialization and cut and sew her own clothes. It is also notable that she used patterns from Western sewing magazines that her father had picked up when the National Opera toured abroad. Her friends were so impressed by the fashionable Western designs that they, too, were soon sewing their own clothes from Simona's magazines.

Shortages were a significant factor in daily life—not just of "luxury items" like cars but of just about everything of value to consumers. Simona's family never went hungry, but she remembers how bananas and oranges would disappear from markets for months at a time. When Božena went shopping on Saturdays for the Sunday meal, she would determine the menu according to the type and cut of meat available that morning at the market. She, too, would hoard scarce goods when she could, on the assumption that they might not be readily available in the future.

Simona's father was notorious for keeping the WC stocked with several months' supply of a rough toilet paper called Harmanec. Everyone thought he was crazy. Of all the things to hoard! But then the factory burned down and the stock came in handy as shoppers emptied the stores.

The Harmanec paper factory was also a major producer of sanitary napkins. As a shortage developed across the country, the Central Committee called an emergency meeting to determine the best response. The first suggestion was to order other factories to stretch out scarce inputs by decreasing the width and absorbency of sanitary napkins made at other factories! In the end, however, the committee bought napkins from neighboring Austria.[33]

Over time, shortages shaped social interaction and attitudes. People began to look at their workplace for insider resources to be traded or used. The workplace thus became a "positional resource" that could help one cope with constant shortages. As often as not, one made these work-related resources available to others without a quid pro quo. Reciprocal cheating—or providing something for others with the understanding that they would someday provide something for you—became a basic moral-cultural understanding of society. A common saying emerged: "*If you don't steal from your factory, you steal from your family.*" Under this system, one's wealth and opportunities came less from hard work—which was poorly rewarded—and more from the resources available from one's extended social network. What we might call "corruption" was often *morally expected* and informally valued.

In Slovakia, the word for an insider connection is *známosť*. Under communism, those with a great deal of *známosť* did better than those without. But virtually everyone had it somewhere, because virtually everyone had a link to the state-run economy. Being a top party member was kind of like carrying a *známosť* credit card—a permit to empty any cookie jar appropriate to one's rank in the party. Party members could always jump to the head of a line by waving their credentials—or at least that was Božena's impression. Needless to say, this sort of party *známosť* was resented by those who didn't have it.

Personally, Božena would have loved to have *známosť* with the butcher, but she did not and therefore had to settle for just being extra polite in the hope that he would not give her the worst cuts of meat. The butcher was one of the most powerful people at the market. Božena's personal *známosť* came from her students' parents at the middle school where she taught. I saw this in action long after the fall of communism when I naively booked a research trip from Slovakia to Ukraine without getting the requisite visa. With only two days to go before my trip, I discovered that the normal visa process took one to two weeks to complete and that there was no way to expedite it. Božena took care of me though. The morning after my discovery, she took my passport to her middle school. When she got home, she told me to report to the Ukrainian embassy's side gate the next morning at exactly 10:00 a.m. with two bottles of Slovak champagne. It turned out that one of her students was the child of a Ukrainian diplomat. The next morning, with a mix of embarrassment and relief, I walked past the long embassy line, rang the buzzer, and right there at the door exchanged the champagne for the passport and visa. No one in line objected, but there were some glares—clearly I had some powerful *známosť*.

Czechoslovak party economists realized the basic problems with the command economy model as early as the 1960s, leading to a number of experiments in decentralization in economic decision-making. The Hungarian experiment in decentralized reform communism—known officially as the New Economic Mechanism but colloquially as *"gulas communism"*—was the most notable. Hungary, as well as Yugoslavia, experimented by allowing firms to make their own marketing and production decisions.[34] Communists soon found out, however, that giving greater autonomy to enterprise directors simply allowed them to divert more resources from the official economy to their private networks. In Hungary, David Stark saw personally how more skilled workers frequently won the right to use state factory equipment and labor to work off hours in what were essentially private endeavors.[35] They produced many needed things and helped the Hungarian economy reach higher standards of living than elsewhere, but they also did so by draining resources from the official state economy. Moreover, when firms ran into financial trouble, the state simply bailed them out—creating what Hungarian economist János Kornai has famously called "the soft budget constraint."[36]

By the late 1980s, factory managers across the communist world took this logic to its extreme by using the newly earned right to set up private cooperatives to perform all sorts of services for state companies. Of course, the state company often overpaid for these services, creating another drain on the official economy and eventually bankrupting the state company.[37] We'll return to this practice in the next chapter.

Decentralizing decisions from the planning agency to the factory directors thus ensured that the state economy subsidized the private activities of those state officials with positional power to draw on state assets. Far from improving the efficiency of the state economy, decentralization and partial marketization thus accelerated its decline—which was exactly the reason the party had banned entrepreneurial activity in the first place.

Another important experiment occurred during the Czechoslovak "Prague Spring" of 1968. Again, reformers envisioned the decentralization of decision-making power in the economy and the partial introduction of market mechanisms.[38] The unwillingness of Czechoslovak bureaucrats to release control over enterprises, however, led Minister of Finance Ota Šik and other reformers to support introducing basic civil and political freedom and holding a contested election for party positions. Šik and others, like the pro-reform intellectual Zdeněk Mlynář and the newly elected party leader, Alexander Dubček, reasoned that this was the only way to get entrenched, hardline central planners to release their grip on the economy.[39]

Yet, free party elections and the freedoms of speech and assembly that went with them implied that average citizens could make better decisions through a democratic process than could the unelected communist bureaucrats. Moscow found this unacceptable. The Warsaw Pact invasion of August 22, 1968, put the hard-liners firmly back in control. Šik immigrated to Switzerland.

The bottom line is that *command economies could not transition from growth based on bringing new raw materials, technology, and labor into economic production to growth driven by making better use of these inputs.*[40] Solutions threatened the essential justification for party rule or increased corruption by providing new opportunities for those with "positional resources" to prey on the state economy. All "solutions" eventually raised the suggestion that the real problem was the party's insistence on managing the economy rather than trusting the decentralized, voluntary economic decisions of people. In lieu of such a solution, communist Europe's high postwar growth rates slowly declined as governments ran out of new resources and labor and as communist managers, bureaucrats, and average citizens gamed the system.[41]

One should note, however, a brief exception in the 1970s where many command economies temporarily restored the very high growth rates of several decades earlier. The main causes of the increase in Czechoslovakia were threefold. First, after the Warsaw Pact invasion of 1968, hard-liners raised prices to levels reflecting the product's scarcity. With foreign tanks and soldiers in the streets, no one complained much about more expensive beer and sausage. Yet, this helped stifle demand and kept the stores relatively better stocked than elsewhere. Second, the emergence of plentiful Soviet oil from Siberia gave a lively bounce to growth in the Soviet Union and allowed the Soviets to provide Eastern satellite states like Czechoslovakia with cheaper, subsidized energy.[42]

Finally, Poland, Hungary, Yugoslavia, and others borrowed heavily from Western banks. These credits were in turn made possible by deposits of Arab "petrodollars." Following a quadrupling of oil prices in 1973, Arab oil exporters were making more money than they could spend, so they deposited the surplus dollars in banks in New York and London. With the relaxation of Cold War tensions during détente, the banks happily found new clients for loans in the communist East.[43] Communist countries borrowed liberally. They then used the cash to supplement their people's diets with imported food and to buy efficient new Western machines to improve productivity temporarily.[44]

Czechoslovakia did not borrow as much as its neighbors, but it did borrow.[45] Much of this windfall was subsequently invested in Slovakia— where there were significant political and economic gains to be made by bringing technology to the underdeveloped countryside and by filling the stores with consumer goods. The 1970s in Slovakia were thus relatively prosperous, forward-looking years. Simona's grandmother, Štefania, benefited from investment in mechanized milking equipment for her dairy farm. By the end of the decade she was using machines to do the work of many of the dairy laborers of her childhood. Štefania's daughter, Božena, graduated from college, married Ferko, and began teaching middle school math in Bratislava. Even though she was a younger teacher, their combined salaries were enough to buy an apartment, purchase a car, and take a family vacation to Bulgaria. For Slovaks like Štefania, Božena, and Ferko, the 1970s were good years.

Yet, Soviet subsidies and loaned petrodollars bought Slovakia only a decade of rapid growth. They did not solve the basic problem of the command economy. With Slovak labor mobilized into industrial production by the end of the decade, the return on new capital declined under the crushing illogic of the command economy. Stagnation set in by the mid-1980s.

By 1989, communism had run its logical course in Central Europe. Simona's family wasn't badly off, but they were eager to see the system go. Their car-buying fiasco was only symptomatic. Most of all, they were sick of participating in the public lie that the party still deserved to be in charge.

Four months after the Warsaw Pact invasion of August 1968, the comedians Milan Lasica and Július Satinský did a sketch in which they discussed the art of playing make-believe. The scenes they played out were silly enough not to be threatening to the state.[46] But anyone with a critical mind got what they were *really* saying. Indeed, after the invasion, everyone was asked to play make-believe or pay a high cost for not doing so.

In the privacy of his own home, Simona's father would rant about the "unbelievably stupid and arrogant communists!" At work, however, he called everyone "comrade" and played the loyalty games expected of him by the state. This was a morally sickening charade, one he cast off with great enthusiasm.

Indeed, the communists' legitimacy story had deteriorated from an inspired, if coercive, vision for the future to a set of self-referential tropes requiring endless repetition that even party members didn't believe. While average citizens pretended in public as if the lie were true, virtually no one really believed that this particular group of unelected technocrats could or should manage political and economic affairs on their behalf. The Velvet Revolution thus gave Ferko, Božena, Simona, and their many friends and family the opportunity to finally stop making believe and openly say what they really felt. In response, the communists had nothing to say in their own defense. They too had lost faith. Bereft of any workable legitimating ideas, citizens simply removed them from power.

CHAPTER 3

Neoliberalism

Why BMWs Don't Just Randomly Explode!

*Jiři conspires against the state . . . A BMW blows up . . . Liberals
make people rich, and poor . . . About those Hugo Boss Suits . . .
Two cheers for democracy . . . The great shark feed . . . Slovakia's
privatization rip-off . . . Paranoia in the Hotel Družba . . .
Who killed Remiaš?*

PREFACE: There was something hopeful about the way Central Europeans
gravitated toward the Lockean state in 1989. I remember my conversation
with Jiři in that smoky, crowded Prague pub on the November 3 night when
it all began to unravel. Yes, communism needs to go, I agreed, but please
don't be so naive about unbridled capitalism. Don't give up, I recall saying,
on seeking a state that cares as much about protecting people as it does
property! Jiři dismissed me immediately. That would require allowing the
same old self-serving bureaucrats to have too much power in the new era.
Better, he whispered quietly over his beer, to keep them weak, ineffective,
and out of his life.

It was my first real-life encounter with the paradox of state power.
Czechs and Slovaks like Jiři were burned out on the state, to put it mildly.
They'd had it with communist bureaucrats micromanaging their lives. The
party had done a poor job of it, and so many party members were obviously
only in it for themselves. People like Jiři favored a state where bureaucrats
would have less power.

The paradox was that when communism collapsed, the state needed
to do nothing less than transform economic and political life. As Jiři so
fervently wished, it had to step back from micromanaging the economy.
But this did not mean that the state could disappear. As noted, liberals
wanted the state to be what David Hume calls "just"—to be a firm and fair

arbiter of the market economy. This requires that the state (1) protects the new property rights it creates; (2) ensures that market transactions are voluntary—not coerced; and (3) legally enforces the independent agreements people make between themselves.[1] In short, to have a market economy, state officials had to be arbiters, not directors, of economic activity. This was exactly the opposite of what the Leninist Vanguard Party had trained them to do.

The first task of creating (and protecting) private property rights was particularly explosive. The state owned nearly everything in Czechoslovakia. Who would get this property? It was a momentous question whose answer would be bitterly contested and would stress democratic institutions. How would the state handle it? Top communist officials would have to leave after the revolution, removed by a controversial new policy of "lustration" (meaning purging or purification), but the bureaucracies would remain.

In addition, democratic elections would produce new top bureaucrats with their own ideas about how an economy should work. This might bear little resemblance to the vision of the liberal economists. How would elected officials choose to distribute state property? How would they envision the state's relationship with the economy? Would they be "directors" or "arbiters"? Democratic politics might not produce free market economics, but liberals fervently hoped they would.

Another unknown was what sort of democracy they would choose. In modern form, the Lockean, property-protecting state is rooted in a liberal democracy in which power is won in regular free and fair elections, where there are safeguards against the overconcentration of power, where the rule of law applies to all equally, and where citizens enjoy full political and civil rights and freedoms. Again, these institutions are a choice, not a given. Would postcommunist electorates choose and sustain them? Jiří did not know it at the time, but he and his compatriots were about to put political and economic liberalism to the test.

This chapter will focus on these challenges and the politics surrounding them. I start with my arrival in 1996 in Slovakia, a country that was then only three years old. It was a time when its market and political institutions were liberal in form but still contested in practice. Much of the stress—but not all—was from the fight over who would get to own former state property privately. Some were winning this contest while many were not. People in and around the government were playing quite hard to be on the winning side. It was, in short, a compressed process of "capital accumulation by dispossession," a contest fought so desperately that it was undermining fledgling democratic institutions. It took a murder for me to begin to catch on to what was going on. So let's start with that.

$$\wp \; c\wp$$

April 29, 1996. I'm living in a Soviet-era concrete dormitory in Bratislava, Slovakia, called the Hotel Družba (meaning "friendship"). It's early evening, and I'm reading an important book called *Privatizing Russia* when an explosion outside bows my window near to the point of breaking. A quarter mile down the street a BMW is flipped on its back—its driver, a man named Robert Remiaš, is dead.

Initial police reports blamed the explosion on a fault in the BMW's fuel tank. Within hours, however, BMW officials angrily asked for clarification. Until then, no BMW had ever simply exploded without a little external assistance. BMW's insistence on a real investigation helped prevent the government from sweeping the event under a rug. In subsequent weeks, the government of Prime Minister Vladimír Mečiar fired two investigators, allegedly for being too diligent. The third obligingly suspended the police inquiry into the murder. Still, the investigator admitted to BMW, around 200 grams of the Czech-made explosive Semtex had ignited the car's propane tank.

Robert Remiaš's murder was likely the result of a conflict between the prime minister and Slovakia's largely honorary president, Michal Kovač Sr. Originally allies, Mečiar and Kovač had fallen out over the future direction of the country. By the time I arrived in January 1996, the spat had gotten out of hand.

My good friend and mentor Kevin Deegan-Krause filled me in on the details soon after I arrived. Prime Minister Mečiar appeared to be at war with the president. Mečiar's secret service no longer offered President Kovač personal protection and Mečiar's government sought to undermine him wherever possible. In one particularly dirty trick, the secret service allegedly drugged and kidnapped the president's son, doused him in alcohol, and dumped him in neighboring Austria. Kevin speculated that the service expected the Austrians to arrest Kovač's son on fraud charges then pending against him in Germany. If that is the case, the plan went awry. The Austrians simply returned Mr. Kovač Jr. to Slovakia. He then went to the independent press with details of his ordeal. Remiaš was most likely murdered for helping independent journalists tie the government to the kidnapping.[2]

Why were the president and the prime minister in such a fight? It boils down to a conflict over power and property. Simply put, Prime Minister Mečiar was attacking the country's fledgling democratic institutions, including his opposition in parliament, the courts, civil society, and even the electoral process. In almost all spheres, Mečiar acted as if he wanted to return to the illiberal model of the top-down, one-party state.

Meanwhile, his government was privatizing state property to friends and allies on terms that angered people whenever they found out the details. Ironically, the book I had been reading the night of Remiaš's death made an amazing statement. It read, "The principal objective of reform was to depoliticize economic life."[3] I admire and learned a lot from this book, yet all I had to do that night was look out the window to see that the depoliticization of economic life was *not* what was happening in Slovakia or in neighboring countries. Indeed, it appeared to me—and the growing scandal around Remiaš's death confirmed it—that high-stakes reforms like privatization were sharpening the political conflict.

I had, at the time, theories to explain this, but they were incomplete. At the time, I was only a few months into my dissertation research. Are political freedom and economic freedom, I wondered, compatible in a postcommunist setting? Many of the learned professors I read at the time expected that, if given time to deliberate, voters would use their political liberties to reject liberal economic reforms if they became too painful. Experience showed, two economic advisers wrote, that "a fragile democratic opening combined with a deep economic crisis is a fertile brew for populist politics. Only decisive actions by a reformist government can keep these populist pressures in check."[4] While certainly not advocating a return to authoritarianism, policy makers and academics began to write about public participation as a problem for the economic reform process and to discuss ways to manage it better or to circumvent it altogether.[5]

Mečiar's illiberal behavior helped us to understand how this was incomplete. He certainly had populist leanings and the support of many voters who had been hurt by economic reform. But the broader lesson was that it wasn't society that was the biggest danger to liberalism but rather the politicians and their allies. To understand why, however, we first need to explore the sorts of economic reforms being applied all over postcommunist Europe at the time, and then we need to look more deeply into why someone connected to the government of Vladimír Mečiar was allegedly willing to murder Robert Remiaš.

THE LIBERAL BLUEPRINT: Why would scholars have expected voters to reject economic liberalism? The answer is that liberal economic reforms can be painful for many. In the 1990s, there was already a lot of experience with this. The fall of communism came after a decade of deep financial crisis in state-directed economies around the world. Many of the economists I encountered in graduate school prescribed some variant of economic liberalism as the cure. Everywhere one looked—whether it was to international financial organizations like the World Bank and the International Monetary Fund (IMF) or to leading programs in economics like Harvard or the University of Chicago—economic liberalism dominated discussions about how to structure the relationship between the individual and economic activity.

Economists and policy makers diverged widely over the details of reforms, but most policy makers agreed that economies performed better when citizens had individual responsibility for ensuring their own economic well-being and more choices to secure it. Because this loose consensus was so strongly associated with the IMF, the World Bank, and the US Treasury—all DC-based institutions—it came to be called the Washington Consensus.[6]

Support for the liberal blueprint in Czechoslovakia was remarkably strong. While there were many disagreements over timing and the role of the state, few disagreed with the need to introduce a market economy and integrate this economy into global markets abroad. Yet the changes required could not have been more stark. Rather than having one's economic well-being brokered by the state, as it was under communism, one would now have to do much more of the brokering oneself. Indeed, economic liberalism functions by attaching clear consequences to one's choices and then letting one's own self-interest do the rest. Feel like slacking off at work? Under communism, that was relatively normal and sometimes even accepted. Under capitalism, it is often a surefire recipe for getting fired. After all, your boss also faces consequences. If you can't help them succeed, they too will soon find themselves out of work. Consequences ensure that people's hard work is duly rewarded—or the lack thereof, punished.

The rub is that liberalism also entails a politically challenging return to inequality. People can do quite well under the competitive conditions of liberalism, but they can also do quite poorly. Moreover, it is generally predictable who these winners and losers will be. To succeed in the globalizing market economy of Czechoslovakia in the early 1990s, for example, *it really helped* to be young, educated, able to speak foreign languages, and living in or near one of the major cities where most of the jobs were being created.[7] And, as we shall see, the bureaucrats of the old communist system and their children possessed some important advantages as well.

Opportunities (and the distribution of familial burdens) were also gendered and racialized. So, opportunities to do well in the new market economy affected men differently than women. The Roma were particularly disfavored by being at the intersection of several forms of disadvantage, including intense racial prejudice and discrimination, poverty, and few meaningful educational opportunities.

The path to "real consequences" began in earnest in Central Europe between 1990 and 1992. Every country did things differently, but most had the advice of Western or Western-inspired economists, like Harvard's Jeffrey Sachs. Sachs advised multiple governments on economic reform and successfully lobbied Western governments to reduce billions of dollars in foreign debt owed by postcommunist countries, especially Poland. With an ironic nod to Lenin, he summarized the advice he had given governments, and especially Poland, in a series of lectures, the first of which was entitled "What Is to Be Done NOW?"[8] If you'll recall, *What Is to Be Done?* was the name of the 1902 monograph in which Lenin laid out his case for the Vanguard Party. Sachs's obvious point in choosing the title was that Lenin's Vanguard Party had left a mess that economic liberals would now clean up.

Yet the title also implied that, like the Vanguard Party before him, Sachs now knew exactly what to do. This top-down self-confidence was typical of the Washington Consensus. Advocates often referred to themselves as "doctors" dispensing painful medicine referred to as "shock therapy," that their sick patients needed to get well. "There is no alternative," intoned British prime minister Margaret Thatcher. Later, economists didn't even bother spelling it out: "T.I.N.A.!" they would say with a dismissive wave to those with objections.

This arrogance did not necessarily make the economic advice bad, but it did set the stage for an ongoing tension between economic policy makers and the democratic choices of peoples. What if elected representatives chose different treatment doses, timing, or even alternatives? From the economic certitudes of the Washington Consensus emerged temptations to stealthily pass reforms right after the revolutions—to make changes before jubilant people knew what was really happening; to isolate important aspects of economic decision-making solely within the executive; or to embed national economies so deeply into international markets and European conditionality that heterodox policies would become unthinkably painful. The goal was to deny populists the opportunity to derail market reforms—but this meant concentrating the power to make economic decisions into fewer hands.[9]

So, what were these reforms? For convenience, I have grouped them into four major categories.[10]

1. MACROECONOMIC STABILIZATION: The most dramatic initial change that Sachs and many, many other economists recommended was macroeconomic stabilization, an effort to put government spending on a sustainable financial footing and stabilize prices for goods and services at levels reflecting their relative scarcity. This was to be done largely by releasing prices and restraining government fiscal and monetary policies.

Czechoslovakia had a very successful macroeconomic stabilization policy. Policy makers did most of the things the economists advocated, and they cemented them in place by giving citizens the right to convert their Czechoslovak crowns into foreign currencies at a rate that started around the black market price I had paid for crowns just over a year earlier. Should some future government decide to pay its debts by printing money, citizens would be free to convert their money into dollars, deutsche marks, or some other foreign currency. The resulting "run" on the Czechoslovak crown would lead to a collapse of its value and make everyone poorer— something most democratic governments would try to avoid. So, the government behaved itself by protecting the value of people's cash. Given what happened in Russia and Ukraine, this was a resounding success. But more on this later.

Stabilization still came as something of a moderate shock to Simona's family. Given the problems with hidden inflation that her family experienced during its car-buying fiasco, the obvious thing for policy makers to do was to free prices. Shortages and lines would then be replaced by higher prices. This burst of inflation would sop up all the extra money the family had saved to purchase future goods or services. But it would also make many meaningful items, like the new Lada Samara that Ferko wanted to buy, more immediately available. This was known as price reform.

Yet, economists also feared that if everyone was expecting prices to go up indefinitely, workers and businessmen would demand that this future increase be considered in their wages and other contracts. There was also risk that sellers would withhold their products in the expectation that they'd be able to get a better price a little later. Inflation, defined as sustained price increase over time, would then get built into the new economy, a phenomenon called **inflationary expectations**. The trick was, therefore, to limit the amount of new money available to people to access available goods. It was thus actually *policy* to limit the growth of pensions and state salaries to a rate *below* inflation. As pensioners and state workers had less money available to chase goods, retailers would have to stock the shelves and restrain future price rises to attract customers. Inflation would fall and prices would eventually stabilize. Macroeconomic stabilization thus called for dramatic cuts in government spending and an official incomes policy of *keeping state wage and pension increases to levels below inflation.*

Led by Minister of Finance **Vacláv Klaus**, the Czechoslovak federal government released prices on January 1, 1991. Božena and Ferko felt the pinch immediately as the price of basic items like meat and bread doubled and then quadrupled while their incomes stagnated. There were now plentiful cuts of beef and tropical fruit to be had in the stores but much less money with which to buy them. For Božena, macroeconomic stabilization meant switching to cheaper meats like pork or chicken and adding carbs at the expense of protein.

One might wonder, therefore, what good price liberalization did for the individual. Božena's answer is remarkably close to Sachs's.[11] Over time, the real value of her income stabilized and began to move more in sync with price rises. Now she had the triple advantage of immediacy, quality, and choice of goods in the stores. Under communism, her income was not the real measure of her purchasing power. Yes, beef was cheaper then, but decent cuts were only available if one was ready to get an early start to the market on Saturday or wait in a line to buy them before they ran out. Now more expensive cuts were always available and there was no line. Božena instead usually bought the cheaper cuts. But, perhaps more importantly, had the command economy remained in place as it functioned in the 1980s, *Božena would have spent at least four months of her waking life between 1991 and 2019 physically standing in wait*—and that is no exaggeration.

Yet, macroeconomic stabilization impacted women differently in other ways. Women like Božena tended to be employed in sectors, such as education and health care, which were not only less well compensated by the state but also more likely to suffer from spending freezes or cuts. In addition, according to research by Zora Bútorová and others, the market economy turned out to be as dependent on the unpaid labor of women as the command economy had been—if not more. Indeed, in choosing which government programs to cut, policy makers appeared to expect women to freely provide services to the family that the state had provided under communism—a rarely acknowledged form of unpaid labor that kept the economy running. Macroeconomic stabilization thus intensified the "double burden." Nor, according to research by Bútorová's team, did men step up to share more of the domestic work. The prevailing view remained that it was up to the woman to care for the household even if she had a formal job.[12]

2. TRADE LIBERALIZATION: The second major category of liberal reform was trade liberalization. As freed prices, government spending cuts, and incomes policy reduced the Czechoslovak citizen's ability to buy things, more goods and services were made available for foreigners to buy, including Czech and Slovak labor and, over time, property. This began the process of introducing the Czechoslovak market to the global markets of Western Europe and beyond. To accelerate this process, the government drastically reduced external trade barriers and removed many impediments to foreign direct investment, defined as the foreign acquisition of a significant ownership stake in a domestic company, usually of 10 percent or more. At home, trade liberalization policies broke up state retail and wholesale monopolies. In principle, they also encouraged entrepreneurialism—allowing anyone to go into business for themselves.

I write "in principle" because first—and just as Jiří and liberal economists like Jeffrey Sachs worried—these entrepreneurs had to get all the requisite "permissions" from state bureaucrats, those who had yet to get Locke's memo that the role of the state was to protect property holders, not shake them down. Organized crime also became a threat to trade liberalization. Criminals sought to limit market access only to those endeavors that paid them a "protection" fee. They thus limited voluntary exchange and threatened the security of property rights through violence, threats, and bribery.

Virtually everyone who spent time in the region in the 1990s probably has an example. In 1992, my former boss took a short-term contract as a personnel consultant in Moscow for a US-based food company. His task was to find talented local executives to run the new Russian subsidiary. He succeeded in hiring the top executives, but later he learned that his new CEO had disappeared.

After two weeks, the missing CEO surprised the US headquarters with a frantic phone call from "somewhere in Russia." I imagine it started with, "I've managed to secure an excellent delivery company. I am faxing you the contract." The American executives had been planning to build their own delivery network to get their product out to Russian stores. But to save their employee's life, they signed the papers and used the kidnappers' client company for the next few years. The CEO was quickly released.

Slovakia was never so wild, but criminality was (and is) still an issue.

In Bratislava, I grew to be acquaintances with one of the beefy, bald guys hired to "protect" my favorite bar. One day he was gone—replaced by another group of beefy, bald guys and a few new bartenders. In the two or three days between visits, my bar had been forcibly taken over by a rival "security company." The new guys were not so nice, so I stopped going.

Nevertheless, trade in Czechoslovakia grew rapidly, and Czechs and Slovaks began to reacquaint themselves with market competition. This had important cultural and social ramifications. For example, the unequal relationship between Božena and her butcher slowly changed. *Známosť* ("connections") no longer mattered all that much on the market. With new butchers setting up in the city, she searched for a butcher who did not take shortcuts by disguising bad cuts as good ones or by shortchanging her on weight. It took a while for merchants to begin to realize that a good reputation could contribute more to their profit than ripping off and insulting their customers.

Ironically, McDonald's led the way with clean new restaurants, unique food, and a local staff who smiled and treated customers politely and respectfully. From Moscow to Budapest and even Bratislava, the opening of a McDonald's produced a long line of customers eager for something different. Everyone suspected the smiles on the staff were required. It did not seem natural at first, but the example slowly caught on in the service industry.

Indeed, throughout the 1990s, a cultural battle raged between consumers who wanted to be treated better and old-style providers who continued to act as if their position entitled them to behave otherwise. Where penalties for failing in competition existed, as in the growing number of retail trades and services, the customers gradually began to win. Where they did not, as in the large state bureaucracies, public officials made life difficult for anyone who needed their services or permits. Sadly, many of these bureaucrats are *still* in their stuffy offices making people's lives miserable.

3. STRUCTURAL CHANGE: A third area of reform in the 1990s was known as **structural change.** The most important component was to make enterprises more sensitive to market incentives by replacing an indifferent state owner with a profit-oriented private owner—a process called privatization. To make sure this transformation was thorough, many economists advocated stiffening the spine of the market economy by privatizing state commercial banks. Private bankers would also want to make a profit and were expected only to loan money to firms that could demonstrate the ability to pay the money they borrowed back with interest. State banks, reformers feared, would make loans according to political criteria and might let really good new businesses die for lack of credit.

Equally important was to create some form of bankruptcy law that would establish the threat that deadbeat firms could be taken over by their creditors—their assets liquidated and their workers "released" (fired) to find jobs in a productive part of the economy. Many economic liberals shrugged at the potential for social disruption that this would lead to. To his credit, Jeffrey Sachs promoted a social safety net to catch those on the losing end of the transformation.[13]

Liberals celebrated the market's life-changing disruptions as part of what Joseph Schumpeter once called "creative destruction."[14] When businesses were killed off by competition, new entrepreneurs would step in to hire their laid-off employees and buy some of their unused assets—often tweaking, rethinking production, and investing in technology in ways that posed an existential threat to other firms. Old companies would give way to new, more productive ones that would offer both cheaper and better products. After switching to the new companies, customers would have more money left over to spend on other things. Economists call this "trade creation." The messy deaths of old firms at the hands of superior competitors created new wealth and improved standards of living. Advocates of creative destruction and trade creation would point out that the unemployed South Carolinian textile workers of the late 1990s have made it possible for us to buy high-tech cell phones today.

The liberal blueprint thus envisioned creating a Darwinist economic system that kept prices down, improved the selection and quality of goods and services, and, most importantly, created a dynamic life cycle of competition and innovation that would drive sustained growth in competitive global markets. This was expected to be a marked improvement on the old communist mode of growing by extracting more resources from the earth and more labor from society.

4. STATE CAPACITY: Finally, to ensure all this flowed smoothly, liberals recognized the absurd need for *both* a rollback and a strengthening of the state. On the one hand, the state needed a capital-friendly legal infrastructure, complete with police, courts, and prisons, to ensure that property rights were protected and contracts enforced. On the other hand, the state's capacity to interfere in the economy had to be drastically reduced in scope through bureaucratic retrenchment—an effort to get rid of all those state officials who made the life of citizens and entrepreneurs difficult rather than easy.

Liberal reformers thus understood the paradox of the state—that the state is both necessary to functioning capitalism *and* threatening to it. They were well aware that throughout postcommunist Europe, state bureaucrats used their office solely to control citizens' access to state goods or services, by, say, making their stamp of approval prerequisite to opening a new store or, to take an example from my wedding with Simona, setting up a sobriety checkpoint just down the street from our reception to extort $20 bribes from exiting guests who did not want to take the breathalyzer test.

As steps toward markets began, this middle generation of *apparatchiks and police*—the B-team of communism—hoped to turn their positional capital into cash. The B-team instinctively rejected the lessons of John Locke: They acted as if the state existed to enrich themselves at the expense of citizens. They drew riches from merely occupying their positions in the same way a landlord draws rent from his tenants. For this reason, economists call them **rent seekers**.

Liberal policy makers distrusted measures that might enhance the power of state bureaucrats. They recognized that a market economy would eventually require strong state institutions to protect property, facilitate voluntary exchange of goods and services, and enforce contracts. Yet in the short term, they felt, responsible institutions would be hard to establish due to the relentless rent seeking of the B-team.

In Czechoslovakia and elsewhere, reformers like Minister of Finance Václav Klaus chose instead to nourish **entrepreneurs** through the policies of trade liberalization and privatization. Entrepreneurs, the logic went, don't like to be shaken down by bureaucrats, and without entrepreneurs, economists Andrei Shleifer and Robert Vishny later wrote, there would be no one to resent the "grabbing hand" of the state.[15] The bet was that entrepreneurs would organize and force the state to restrain itself. They would, in other words, become a driving force for Locke's contractual government—one in which the enfranchised used their control over the parliament to limit the state's predatory instincts. The path to real democracy and a robust market economy was to create a capitalist class as fast as possible.

Yet the lived experience was much more complex. Simona recalls her parents' surprise in the early 1990s as their neighbors, some relatively average B-level communist bureaucrats, suddenly produced the cash to purchase a grocery store! How, Božena and Ferko wondered, could these officials possibly have earned that much money on their meager state salaries? This was their first encounter with what became a familiar phenomenon in postcommunist Europe: the $30,000-a-year bureaucrat in a tailored Hugo Boss suit and a late-series black BMW sedan. They were among the first to figure out how to become postcommunist millionaires.

For very obvious reasons, these particular entrepreneurs probably *distrusted* the rapid introduction of a Lockean-style, law-abiding state. Far from demanding a better state, they actively collaborated in its corruption. After all, that's how they were getting rich!

Bureaucrats turned entrepreneurs were not the only ones to cash in on their positions. As markets and private property were introduced, many state officials in the command economy benefited from a scam they ran called spontaneous privatization. This was the means by which the top manager of a state-owned factory (let's call him Pavol) transferred the state's wealth to himself. There were many ways to do this—and the more complex, the better. Complexity made the cheating harder to discover.

To see how it worked, let's take the fictional (and, believe it or not, simplified) case of Pavol, the manager of a state-owned factory. Toward the end of communism or soon after, Pavol suddenly found that he had more freedom to make decisions about where to buy materials for his factory and where to sell the products that his factory produced. Given the new freedoms, Pavol decided to do business with a friend (let's call her Katka) who had just set up her own private company. One night, over drinks, Pavol agreed to sell his products to Katka at a big discount and to buy products from Katka at inflated prices. His state company began to lose money while Katka's private company made large profits.

Why would Pavol do this? Chances are that Katka had found a way to cut him in on the large private profits she made by trading with his company. One possibility is that Katka's private company was owned by a foreign company registered in Malta. Katka owned 50 percent of the Maltese company while the other 50 percent was owned by two companies in Switzerland, which were owned by a couple of companies in Cyprus, which in turn also had external owners. These companies did not produce anything. Really, they were just legal entities, often referred to as shell companies, created on paper and located in a small office in a country where regulation was light, taxes were low, and few questions were asked. In the early 1990s, it was almost impossible to trace who held the strings of this web of ownership, but if one had been able to do it, one would have discovered that Pavol owned the other 50 percent of Katka's foreign company.

Through this scheme, Pavol and Katka got very rich while the state-owned enterprise languished. Ironically, when the state-owned enterprise could not pay its bills, Pavol may have even asked the state for subsidies and loans "to help him make the transition" to a market economy and to keep his workers employed.

I like to call private trading firms like this **vampire companies**, because they sucked cash from the state like blood from a tragic goth teen in a third-rate novel. Vampire behavior occurred everywhere, but since such practices were hard to justify to the public, it especially flourished where the independent press was weak, where managers could skirt the rule of law, and where politicians were more immune from public outrage. Vampire companies were particularly pernicious in Russia and Ukraine, where communist elites had not been displaced through a popular anti-communist election.[16]

Recall that, at the outset of my research, I was told to expect that democratic freedoms would be a problem for economic reform. By the mid-1990s, political scientist Joel Hellman began to show how vampire companies and rent-seeking bureaucrats flourished in *less* competitive democratic settings. So, it turned out that our expectation about the tensions between market reform and democracy was wrong: fewer scandals were happening where democratic competition was more robust. Democracy allowed citizens to gather more information about the scams, and it gave them a chance to dislodge the scammers' political patrons through elections and other means. Hellman showed that the quality of economic reforms was directly correlated to the competitiveness of democracy.[17]

In hindsight, this should not have been a surprise to liberal political economists. After all, we had all read Adam Smith, who repeatedly warned about corporate scams in *The Wealth of Nations*. Businessmen in the same line, Smith famously wrote, "seldom meet together, even for merriment and diversion, but the conversation ends in a conspiracy against the public."[18] Here now, in postcommunist Europe, were some of the grandest conspiracies of all time.

Sadly, there was at least something predetermined about this. Unless the fall of communism had produced a real, one-time replacement of political elites and relatively strong democratic institutions, the old elites remained to take advantage of their positions during a time of rapid change. Located in state enterprises, banks, and powerful bureaucracies, they became part of a vicious cycle in which the monopolized production of private capital reinforced monopolized political power, which delivered the policies that monopolized the future production of capital. This was a hard cycle to disrupt and, as we shall see in later chapters, often required civic mobilization, external incentives, foreign assistance, and luck to break. Even this often failed.

In Czechoslovakia, by contrast, citizens drove hard-line communists out of power in the Velvet Revolution of 1989 and established a new political elite in a free and fair election in summer 1990. Economic reforms began in earnest in 1991 with price releases and the beginning of trade liberalization.[19] But Slovakia's heavier reliance on large, uncompetitive heavy and defense industries meant that many more Slovaks than Czechs were being laid off from their jobs. This stoked the fire of a growing Slovak nationalist movement that could argue that Slovak self-determination would allow Slovaks to design a reform program more appropriate to Slovakia's special conditions.[20] In 1992, a democratically elected nationalist coalition secured control over the Slovak Republic government. When it could not come to an agreement with their Czech counterparts, it negotiated a peaceful breakup of Czechoslovakia on January 1, 1993, known as the "Velvet Divorce."[21]

The new Slovak government of Prime Minister Vladimir Mečiar inherited a federally administered, large-scale privatization program that his key supporters in the heavy industrial sectors hated, since it preferred strangers over themselves as new owners. Accordingly, Mečiar sought to disrupt and then replace the federal program with something that served his supporters and governing coalition better.

The federal program that Mečiar dismantled admittedly had significant flaws. In the mid- to late 1990s, I interviewed several dozen Czech and Slovak economists, administrators, and others, and I read some remarkable books and articles by economist Karla Brom and political scientists Mitchell Orenstein and Hilary Appel, among many others. Stopping the spontaneous "vampire" practices that emerged after the fall of communism was one of the major reasons that policy makers, like liberal Czechoslovak finance minister Václav Klaus, felt they had to privatize as quickly as possible.[22] Yet, Klaus was well aware that privatizing to a select few would be politically unpopular.

As Orenstein pointed out to me early in my research, the distribution of everyone's state property to some—but not others—was a politically contentious, zero-sum contest. His own research and that with coauthor Brom demonstrated how Klaus's privatization team reduced this intense distributive conflict with a privatization law that promised to make *everyone* a small winner. First, they transformed most state-owned enterprises into joint stock companies. For a $30 administrative fee, adults could then buy something called a "voucher," which they could use to bid on shares in the joint stock companies. If many people bid on the same company, one would receive a smaller portion of the shares available, and presumably the subsequent price of those shares would be higher on the stock markets being set up in Prague and Bratislava.

Despite the fee, the program really was a huge property giveaway to citizens. If one added up all the processing fees, one could buy a significant portion of the Czechoslovak economy for a fraction of its real worth. Even if one took an extraordinarily pessimistic view of the value of Czech and Slovak firms, this was a very large discount.

It did not take long before a young entrepreneur named Viktor Koženy figured out that he could buy vouchers from citizens for cheap and then combine their bidding power to get a concentrated share of very valuable state-owned companies for a fraction of their real value. Others quickly got into the game as well. In spring-summer 1992, a new class of financial intermediaries emerged—established by young, outsider entrepreneurs like Koženy, managers from the state banks, company employees, and the state-employed enterprise managers themselves. In the fall, actual privatization started, and these new financial intermediaries gained control of large parts of major Czech and Slovak firms.

Voucher privatization divided ownership of the firm into many parts, each now controlled by a different owner. The state usually reserved a large share for itself, as did the company managers and their employees. Ownership of large portions also went to the new investment companies that had purchased citizens' vouchers. Some of these investment companies, moreover, were owned by banks that had been loaning the companies credits that they now wanted repaid. Finally, individual citizens who had not given their vouchers to an investment company had tiny shares for themselves.[23]

One would have expected the new owners to cooperate to improve their companies and thus raise the value of their shares. Surprisingly, however, over time the opposite happened. By the mid-1990s, as the World Bank's chief economist, Joseph E. Stiglitz, pointed out, many citizens found they could not sell their new shares at any price.[24] Something was terribly wrong.

Why? The answer lies in the paradox of state power and especially the liberal reformers' deep distrust of postcommunist bureaucrats. As noted, the policy makers trusted businesspeople more than they did state bureaucrats and thus refused to give their state institutions adequate power or resources to regulate the intermediary companies or the new markets in shares. The liberal reformers' distrust of the state meant for a regulation-light environment in which distinctly unethical practices became the norm. It was somewhat like giving rival bands of jewel thieves the keys to

Tiffany's and removing the guards. If one owner could gain control of 51 percent of the shares—although it was usually much less due to the collusion, exclusion, or disinterest of other owners—that person could then use vampire techniques to steal the valuable assets from the firm. This was an outright form of theft.

Imagine investing $1,000 in Apple stock only to be told a month later that Apple's managers had transferred all of the valuable assets to their own company, making your shares worthless! In the Czech and Slovak Republics, tens of thousands of people had this experience. Most never found out where the value had gone. All they knew was that suddenly no one wanted their shares. And, of course, the mindset of the government regulators was to chalk this zero-sum carnage up to the necessary and inevitable process of property consolidation.[25]

As Stiglitz observed, consolidation of control over a Czech company in the early 1990s paradoxically rendered everyone else's shares "illiquid," meaning that one could not find a buyer for their shares at *any* price.[26] Potential buyers realized that the game was over and that the real value of the company—the cash, machinery, technology, and inventory—would quickly be transferred to the controlling owners' private holdings. This threat provoked owners into a sharklike feeding frenzy, a first-strike temptation for owners and managers to "tunnel" out the value of the company before they lost the ability to do so and some other group did it. Indeed, the word "tunneling," used in this sense, is a 1990s Czech invention.

Sadly, the average citizen had very little information by which to make informed moves, and many got ripped off while the state did little more than shrug. Most hurt were the citizens who invested their vouchers themselves or who traded them for a small ownership share in a financial intermediary rather than for a cash payment.

Simona's mother and grandmother, Božena and Štefania, wisely got out of the voucher privatization game immediately and sold their vouchers right away to Koženy's fund, Harvard Capital. Their immediate payout was 10,000 crowns in cash, or *10 times* the administrative fee they paid for the voucher, well over twice their monthly paycheck. It went a long way to taking the sting out of recent price rises.

Ferko, by contrast, was still smarting from his great car-buying fiasco. Then he got talked into investing in a fund that would be used to support Simona's youth choir. Government spending cuts had axed most spending for culture, so Simona's choir had to fend for itself. For a while, the fund helped pay the choir's expenses, but something happened along the way and the parents lost their investments. The most likely scenarios are either that the fund's companies were "tunneled" by their management or that the fund owners transferred the valuable shares to themselves using vampire techniques. Either way, Simona's dad was robbed. It's telling of the times that he never quite figured out how or by whom.

This was infuriating, but there were few state officials to appeal to, and many of them did not even see the practice as wrong. I interviewed the chief market regulator in Prague the day after Václav Klaus, now the Czech prime minister, fired him some say for suspected corruption. Before he was fired, he thought his job was to "turn out the lights" on the unsavory practices that went into the proto-capitalist process of "creating a new entrepreneur class." He did not seem concerned about people who got ripped off. As he packed up his desk, he told me apologetically, "It's like a lottery—it's up to you to decide how you will play the game. Don't expect we will arrange everything for you."[27]

Recall that another liberal expectation was that these new owners would support the creation of a Lockean state—one that would handcuff government bureaucrats with representative politics, independent media investigations, and the rule of law. Think about it. If you've made your first $10 million by ripping off others, do you really want your democracy to be robust? No, it's quite likely that you and others will buy media outlets to control available sources of information. You'll also find someone to run for office to ensure that the "reformers" don't do anything politically that will hurt your newfound gains. In short, you'll fight to ensure that the real practice of politics underlying the new democratic institutions is permanently tilted sharply in your favor. The most powerful players were working hard to keep the political lights off!

The process of extinguishing the lights was in full swing when I arrived in Slovakia in January 1996. As the fight over property and politics was reaching its height, Slovakia's democratic future was deeply imperiled. Vouchers, it turned out, were only the *first stage* in the great privatization robbery in Slovakia. From its inception, Prime Minister Mečiar had complained about the problems of the voucher program. During his second and third terms, however, privatization policy came under his control, and he was able to do something about it. I arrived in Slovakia just in time to see how "his fix" worked in practice. I quickly noticed that it was somewhat akin to "privatizing the privatization process" to the benefit of his family, friends, and allies. This process took "everyone's" state property and gave it to the politically connected for prices that were usually a fraction of the assets' real values.[28] Obviously, such wholesale robbery would not be very popular were it to be exposed to voters, so Mečiar and his allies led the fledgling country through a morass of nationalist-tinged obfuscation that justified attacks on the country's democratic institutions under the guise of protecting Slovaks from their enemies at home and abroad.

And this is where the ill-fated Robert Remiaš comes back into our story. Slovak president Michael Kovač did not have much formal power over Mečiar's government, but even as a largely ceremonial public figure, Kovač could use his position to expose the misdeeds of the prime minister's government. He began to do so in March 1994 and, like a woodpecker, hammered out a beat of criticism until his presidential term ended. Among his litany of accusations were attacks on Mečiar's privatization policies. In return, Mečiar unleashed his secret service on the president and any others who threatened his power, including, allegedly, poor Robert Remiaš, whose demise began this chapter.

Even I did not escape some very minor secret service harassment. After a night of drinks with a journalist who was looking into the plight of Slovakia's small, harassed Ruthenian minority, I was treated to a loud 5:00 a.m. knock on my apartment door. By the time I stumbled to open it, the knocker had retreated down the hall. He was a big, burly guy who stared at me with contempt, took a last pull on his cigarette, and walked off into a stairwell. Half a year later, my deepening inquiries into Mečiar's privatization policies got my phone monitored—something made perfectly clear by the loud sound of breathing on the line after my parties had hung up the phone. Obviously, their goal was to intimidate, not gather information. *I* had nothing to reveal. The real secrets were theirs to keep.

Mečiar's government abused its power in many other ways as well. This included illegally kicking an internal party dissident out of parliament, preventing opposition parliamentarians from sitting on key oversight committees, monopolizing the state media for partisan purposes, compromising the independence of the courts, politicizing and corrupting government procurement, harassing critical civic activists, and challenging the country's ability to hold free and fair elections.[29]

Slovakia's democratic credentials took such a hit that the country was downgraded from "free" to "partially free" in Freedom House's rankings. As we'll see in chapter 6, Slovakia was also excluded from negotiations to join the EU and NATO in 1997, a slight that helped mobilize Slovakia's youth against Mečiar in the 1998 election. Many feared that Slovakia would lapse into what political scientists Lucan Way and Steven Levitsky would later call competitive authoritarianism, a regime whose democratic processes are so compromised that the outcomes of elections, while still uncertain, are tilted sharply in favor of the incumbents.[30]

Meanwhile, Mečiar's political "cronies" used their growing control over political power to commit some of the more outrageous robberies in Slovakia's history. Perhaps the most notable was the looting of Slovakia's largest industrial enterprise, VSŽ, the East Slovakia Steelworks, documented in detail by Slovak economists Ludovít Hallon, Miroslav Londák, and Adam Hudek. In 1995, Mečiar's government sold a controlling share of the firm to his friend and former minister of transportation Alexander Režes for a pittance. But Režes was never 100 percent owner of his firm. Not content with sharing profits with other owners, including the state, he created his own network of "vampire" trade companies that served as gatekeepers for many of VSŽ's purchases and sales.[31]

Režes was most likely not the first entrepreneur to have gotten rich by trading with VSŽ. Indeed, as early as 1993, Mečiar's minister of finance accused opposition-linked VSŽ officials of using their own vampire company to acquire VSŽ cash.[32] But then Mečiar replaced them with loyalists like Režes, who allegedly did the same thing on his behalf.

Režes's network was thus simply postcommunist business as usual. But Režes also took it to a new extreme for Slovakia—aided by compliant government institutions and a state media that contextualized theft or looked the other way. By 1997, VSŽ was running short on cash—forcing Režes to find new ways to steal. He turned to government connivance to gain control over one of Slovakia's leading commercial banks. This provided new cash to VSŽ that probably ended up in vampire company accounts. But the bank soon ran out of money and had to be taken over by Slovakia's politically independent central bank, the National Bank of Slovakia (NBS).[33]

In their thirst for new sources of cash, Mečiar's businessmen began pressuring the NBS to "cooperate" with their indebted companies by giving them big loans through the banks.[34] Fortunately, Slovakia's democratic framework was still strong enough to prevent this from happening. In 1997, the government only narrowly failed in an attempt by parliament to gain direct control over the politically independent NBS. Had this happened, it is quite likely that Mečiar's governing coalition would have ordered the NBS to print money to "bail out" Slovakia's indebted banks and their controlling enterprises. Companies promoted the NBS takeover, promising to use the loans to help them get through difficult times. Critics, however, feared that the money would simply end up feeding the owners' networks of thirsty vampire companies. This would have also been inflationary. In Russia, ample central bank credits between late 1992 and 1994 helped blow up Russian prices like a marshmallow in a microwave. Inflation rates topping 1,000 percent devastated the Russian middle class as growth in their pensions, wages, and savings failed to keep pace.[35]

The most important watershed in Slovakia's postcommunist economic development is therefore the mass civic mobilization and defeat of Mečiar in the 1998 parliamentary elections. In the face of new rules and practices that threatened a free and fair election, 84.4 percent of the Slovak population voted—led by young, first-time voters driven by their desire to become EU citizens. Mečiar wisely decided to step down rather than try and steal the election. Before doing so, however, he granted government officials—including himself—amnesty for any crimes tied to the death of Robert Remiaš. As of this writing, neither Mečiar nor his secret service director, Ivan Lexa, have been called to account for Remiaš's murder.

CHAPTER 4

Nationalism

*Liberalism's Evil Twin Screws Up
the Enlightenment*

*Fukuyama tries to cancel your philosophy class . . . That "warm,
fuzzy we-feeling" . . . Nationalism soup . . . Ethno-nationalism
and existential angst . . . Hungary's controversial language
curriculum . . . President Wilson flunks a geography test . . . Fascists
crash Slovakia's birthday party . . . Tito's proletarian nation . . . Alino
and Ferko have some wine—and help break up Czechoslovakia.*

PREFACE: Communists claimed to have a monopoly on the truth. The
"truth" justified their exclusive hold on power. The communists' claim,
however, took some significant hits in Central Europe and by 1989 lay
abandoned, lifeless and despised, along the region's historical pathway.
What filled the void in the scramble to justify rule?

The passing of communism gave way to a battle of conflicting new
narratives of power. The dominant narrative was liberal. The tone had
already been set by Francis Fukuyama, who in his essay "The End of History" argued that the liberal principle of freedom had fully triumphed in
history's ideological wars; it could not be improved upon. Liberalism was,
and would remain, logically, morally, and empirically better than any other
"ism" humankind's best minds could dream up. With the answer to all of
society's biggest questions now embodied by some contemporary combination of liberal democracy and freer markets, Fukuyama wrote, history
had come to an end. There were no big questions left to argue about.[1]

In Czechoslovakia, liberals echoed Fukuyama's claim and proclaimed
a triumphant "return to Europe"—the wealthy, liberal homeland to which
they had once belonged. They argued over the exact details, but most

agreed that leaders should aspire to market economics, democratic politics, and integration into Western Europe's two most important "clubs," the European Community (which became the European Union in 1993) and the North Atlantic Treaty Organization (NATO). NATO is a US-backed alliance of collective defense in which an attack on one is considered an attack on all.

Yet it did not take long for alternative narratives of power to emerge. Simona first noticed something new was afoot during the Velvet Revolution when a neighbor, the son of a prominent communist, joined demonstrations with the banned flag of Slovakia's World War II-era Nazi puppet state. Where would a communist get such a thing, Simona wondered? That flag and the many more that emerged in the next few days immediately put people's new commitment to freedom of speech to the test. Could people use this troubled old symbol openly? Would democracy bring a new generation of fascist troublemakers to power via the vote? Liberals began to sound the alarm about resurgent nationalism.

Given the increasingly violent unraveling of Yugoslavia, they had good reason to be nervous. In 1989, Serbian aspirations for hegemony over Yugoslavia's communist institutions were dissolving the glue that cemented the federation together. Meanwhile, under conditions of growing political competition, local politicians harnessed national fears and aspirations with the hope of riding them to power in elections.

It was already violent. In March 1989, Serbian police had occupied the Autonomous Republic of Kosovo over the protests of its large Albanian majority. In just over a year, there would be a small war in Slovenia followed by major wars in Croatia and Bosnia. By 1995 Yugoslavia's collapse had produced as many as 140,000 dead and over 4 million displaced from their homes while leaving much of the new countries of Bosnia and Croatia in ruins.[2]

What happened? Well, obviously history had not ended. Like many liberals in 1990, I had come to think of nationalism as an outdated doctrine of the conservative political right that is prone to extremism. What I did not understand—and what my reading of Fukuyama failed to tell me—is that nationalism and liberalism are siblings, born of the same Enlightenment parents and educated in the schools of the French and American Revolutions. When Central Europeans reopened their homes to liberal politics in the late 1980s, nationalism slipped in quietly behind.

This chapter and the next one explore the intersection of political liberalism and national identity, first in Czechoslovakia, where it contributed to the peaceful breakup of the state, and second in Yugoslavia, where the foundering of communism and liberalism alike led to a militarized melt-down of murder, sexual assault, genocide, and dictatorship. These two chapters are accordingly going to be complex and at times disturbing. I begin this chapter with some introductory concepts about nationalism and national identity and then take an introductory dive into regional history to demonstrate how Central Europe's nationalist and liberal projects have developed in tension with each other. This section is long, but it covers crucial events in Central Europe. It also helps explain why liberalism in Central Europe has had such a troubled history. I will conclude with an exploration of the breakup of Czechoslovakia.

In the next chapter, we'll turn to the breakup of Yugoslavia using a feminist lens that helps explain how a national feeling of belonging can become dangerous and why it can violently spill over into arguments over gender and sexuality. Later chapters will explore the aftermath of these splits.

Nationalism, as Ernest Gellner famously put it, is the doctrine "that the political and national unit should be congruent."[3] Scholars may disagree over definitions and the origins of nationalist sentiment, but most would agree that nationalism as a political movement flowered into importance in the late 18th and 19th centuries as part of the Enlightenment's radical challenge to the ancien régime of aristocratic privileges. Following the American and French Revolutions, liberals made two radical claims. First, they asserted, political institutions must emerge from, and be held accountable to, the will of "the people," and not from the will of the monarch. Second, they added, these sovereign "peoples" should be organized by nations.[4]

It was the second assertion—that *nations* are the natural unit of popular sovereignty—that most challenged Central Europe's liberals in the 1800s to the early 1990s. There were then as now very few easy answers to the thorny problem of how to determine the cultural and political boundaries of the region's nations. Still, liberals were attracted to the national project of creating a unified people who would form the basis of a modern Lockean state. With a national identity cohering around a state-supported language, capitalism would be more effective. Factory workers would be able to follow the instructions of their bosses; businessmen could negotiate and trade; the rule of law would be easier to follow if the courts and subjects communicated easily; and representative parliaments would function better if they legislated free from ethnic minority factionalism. And, of course, the association of the state with what my friend Karen Ballentine used to call "that warm, fuzzy we-feeling" of national belonging would provide states with legitimacy—the voluntary cooperation of subjects with the state's political order.

Yet, there was a problem with this homogenizing state development project, according to Gellner. It naturally provoked existential anxiety among those nationalities without a modernizing state to protect them. As Gellner put it, "Not all societies are state-endowed."[5] This was particularly true in Central Europe. There, historian John Connelly has observed, people have a "particular sensibility" about national identity. For most of the 19th century, ethnic minorities had to deal with large empires intent on homogenizing their states around the German or Hungarian language. Slavic and other nationalists in the region thus came to embrace the cause of national self-determination from a sense of existential dread. Without a political unit to recognize and protect them, they feared that their culture and language would eventually disappear.[6]

A nation exists, according to Gellner's tentative and spare definition, wherever two or more individuals share a culture and recognize each other as belonging to the same nation.[7] Benedict Anderson locates the West European and colonial origins of nations in the printed word—a modern linguistic vehicle for sharing the historical narratives, contemporary experiences, and cultural inheritances that produce a community's mutually intelligible discursive practices. Nations are, in short, a form of imagined community where two people who have never met will recognize each other as belonging to a broader group.[8]

Anderson's concept is an important corrective to primordialism, the conceptualization of the nation as a stable, unchanging actor over time and the root cause of politics rather than its artifact. The primordial view is that nations regenerate themselves across time through biological reproduction or via some mystical spirit, which infuses generation after generation with common characteristics, loyalties, and understandings. One is either "of the nation" or outside of it. Primordialists thus see the nation as one of life's fixed causal factors.

Anderson, by contrast, encourages us to think of national identity as something that is more fluid—the modern result of language, communication technology, and an evolving complex of social behavior. Yet, if identity is like a fluid, it's thick and sticky. Politicians are not free to "imagine" a nation from whatever ingredients they have handy. As Anthony D. Smith points out, to be politically successful, nationalists' messaging must be sufficiently consistent with the shared narrative to have "popular reso-nance."[9] This is a complex way of saying that nationalist politicians must have a populist touch; they must develop their appeal in an ongoing recip-rocal conversation with their audience. Nationalist leaders not only shape the nationalist sentiment but also feed on it by adopting their rhetoric in response to the most vigorous applause. Building a nation requires some significant social skill and local understanding.[10]

Central Europe's liberals produced many artless nationalists, most of whom had to spoon up their syrupy identity soup alone because no one else wanted it in their bowls. A simple glance at the history of Central Europe since the French Revolution provides a long litany of such failed experiments: In the late 1700s, Austria's Habsburg rulers tried to make Germans out of Hungarians and Czechs. In the 1800s, Hungarians tried to make Hungarians out of Slavs. In the 20th century, Slavs tried to create pan-Slavic nations out of Slovaks and Czechs in Central Europe and from Croats, Serbs, and Slovenes farther south. All of these colonizing assimila-tion efforts failed and, in many cases, resulted in state repression, conflict, and even genocide.

To understand these tensions better, we now dip into Central European history from the mid-1800s to the end of communism, with a focus on the Kingdom of Hungary, whose policies helped spawn Czechoslovakia and Yugoslavia. This will be a necessarily cursory swim and a surprisingly dry one for being so soaked in history. Students who would like more detail should consult the sources in the notes, starting with John Connelly's truly marvelous 2020 book, *From Peoples into Nations.*[11]

CENTRAL EUROPE'S MULTIETHNIC HIERARCHIES: Before 1867, the Kingdom of Hungary was a subordinate unit of the Habsburg-ruled Austrian Empire with some privileges of self-rule. Its territory included the contemporary countries of Hungary and Slovakia and large parts of Ukraine, Croatia, Romania, and Serbia. Ethnically, the plurality of Hunga-ry's population, and most of its ruling aristocratic class, considered them-selves Hungarian (ethnic "Magyars") and spoke the Hungarian language. However, the peoples of Hungary also included ethnic Slovaks, Ruthe-nians, Romanians, Croats, Serbs, Germans, Roma, and Jews, among others. These peoples were cross-divided by class, dialect, and religion, but com-bined they made up a slight majority of the kingdom's population. Hun-garian elites treated these minority peoples with racist contempt, loaded with existential angst. Indeed, Slavs were numerous enough to be a threat to the long-term survival of the Hungarian nation.

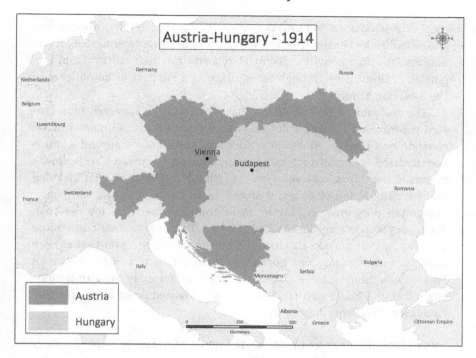

Challenges to Hungarian national survival, however, came from Austria. In the early 1780s, Austria's German-speaking Habsburg rulers demanded that Hungarians speak German in official settings and conduct much of their official business in Vienna. Proud of their culture, their language, and their 800-year-old kingdom, the Hungarian aristocrats resisted bitterly and fought hard for greater autonomy and the right to use Hungarian in state matters.

Yet, Hungarian linguistic demands alienated non-Hungarians within the kingdom. Slavic clergymen wanted a literate flock, able to read the Bible and do business in their own dialects. In the early 1800s, Slavic-speaking intellectuals like the Slovak Jan Kollár and the Croat Ljudevit Gaj found a basis for thinking about identity in the work of German philosopher Johann Gottfried von Herder. Herder rejected the Enlightenment idea that languages were interchangeable systems for communicating rational thought. Rather, to quote historian John Connelly, he celebrated each language as possessing unique value as "a sacred repository . . . through which the Almighty revealed his will for humanity."[12]

Kollár and Gaj came to argue that just as there was a German linguistic nation underlying the crisscrossing borders of Europe, so too were there Slavic nations in Central Europe. These nations, however, lacked states and risked extinction as their peoples became assimilated. Slavic nationalists thus sought existential security for their cultural and linguistic communities through recognition and support at some level in the Austrian Empire.[13]

The question of how to define Slav communities, however, soon created controversy. Kollár's solution was to unite Central European Slavs, consisting of Czechs, Moravians, Silesians, and Slovaks, around a single standardized Czech dialect and demands for a recognized Czechoslovak nation. In the 1840s, however, a group of Slovak intellectuals that included Ľudovít Štúr, Milan Hodza, and others began to challenge this response. Hungarian pressures on Slovaks to assimilate were more intense than Austrian pressures on Czechs, Štúr argued. To preserve their culture and language, he felt Slovaks had to standardize a language closer to their own dialects.[14] Similar tensions shaped the debate among South Slavs, with tension emerging between pan-Slavs like Gaj and early Serbian nationalists and to a lesser extent Croatians, who wanted some form of sovereignty for their own community.

REVOLUTION, LIBERALISM, AND NATIONALISM: In 1848, the peasants, workers, and middle class of Europe challenged aristocratic privileges across the continent. In Hungary, nationalist gentry led by Sándor Petőfi, Lajos Kossuth, and others demanded liberal constitutional autonomy for Hungary within the Austrian Empire. The Habsburgs were already under significant pressure from a rebellion in Vienna. In the spring, they thus felt pressured to grant Kossuth and the Hungarian national movement several liberal concessions, including a bicameral parliament, equality before the law, a free press, the limited extension of religious freedoms, the right to vote for male property owners, the right to buy and sell land, and an end to peasant servitude.[15] These went a long way to establishing liberal governance in Hungary. Yet, Kossuth and other reformers were also explicit that Hungarians were the sovereign people of the realm and that Hungarian would be the lingua franca of the region. This did not please the Slavs within the kingdom.

Similarly, a revolutionary convention of German liberals and socialists in Frankfurt proceeded from the assumption that the German nation would dominate any democratic bodies that might emerge from the revolution. This alienated the Czech liberals who attended. In short, while German and Hungarian rebels were willing to challenge the worst excesses of the old aristocratic order, they also continued to assume that it was the duty of the region's Slavic peoples to shake off their "inferior" ethnic identity through assimilation—starting with the adoption of the German or Hungarian language. The rebelling liberals simply could not understand why a Czech or a Slovak would not aspire to be part of a culturally and linguistically German or Hungarian nation.[16]

Soon after the spring reforms, the Hungarian parliament (or Diet) declared full independence from Vienna in the name of the sovereign Hungarian people. Unsurprisingly, Štúr and other Slovak nationalists responded with a bid to carve an autonomous, nationally sovereign Slovak state from the northern Hungarian reaches where they lived. With some Habsburg support, the Slovaks met in Vienna to create a Slovak National Assembly and a volunteer militia to defend the new state from Hungarian suppression.[17]

These efforts failed. Kossuth's uprising ended in 1849 with the assistance of Tsarist Russia and a Habsburg army led by the Croatian pan-Slavic leader Josip Jelačič.[18] For the next 18 years, Vienna administered Hungary directly. The Habsburgs granted ethnic minorities some minor concessions. Yet, German-speaking liberals in Vienna also feared the emergence of pan-Slavic national movements and proved as suspicious of Slavic nationalists as the Hungarian aristocracy.

AUSTRIA-HUNGARY, 1867-1919: Habsburg control over the empire weakened again after Austria's defeat in the Austro-Prussian War of 1866. The Compromise of 1867 reconfigured the Austrian Empire as a dual state called Austria-Hungary. On paper, it was a victory for liberalism. The Hungarian Diet gained control over Hungary's internal affairs while the Habsburg monarchy controlled foreign policy and promoted a single internal economy. Formally, at least, citizens had substantial civil rights, equality before the law, and parliamentary representation. Yet, in reality, parliament disproportionately represented the interests of the large landowning Hungarian aristocracy and industrial leaders, few of whom had respect for democratic rule, ethno-national minorities, or the Hungarian peasantry.

Slavs in Croatia secured some national rights as a self-governing nation represented by its historical assembly, the Sabor. Elsewhere, however, the state treated minorities as ethnicities rather than as nations. The distinction gave them some recognition but no right to self-determination. Assimilation remained the best personal advancement strategy.[19] Meanwhile, German liberals in Vienna defeated a promising reform for the Czech lands that would have guaranteed German-Czech bilingualism and a level of autonomy in Prague. The defeated provisions arguably would have gone a long way to diffusing growing German-Czech rivalry in the Czechlands.[20]

Slovak and other minority nationalists in Hungary also suffered setbacks. After 1875, policy mandated that local educational and administrative authorities conduct most affairs in Hungarian.[21] As a new generation of Slavic nationalists took up the fight for survival in the face of German and Hungarian liberal chauvinism, a vigorous debate reemerged over where Slavic sovereignty should lie—within the *individual* Czech, Slovak, Croatian, Slovene, and Serb nations or across them in the form of unified pan-Slavic states.

Germany and Austria-Hungary suffered a debilitating defeat in World War I. By the end of the war, some Hungarian elites belatedly concluded that Hungary could never flourish as a successful modern state without offering linguistic, cultural, and political autonomy to its national minorities. Yet, subsequent discussions to redesign Hungary along ethno-federal lines did not gain the support of the elite and, in any case, came too late.[22] According to Connelly, the Hapsburg monarchy was "beyond salvation, unable to produce a structure that would satisfy its various components."[23] Meanwhile, the war had produced powerful new ties of convenience between the Allied victors and Slav and Romanian nationalists.

With French support in 1918-19, Czech, Slovak, Romanian, and South Slav forces seized control over Slavic- and Romanian-speaking lands, but then—with apparent Allied approval—they continued through Hungarian-speaking borderlands to create a "more defensible" frontier along the Danube and elsewhere. The incursion helped radicalize domestic Hungarian politics along both class and national lines. The main beneficiary was Béla Kun, the new Communist Party leader who promised the redistribution of aristocratic land to the peasants, proletarian rule, and a restoration of control over all Hungarian-speaking territory. Many Hungarians thus supported, or at least tolerated, Kun's Bolshevik 1919 revolution because it offered a way to resist the victorious Allied powers' attempt to divide the Hungarian people. Regardless, after Kun's brief invasion and occupation of parts of Slovakia, a menacing French-led coalition of Allied forces convinced Kun to withdraw. Several weeks later, a Romanian invasion supported by anti-Bolshevik, Hungarian troops forced Kun to flee.[24]

THE INTERWAR PERIOD: The postwar Treaties of Saint-Germain-en-Laye (1919) and Trianon (1920) dismembered Austria and Hungary, respectively. The treaties created Czechoslovakia by fusing the Czech lands (parts of Silesia, Bohemia, and Moravia) to Slovakia (formerly

"Upper Hungary"). Austria also lost Galicia and part of Silesia to a newly independent Poland, its southern alpine and littoral regions to Italy, and the coastal region of Dalmatia to a new state called the **Kingdom of Serbs, Croats, and Slovenes** (already referred to as Yugoslavia). The new kingdom received the mixed ethnic South Hungarian region of Vojvodina and part of Bulgaria. Meanwhile, Romanian demands for an economically feasible and militarily defensible state secured its control over Transylvania with its large Hungarian-speaking population.

Everywhere one looked at the map of the former Austria-Hungary, the new states made minorities of the peoples of the former ruling nations. The Treaty of Trianon alone located 3 million of 11 million Hungarians "abroad," that is to say, outside the new Hungarian borders. The Treaty of Saint-Germain-en-Laye similarly "stranded" 3 million, mostly reluctant Germans inside the borders of Czechoslovakia. Moreover, about 10 percent of the population of Slovakia was now ethnic Hungarian—a proportion that persists today. President Woodrow Wilson's promise "that every people has a right to choose the sovereignty under which they shall live" had been pragmatically disregarded over the explicit objections of Austrians, Germans, and Hungarians throughout the region. Remarkably, Connelly has found, Wilson was kept ignorant of the real size of Czechoslovakia's German population by both his key adviser and future Czechoslovak president Tomáš Masaryk.[25]

The new states of Yugoslavia and Czechoslovakia were controversial even among the Slavs they were created to represent. Over the next 20 years, a plurality of Slovak Catholics voted repeatedly for the Hlinka Slovak People's Party (HSĽS), a party that resented Prague's dominance of the new state almost as much as its founders had resented the rule of Budapest before. Organized around **Andrej Hlinka**, a Catholic priest, the HSĽS fought for traditional Catholic values, sought changes in rural land reform, rejected the existence of a single "Czechoslovak nation," and correspondingly sought to reestablish Czechoslovakia on the basis of an equal federation of the Czech and Slovak peoples.[26]

The new state of Czechoslovakia was thus vulnerable to disruption from both within and without.[27] In March 1938, citing German self-determination, Adolf Hitler occupied and annexed the state of Austria. At the **Munich Conference** of September 1938, the leaders of France and Britain granted Adolf Hitler's demands to let Germany absorb the largely German-speaking **Sudetenland** of Czechoslovakia. Similarly, pressure from Italy and Germany forced the Czechoslovak government to cede most of Slovakia's Hungarian-speaking regions to Hungary. Unsurprisingly, these steps met with the broad approval of the regions' German and Hungarian populations.

In March 1939, Hitler summoned Hlinka's successor, Jozef Tiso (also a Catholic priest), to Berlin and urged him to declare Slovakia's independence from Czechoslovakia. In the following days, Slovak parliamentarians agreed, fearing that if they did not comply, Hungary and Germany would divide Slovakia between them. The next day, Hitler's troops occupied the remainder of the Czech lands. A week later, Hungarian soldiers forcibly expelled the Slovak military from Slovakia's eastern, ethnic Ruthenian territory.[28]

Similar to Czechoslovakia, the post–World War I Kingdom of Yugoslavia had a short lease on life. Established in 1920, the new state located its legitimacy in the South Slav "nation," and its constitution explicitly stated that the Serbs, Croats, and Slovenes were "one people." Many Croat nationalists, however, considered the single "Yugoslav nation" to be no more than a fig leaf for Serbian control. Indeed, Serbia's ruling Karadjordjevic family ascended to the throne of the new constitutional monarchy. Far more disruptive, however, was Serbia's demographic weight in the new kingdom. In the founding elections, Serb politicians wooed enough Bosnian Muslims and Slovenes to their side to create a constitution stipulating a unicameral parliament.[29] Without a separate house that weighed ethnicities more equally, the unicameral legislature produced Serbian prime ministers and cabinets and a Serbian-dominated officer corps and civil service. Similar to Slovakia's HSĽS, the Croatian People's Peasant Party (HPSS) waged a frustrating campaign for Croatian self-determination.

In parliament, Serb nationalists shared HPSS skepticism about the existence of "one" South Slav nation but instead agitated, with some support from the Serbian Orthodox Church, for a Great Serbia that would incorporate Serbs in Croatia, Bosnia, Dalmatia, and elsewhere into one Serb-dominated state. Politics soon became violent. In 1928, a pro-Serb Montenegrin delegate shot Croat leader Stjepan Radić on the floor of parliament. He died soon after. This led King Alexander Karadjordjevic to suspend the body and rule as a dictator. In 1934, he was assassinated by a Bulgarian with links to the Ustasha, a radical Croatian separatist movement suffering from the fascist fantasy that the Croatian nation had superior genetic origins in Aryan "blood."

Croat leaders subsequently reached an agreement (the Sporazum) supporting a federalized Yugoslavia, but World War II intervened. Ustasha leader Ante Pavelić emerged from exile in the wake of the German invasion of Yugoslavia in August 1941 to lead the Nazi puppet state of Croatia. Germany occupied the rest of the state.[30]

WORLD WAR II: For both Yugoslavia and Czechoslovakia, World War II was an unmitigated disaster. The Slovak and Croatian governments of Tiso and Pavelić were closely linked to Hitler's Germany and complicit in both German atrocities and crimes of their own making. Tiso ruled Slovakia with some popular support as a HSLS-led, pro-German dictatorship. He oversaw the exportation of Jews, Roma, and others and arrested and imprisoned opponents. In 1944, Tiso's democratic and communist opponents in the Slovak military launched the **Slovak National Uprising.** The uprising failed but forced Germany to divert troops to occupy the country for the remainder of the war.[31]

Czechoslovakia was restored after the war, but the new government joined in with other postwar states in controversially purging their borders of their suspect minorities. In 1946, the Beneš decrees expelled 2.5 million Sudeten Germans and as many as 40,000 ethnic Hungarians. At least 19,000 died in the process, accompanied by mass dispossession of property, starvation, disease, summary executions, and sexual assault.[32] In February 1948, the Communist Party took full power in a coup with Soviet backing.[33]

In wartime Croatia, Pavelić's Ustasha ruled through the terror of fanatical racists, opportunists, and criminals. The Ustasha enthusiastically deported Jews to Central European death camps and murdered many directly. They also considered Serbians to be a genetically distinct, alien population polluting the Croatian nation. The number of their victims is a source of contention, but a recent study reports that the Ustasha killed over 300,000 Serbians in Croatia—about 17 percent of the prewar population. At the very least, 85,000 Serbs, Jews, Roma, Croats and others were murdered at the Jasenovac concentration camp, with thousands more killed at camps and execution sites throughout the country.[34] Ustasha victims often also included moderate Croatians who opposed them. In Bosnia, Ustasha ideology protected Muslims, some of whom joined units that attacked Serbian families in their homes and villages, but many Muslims also fought against the Ustasha.

Ustasha and German brutality fueled resistance from two groups, Serb Royalists (referred to as **Chetniks**) and a communist **Partisan** movement headed by Marshal Tito. The Partisans drew support from across Yugoslavia's ethnicities and included Muslims and Croats. The Serbian Chetniks, on the other hand, often espoused rhetoric demanding Serbian national racial purity and the need to re-create a Serb-dominated Yugoslavia with ethnically pure Serbian zones stretching across Bosnia to the coastal region of Dalmatia. Chetnik forces were accordingly brutal toward Croats, Muslims, and, frequently, Serbian moderates. In Foča, a town in Bosnia, a Chetnik unit killed over 2,000 Muslims in August 1942.[35] As the war progressed, the United Kingdom threw its support behind Tito's Partisans. Soon after the end of the war, the communists edged out the restored monarchy and established the Socialist Federal Republic of Yugoslavia.[36]

THE COMMUNIST ERA: Communism in both Czechoslovakia and Yugoslavia offered a new solution to the old question of popular sovereignty. The communist states could locate their legitimizing sovereignty in the will of the proletariat, not the nation. Nevertheless, both states struggled with national tensions—often emerging from within the ruling communist parties. The parties periodically repressed their national-oriented cadres, but in the 1960s, demands emerged for greater federalization. Constitutional changes in 1968 (Czechoslovakia) and 1974 (Yugoslavia) created stronger republics, rooted in national sovereignty of constituent peoples. Despite these formal changes, real power was held by the federal-level communist parties in both countries. This served as a break on centrifugal nationalist pressures until the late 1980s.

$\wp$ $\wp$

If anything can be gleaned from this necessarily brief and partial history of Central Europe, it is that political liberalism has been congenitally vexed by nationalism. With the restoration of political freedoms in 1989, it is thus not surprising that tensions reemerged from the confluence of newly empowered democratic assemblies and those with rival conceptions over who should be the sovereign peoples of the state. For many politicians, the tensions posed new challenges in constitutional design and language and cultural policies. For all too many others, however, they provided an opportunity: a chance to distinguish oneself as a patriot in a crowded new field of political competitors.

The trend was ubiquitous in the region, but in both Czechoslovakia and Yugoslavia, it contributed to the breakup of the country. Each was formally structured as a federation. Therefore, a simple explanation for the breakups is that nationalists gained political control at the constituent republic level and used that to break up the larger federation. This did not require virulent national fanaticism to function. Indeed, while the rise of Slovak nationalism contributed to the split in Czechoslovakia, the most nationalist voices failed early to catch on with the Slovak public. They were simply too extreme to rival the liberal, pro-European aspirations then sweeping the region.

Slovaks were more united in their concern about the disproportionately heavy price Slovak workers and enterprises were paying in the economic transformation. This came to serve as a wedge between national-oriented politicians and pro-federation liberals. A sort of "reasonable nationalism" emerged in Slovakia in 1991-92 demanding greater autonomy over economic decisions along with more respect for Slovak culture and language. This nationalism carried little real animosity for Czechs or Hungarians. Rather, it asked that "a Slovak perspective" be heard and respected in Czechoslovak politics.

Nevertheless, there were enough ethno-nationalists backing Slovak independence on cultural grounds to give people pause. Over 20 percent of Slovak citizens belonged to one of the country's major non-Slovak minorities: Hungarians, Jews, Roma, Ruthenians, and others. Each community had a story of conflict with Slovak nationalists in the past. Most notably, Slovakia's willing participation in the Holocaust in spring 1942 was inconvenient for the nationalists' story in the early 1990s. The most ardent Slovak nationalists, some with links to the wartime state, cherry-picked Slovakia's history in ways that ignored, minimalized, or misleadingly contextualized such events. Some nationalist intellectuals reorganized history to portray Slovaks as an ancient, Slavic people thwarted early in their national aspirations and victimized ever since by their many enemies, including the Czechs, Hungarians, and Jews within.

In 1990, a small group of politicians and cultural leaders demanded a new language law making Slovak the exclusive language of the Slovak Republic to the detriment of Czech and Hungarian. It was a potentially explosive moment, one that threatened to turn Hungarian resentments about the Trianon dismemberment into a real movement to dismember Slovakia. Fortunately, Slovak prime minister Vladimír Mečiar came down at the last minute against the more exclusionary language law, even calling one of its architects a "dangerous nationalist."[37] The ensuing law could have been much better than it was, but the importance of Mečiar's decision cannot be understated. When elites finally did split the state, Slovakia's Hungarian minority did not try to leave.

Simona's generation had to deal with this reemergence of nationalism. As new opinions tumbled out at the dinner table among friends and family, people took sides. The result was many painful and divisive conversations. Simona was happily touring California with friends and missed most of it. Back home, however, her family split on the issue of independence. Simona's grandfather Izidor could not see how an independent Slovakia could survive—especially with resurgent Hungarian nationalists again assailing Trianon. If Slovaks left Czechoslovakia, couldn't Hungarians leave Slovakia? He remembered before World War II when Hungary reincorporated the Hungarian-speaking parts of Slovakia with the backing of the Italians and Germans and then seized Eastern Slovakia by force. He and many of his generation became staunch pro-Czechoslovak federalists.

A generation down, Simona's uncle Alino—a former communist lawyer—and her devout Catholic father overcame their past animosity to bond over their mutual support for separation. "Alinko," Ferko would say with warmth and increasing fuzziness after each glass of wine, "who would have ever thought we could become friends!" Their mutual love of Slovakia and Slovak culture brought them together.

Many Slovak politicians fell somewhere between Izidor and Ferko. They wanted devolution of federal powers to the Slovak government. Yet transferring economic control from the federal government to the republic-level capitals in Bratislava and Prague was the Czechs' worst-case scenario. The result was a standoff.

On December 8, 1991, in the Soviet Union, Russian president Boris Yeltsin had led a group of national republic-level presidents in dissolving the federal Soviet structure above them—creating 15 new sovereign states from the carcass of the Soviet Union. It was as if the governors of New York, California, Florida, and Texas had dissolved the United States! The majority of Czechs and Slovaks did not want this. Polls at the time revealed that over 70 percent of the Slovak population opposed separation. That was a large number, approaching the majority that rejected communism. Yet, despite the fresh experience of civic mobilization during the Velvet Revolution, this majority now failed to defend itself.

Simona returned from California to find a confused cacophony of views. Public opinion was in favor of remaining together but also far apart on what Czechoslovakia should look like. Negotiations in summer 1992 pitted the Slovak negotiators' demand for a weak Slovak and Czech confederation against the Czech negotiators' demand for a strong, centralized Czechoslovak federation and a continuation of the federal economic reform program. Faced with irreconcilable alternatives, the prime ministers converged on their mutual second choice: to simply shake hands and agree to build independent states. The federal parliament acquiesced, and the date for the "Velvet Divorce" was set for January 1, 1993.[38]

Many found it outrageous to dissolve the state without a referendum, but to take to the streets against the elite decision to split the country, average citizens had to feel validated in their views. Instead, every discussion became long, divisive, and tedious. Perhaps as a result, the divorce proceeded virtually unopposed by public protest. Recalling the 1938 Munich Conference, many observed that once again a momentous decision had been made "*O nás, bez nás!*" (about us, without us). Yet in the villages and towns, there was no outrage, no moral shock—only the muted sadness of parting friends; each side tended to side with their politicians in blaming the other.

This is not a pretty story—especially given the havoc wreaked by Prime Ministers Vladimír Mečiar and Vacláv Klaus in the ensuing years—yet many also sighed in relief. It could have been much worse. While Czech and Slovak politicians dismantled their country peacefully, another federal state, Yugoslavia, was tearing itself apart at the point of a gun. By the end of 1992, Yugoslavs were waging their third conflict in two years, with a fourth conflict just about to start. By this standard, the breakup of Czechoslovakia was a resounding success.

CHAPTER 5

Ethnic Conflict

The Breakup of Yugoslavia

Tito dies . . . The new enemy map . . . Why nationalists want to control your sex life . . . A Serbian memorandum . . . Reproductive anxiety and Milošević's rise to power . . . Existential angst . . . Slobo becomes a Serb . . . War in Croatia . . . Haris becomes a Muslim . . . War in Bosnia . . . Genocide and sexual assault . . . Angels perform Brecht in Belgrade . . . Croatia's witches cast a spell . . . NATO bombs for peace? . . . The Dayton Accords.

As with the breakup of Czechoslovakia, one cannot explain the wars in Yugoslavia without reference to the content of its history and the perennial tensions between nationalism and liberalism. In 1990, anyone over age 50 probably had some firsthand memories of World War II, and these memories were very much in play as Yugoslavia splintered. Despite the intervening efforts of Tito and the Yugoslav Communist Party to forge a collective proletarian identity around the concepts of "unity and brotherhood," the region's aspiring politicians did not have to dig too deeply to uncover real fears and resentments.

However, there were many other factors in play as well. Like the Soviet Union and Czechoslovakia, Yugoslavia was a federation. As we can see from the map below, after Tito's reforms in 1974, Yugoslavia had six republics, each with a different ethno-national majority that controlled many affairs from the local republic's capital. The republics had a great deal of autonomy but also answered to the federal Yugoslav government, based in Belgrade; the unified Yugoslav National Army (JNA); and the discipline of the federal-level Communist Party. To participate in politics in any meaningful way, one had to be a member of the party, and that meant following the party line once it was established. Therefore, while the federation

looked loose on paper, a unified, top-down organization, disciplined by the enormously important persona of Tito, tied it all together.

Tito, however, died in 1980, leaving in charge an eight-person, rotating presidency representing the federation's six republics and two autonomous republics. Their first challenge was economic. Rising oil prices and a US-driven rise in international interest rates created an enormous financial crisis. Higher interest rates meant that Yugoslavia was now having difficulty paying back the loans it had taken from Western banks. With no new loans coming in, the government turned to the IMF for support. In return, the IMF recommended that the government cut spending. This hurt. By 1983, the country stopped growing entirely. Austerity exacerbated old tensions around economic fairness between the republics.[1] Croatian and Slovenian officials complained that too large a portion of their companies' taxes were being spent to subsidize poorer regions. Meanwhile, officials from the poorest region, the Autonomous Republic of Kosovo, complained that they were sinking back into poverty.

Tito's death and the lasting economic crisis helped undermine communism as a legitimating principle and blurred cadres' loyalties. In the mid-1980s, republic-level communist politicians began to assert greater independence from their bosses in the federal Communist Party. First in Serbia, and then elsewhere, they began to challenge the Yugoslav communist "imaginary."

A political imaginary is a term used by Susan Buck-Morss to denote the imagined map that politicians use to position people on the political landscape. Each map has at least three players: (1) a common enemy to fear and resist, (2) a political collective to protect from the enemy, and (3) a protective leader who promises to lead and defend the collective from its enemies. Under communism, Buck-Morss argues, the Communist Party was the protective leader. Its mission was to ensure the victory of the political collective, in this case the proletariat, from the class enemy—both globally and at home. Given the Marxist belief that capitalism's flaws made the enemy collapse inevitable, Soviet communists were usually more interested in buying time until capitalism weakened than in embarking on a risky project of conquering its physical space.[2]

As the Marxist-Leninist political imaginary lost its meaning in the mid-1980s, aspiring politicians struggled to find a new imagined map. Many found it in nationalism. Upstart cultural leaders and communists began to challenge the federation by speaking for their particular nation, identifying its internal and external "enemies," and portraying themselves as the best candidate to protect it from annihilation. Under the nationalist political imaginary, understandings of time compressed: The nation faced an existential crisis and action needed to be taken *now*.

The nationalist imaginary contained a good degree of fretting about sex. It is a common quirk of ethno-nationalists that they often speak of the nation as a personified being—regenerated each generation through sexual reproduction between conationals. Under such logic, if everyone reproduces with a nonnational, the nation becomes impure and risks death.

It is no sin to be concerned about population, of course. States have a legitimate responsibility to help a population to thrive, and this entails a concern with population health. Yet nationalist politicians' rhetorical obsession with the biological reproduction of the nation erroneously locates culturally constructed ethnonational identities in biological origin myths about ethnic and national differences. It also contributes to what Joane Nagel calls an "ethno-sexual frontier" between nations—an imagined boundary that artificially separates peoples from each other.[3] The ethno-sexual frontier provides politicians a biological realm to protect from the enemy. As Katja Kahlina puts it, women's bodies become "symbolic markers" of the nation's borders.[4] Inside that boundary, patriarchs can be empowered to police the nation's will while women are confronted with a patriotic duty to provide reproductive and emotional labor to secure the future of the nation.[5]

Nagel points out that the frontier is frequently transgressed and often poorly policed. Still, it emerges when women face various forms of pressure from ethnonationalists over their sexual and reproductive choices. This logic can also affect sexual and gender minorities who may be accused of choosing a childless life and denying the "nation" a future.[6] In short, the ethno-sexual frontier generates a logic that can be invoked to repress LGBTQ+ citizens and police the reproductive choices of women.[7]

Gender historian Wendy Bracewell explains in detail how nationalist concerns with ethno-sexual boundaries emerged in the Serbian nationalist narrative in the mid-1980s.[8] Prior to Tito's constitutional reforms in 1974, Kosovo was considered a part of Serbia and was administered directly from Belgrade. Tito's reforms, however, changed Kosovo to a self-administered region of Yugoslavia's Serbian Republic. Ethnic Albanian Communist Party members, who represented a majority in the republic, dominated local governance, which was carried out in the local capital of Pristina. This created tensions with the local Serbian minority, who largely preferred the prior arrangement. It also angered Serb nationalists, who stressed Kosovo's importance as the birthplace of the Serbian nation and as the "sacred" location where the ancient, Christian Serb nation lost its sovereignty in a 14th-century battle with the Muslim Ottoman Turks.

In the 1980s, Serbian-Albanian relations grew increasingly antagonistic. Exclusive nationalist claims and the depressed Yugoslav economy contributed to a mutually destructive cycle of slander, intimidation, violence, and competition for stagnating state resources. Among Serbs, Albanians were the subject of racist discrimination, derision, and the suspicion that some of their real loyalties lay with the neighboring socialist state of Albania, not with Yugoslavia. Meanwhile, Kosovo's local Serb minority felt surrounded by a hostile majority Albanian population that often wished to see them leave. Over the decade, there was a gradual exodus of Kosovar Serbs—usually into the neighboring Serbian Republic.

Scholars often cite 1986 as the beginning of the end of Yugoslavia. In that year, a group of Serbian academics published a "Memorandum" that voiced a previously suppressed narrative of ethnic Serb victimization by other ethnicities under the 1974 federal constitution. The document opened with the assertion that other nations were forcing Serbia to bear disproportionate costs in the ongoing economic crisis. However, it also pointed out that the population of Serbs in Kosovo was declining relative to the Albanian majority and accused Albanians of genocide against the Serbian nation. In Croatia as well, the authors added, Serbs faced discrimination and threats. Indeed, nowhere would Serbs be safe and prosperous in Yugoslavia until they achieved national unity and fairer treatment under a new constitution. New arrangements should give Serbia sovereign control over its autonomous republics in Kosovo and Vojvodina and anywhere Serbs lived in significant numbers. This implied ethnic Serbian control over large swaths of Serbia, Croatia, and Bosnia.[9]

The Communist Party naturally condemned the "Memorandum," yet it was widely read and applauded in Serbia. In 1987, Slobodan Milošević, an ambitious communist politician in the Serbian Communist Party, was assigned to respond to the difficult situation in Kosovo. Milošević did not claim to be a strong nationalist. Rather, he portrayed himself as the best hope within the Serbian Communist Party to protect the Serb people from the threats they faced from others. It helped, of course, to have the plight of ethnic Serbians in Kosovo to point to.

According to Bracewell, Milošević took advantage of a Serbian media-hyped story of a systematic "campaign" of Albanian sexual assault on Serbians in Kosovo. The reports appear to have been exaggerated, if not, in some cases, entirely fabricated. Officially, the rate of sexual assault in Kosovo was no higher than elsewhere in Yugoslavia, which in turn was not out of line with numbers across Europe. It is, of course, possible that Kosovar-Albanian authorities deliberately underreported the number of assaults committed by Kosovar-Albanian men. Bracewell doubts this but points out that, even if one *could* discredit these official numbers, the number of assaults committed by Serbian or Albanian men *within* their own ethno-national groups outnumbered sexual assaults *across* ethnic lines. The media outrage was not because people were allegedly being assaulted; it was because of the allegation that Albanian men were assaulting Serbians. Bracewell asks us to consider why alleged assaults across the ethno-sexual frontier were more concerning to the media than the far larger number of assaults among co-ethnics.[10]

Against this backdrop of ethno-sexual anxiety, Milošević stunned the communist establishment in 1987 by siding resolutely with ethnic Serbian nationalists in Kosovo. At a large rally of Kosovar Serbs, he pledged to protect Serbs from further victimization. Over the next years, Milošević used this promise to purge or sideline moderate politicians within the Communist Party. His moderate rivals, he told the large crowds that attended his rallies, were not doing enough to protect Serbians from harm from other nations in Yugoslavia.

Milošević's party-controlled media fleshed out the story. Much of the reporting focused on the threats and discrimination that ethnic Serbs faced outside of Serbia at the hands of other Yugoslav ethno-national groups. Yet, Bracewell documents how the reporting included a sub-narrative accusing Albanians of forcibly impregnating Serbian women with "Albanian babies"—as if the alleged assaults would impose the father's culture on the child. Doing nothing, the media implied, would lead to the death of the Serbian nation. Genocide, via a combination of sexual assault and larger Albanian families, became a media trope.

The nationalist media narrative thus attempted to enlist Serbian men into a project to protect "their" women from threats "abroad."[11] Serbian women now had to deal with an intensified nationalist anxiety about their dating and reproductive decisions. Before, "Baka" and "Deda" might not have approved of Jelena's new Croatian boyfriend, but everyone would have simply laughed it off as the prejudice of the older generation. Now, with nationalists increasingly policing the ethno-sexual frontier, it could be risky. Perhaps not coincidentally, during the ensuing wars, counselors for victims of sexual assault and domestic abuse in both Serbia and Croatia noted marked upticks in domestic male assaults on women.[12]

Milošević held rallies in the administrative capitals of vulnerable rivals. Pointing to the passionate crowds demonstrating for Serb self-determination within all of Yugoslavia, he bullied and intimidated party leadership in Serbia, Vojvodina, and Montenegro into replacing leaders with those who followed his line on the rotating presidency. In March 1989, he ordered Serbian police to occupy the Autonomous Republic of Kosovo. By 1991, Milošević had become Yugoslavia's most powerful politician with significant influence over four of Yugoslavia's eight seats on the collective federal presidency.

Milošević's rise, however, undermined the unity and legitimacy of the pan-ethnic, federal Communist Party. With the real source of centralized power in decline, republic-level politicians bypassed the party and held multiparty elections for republic-level presidents and parliaments. In 1990, nationalists rose to prominence in Croatia's first multiparty election. The major winner was Franjo Tuđman and his party, the Croatian Democratic Union (HDZ). Tuđman had fought with Tito's Partisans in World War II and had taken part in the liberation of Zagreb in 1945. Yet by the early 1970s, his growing national leanings and pro-Croatian advocacy made him vulnerable to attack. Despite initially receiving some party support, he served a jail term in the mid-1970s for nationalist deviation.

Tuđman reemerged in 1990 to lead a renewed Croatian national movement. His early speeches often made perfunctory reference to Croatian "citizens" (an inclusive term), but he was much more interested in talking about the Croatian *nation*, its 1,000 years of historical accomplishment, and the very real threat of Milošević establishing dominance over the federal institutions of Yugoslavia. Nationalists pointed to the danger coming from separatist Serbian communities on "Croatian" soil and the need to reunite dispersed Croatian people in nearby Bosnia-Herzegovina into one Croatian nation-state.

Ethnic Serbs consisted of 12 percent of Croatia's population. Despite the alarmist rhetoric, the majority did not initially vote for the HDZ's Serbian counterpart—the new Serbian Democratic Party (SDS)—in 1990. Most supported an accommodation with Zagreb if the new government would continue the practice of recognizing Serbs as a "constituent nation" of Croatia with the same privileges as ethnic Croats.

This quickly changed, however. In summer 1991, Tuđman drafted a constitution that made no mention of Serbs as a constituent nation of Croatia. This and many other missteps empowered the extreme nationalists in the SDS, most notably a 36-year-old Serb dentist named Milan Babić. As a child, Babić's father had narrowly escaped execution by his Ustasha neighbors. Now, as Mayor of Knin and a top official in the SDS, Babić equated the rise of Tuđman's HDZ with a return of the Ustasha, the specter of

Jasenovac, and a renewed existential threat to Serbian communities. As Croatia polarized, Babić's irregular police forces prevented Croatian police from entering Serb communities. They also bullied the remaining moderates in the SDS and the Serb community into silence, support, or exile.[13]

Croatia's new leaders had fears of their own. One did not have to be a Tuđman loyalist to be unhappy with Serbian president Slobodan Milošević's rise to dominance within Yugoslavia's federal institutions. By 1990, a federation that once operated to balance power between Yugoslavia's component republics was essentially a Serb dominion. Milošević nearly controlled the presidency, Milošević-aligned officers dominated the JNA, and Milošević agents were covertly arming Babić's forces and other Serb militias in Croatia and Bosnia. All the while, Serb nationalist rhetoric reminded many Croats of World War II's Chetniks.

Independence and state sovereignty over Croatian territory seemed like a preferable alternative to a future of national subordination in a Serbian-controlled federation of republics. Slovenians felt the same way. In spring 1991, they took their relatively homogenous and prosperous constituent republic out of Yugoslavia in a short conflict with only minimal casualties. Croatian nationalists wanted to follow, but Croatia's large, Belgrade-backed Serbian minority complicated matters.

It is telling of the way political imaginaries work that for two of my closest friends from the now defunct Yugoslavia, the conflict began with someone else seizing control over their identity and simplifying it. Losing control over how my friends identified themselves was a prelude not only to their silencing but also to war, the destruction of the complex society in which they wanted to live, and its monopolization by nationalist politicians.

In 1990, my friend Slobodan (Slobo) was a high school student in Zagreb, the capital of Croatia. Slobo never thought much about his ethnicity, but technically he was an ethnic Serb. This led to the following conversation between Slobo and his mom one day after basketball practice in late 1990. To paraphrase:

"Honey, sit down. I have something to tell you." (*Slobo sits*)
"Slobo, you are a Serb, not a Croat!"
"What? No way, Mom! I'm Croat!"
"Well . . . actually, you're not."

Slobo's mother then went on a long, painful digression about family origins, which essentially boiled down to a single issue: due to Slobo's Serbian last name, nationalists would treat him as an ethnic Serb, regardless of how she or Slobo felt about it. Worse, it became clear that his parents' career paths in Zagreb would be limited with an HDZ-led government. Ethnic Serbs, Croatian nationalists pointed out, were disproportionately influential in Croatian government and business. They had more positions than their numbers warranted, and given the climate in Belgrade, they could no longer be trusted with sensitive "Croatian" affairs.

Soon, anonymous threats threatened their physical safety. Many Serbs were fired from their jobs while others left "voluntarily." His parents' own workplace purge took place shortly after Slobo's conversation with his mom.

Slobo knew his name was Serbian, but unlike the nationalists, his identity was civic. Croatia was his home. From his perspective, he lived in Croatia, vacationed on the Croatian coast, dated Croatian girls, and played on the Croatian junior national basketball team. He was Croatian, no less so than any of his friends. The idea that people were telling his parents that they did not belong—that they should go live with "their people" somewhere else in Yugoslavia—was ludicrous, but nationalists were now in charge and made life impossible for his family.

Under intense pressure and with dismal prospects if they stayed, Slobo and his family decamped to Belgrade. They didn't want to leave, and they intensely disliked Serbia's own nationalist leader, Slobodan Milošević. But at least in Belgrade, "just existing" with a Serbian name created fewer problems.

Over time, Slobo embraced his newly assigned "Serbian" identity, attended university, and eventually became an important leader in the student opposition to the Serbian nationalist regime called Otpor (Serbian for "resistance"). In 2000, Otpor made an important contribution to the successful civic uprising that unseated Milošević after he tried to steal a presidential election.

Soon after Slobo left, Croatians voted overwhelmingly for independence in a referendum. Serbian Croats opted to remain part of Yugoslavia, and a desperate, one-sided war broke out along the Serbian and Bosnian "frontiers" of the Croatian Republic. Serbian nationalist militias, backed by the Serbian-dominated JNA, violently expelled tens of thousands of non-Serbs from their communities. As Croatian families fled their homes, Serbian refugees from Croat-held villages and towns often moved in. Retreating police forces initially could slow but not stop the well-armed Serbian forces. Atrocities abounded, including a prelude to the campaigns of ethnic expulsion and sexual assault that would later mark the Bosnian conflict. When the eastern Slavonian city of Vukovar fell to invading forces after a long siege, 260 wounded defending soldiers were removed from the hospital and executed.[14]

Croatia temporarily lost about one-third of the republic's prewar territory. The UN entered in early 1992 and stabilized the new frontiers with peacekeeping troops. The territorial gains did not last, however. Croat forces gained in strength and training. In 1995, Croatia received an influx of weapons from the West and a green light from the United States for a counteroffensive. Aided by NATO air power in late summer 1995, they routed Serbian troops in Croatia and helped break the back of Serbian forces in Bosnia. The campaign included a new round of human displacement, this time focused on ethnic Serbs in Croatia and Bosnia. In 1995, a comprehensive peace agreement was signed in Dayton, Ohio, that restored Croatia's borders.

Most of Croatia's ethnic Serbs, however, were now refugees. While they had a right to return under treaty terms, many simply sold their properties and remained in their new countries. Today, only 4.5 percent of Croatia's citizens claim Serbian identity—a reduction of over two-thirds.

As in Croatia, the decline of the Yugoslav communist party in Bosnia gave way to competitive elections in 1990. Where communists once had a monopoly over power, Bosnian politicians now had to run campaigns in which they told the public a convincing new story about why they should be in power and why others should not. Bosnians voted largely along ethnic lines and elected nationalists.

Nationalism in Bosnia-Herzegovina was particularly fraught with dangers of violence. Bosnian communities, including the capital of Sarajevo, were often richly multiethnic. Nevertheless, backed and encouraged by Belgrade and Zagreb, the newly elected nationalist politicians in Bosnia recklessly promised to "protect" their conationals by carving a "greater Serbia" or a "greater Croatia" out of Bosnian and Herzegovinian lands. This would inevitably require the expulsion of "foreign" nationals, and since most had lived in these communities for decades if not centuries, they would be unwilling to leave voluntarily. As in Croatia and Serbia, Bosnia also had a small minority of blended families or people who did not identify with any ethnicity in particular. What should be done with them? Where did their loyalties lie?

In late winter 1992, Bosnia held a referendum on independence from the now Serbian-dominated Yugoslav federation. With Serbs largely boycotting, the referendum produced a resounding Croatian and Muslim majority in favor of independence. Yet, Serb leaders argued that if Bosnia had the right to leave Yugoslavia, they would assert their right to carve out a sovereign Serbian Republic from Bosnia.

It was no idle threat. Milošević and Tuđman had already met, and despite the growing conflict between Croatia's Serbian nationalists and Tuđman's HDZ government, the two leaders had decided to divide Bosnia between their states. Moreover, for well over a year, Bosnian Serb soldiers in the JNA had been transferring to units in Bosnia. When Bosnian independence came and the JNA left, they would stay behind to form the backbone of the new Bosnian Serb army, units trained and stocked with the armory the JNA would leave behind.[15]

Like Slobo, my friend Haris got caught up in the nationalist reordering of identities. Haris came from a Muslim family in Bosnia. His grandmother had practiced Islam, but growing up in Banja Luka, this "cultural artifact" played a very small role in his life. He considered Muslim traditionalism a "quaint custom" of the past. Similar to Slobo, in friendships and dating, Haris's ethnic identity had carried little importance. Like many in Yugoslavia's Muslim minority, he identified as a "Yugoslav," a civic identity that reflected the unified multiethnicity once promoted by the communist regime that could now serve as the basis for a unified, democratic Yugoslavia. Many of his friends similarly rejected ethnicity and chose to identify as "Yugoslavs," while the more creative claimed to be "humans" or, sardonically, "Eskimos."

Haris's attempt to retain his Yugoslav identity was disrupted at the outbreak of the Bosnian war. After he graduated with a degree in English language from the University of Sarajevo, Haris briefly worked for the Bosnian government as a liaison to the European Community Monitoring Mission. The work entailed interpreting and translating for European monitors, diplomats, and civilian and military officials as they tried to understand the situation, and to defuse escalating tensions.

In March 1992, the job became increasingly dangerous. Militias set up barricades to restrict travel around the country—capped by a tightening blockade around Sarajevo by the self-proclaimed Serbian nationalist government. In mid-April, Haris was assigned to accompany a Canadian official out of town. Only a short distance from downtown Sarajevo, however, civilian-garbed Serbian militia stopped their vehicle and pulled Haris aside at gunpoint. After several tense minutes, the gunmen let him go, but not before they had made it perfectly clear that they considered him a Muslim and thus one of "the enemy." They argued over whether Haris, as a "Muslim prisoner," could be used in exchange for some of the Serbs held by the Sarajevo police.

Nobody asked Haris "what" he was. Had they asked, he would have said he was a Yugoslav. They just inferred his new Muslim identity from the name "Haris" on his government ID.

The complicated prewar, civic identities of Slobo and Haris were a problem for nationalists' political imaginaries. Slobo's and Haris's claims to be something other than a Serb or Muslim muddied the clear categories of "us/them," "friend/enemy," and "traitor/patriot" that the nationalists so badly needed to justify holding onto political power. Here was Serbian Slobo claiming to be a Croat, and there was Haris clinging to Tito's outdated proletarian concept of "unity and brotherhood." If everyone identified like Haris and Slobo, the nationalist imaginary would lose all meaning: There would be no one to "protect!" Therefore, nationalists treated Slobo and Haris and the tens of thousands of other nonconforming people as if they belonged to the enemy side.

Full-fledged fighting and Haris's three-year entrapment inside besieged Sarajevo commenced only a few days later. Haris recalls his brief abduction as the moment that his personal pledge to be "the last Yugoslav" became meaningless. After the checkpoint incident, he no longer controlled his identity. Like Slobo, nationalists with guns would define him as they chose.

In 1993, the old term "Bosniak" was adopted to refer to Bosnians who did not identify as Croat and Serb. Haris did not like it. It was a new imposition, and again he was not asked. Yet as shells devastated his neighborhood and sniper fire claimed his friends and neighbors, he came to terms with his Bosniak identity. Personally, however, he still considers himself a human being of Yugoslav origins—with a fondness for Eskimos.

The Bosnian war began in earnest in April 1992. The ensuing siege of Bosnia's capital city, Sarajevo, was particularly brutal. The Serb separatists took the ridges lining three sides of the elongated city and, using Yugoslav army weaponry, fired flat-trajectory artillery into businesses, apartments, homes, and offices. Sarajevo mounted a defense that was strong enough to prevent being overrun but incapable of lifting the siege. Meanwhile, criminal gangs and militias enriched themselves by smuggling basic supplies into the city for a high price or extorting a percentage of the goods delivered by international aid caravans.[16]

Smaller communities, villages, and towns that were overrun by the Serbian forces fared even worse. Families on the losing ethnic side were usually expelled and often subjected to looting, executions, imprisonment, and sexual assault. Moderate coethnics on the winning side were similarly persecuted for refusing to "protect" the nation from its enemies. Blended, mixed-ethnic marriages and their offspring—of which there were many— found themselves forced to embrace one side of their family or risk being labeled traitors and expelled.[17] This was repeated across Bosnia wherever militias had a military advantage, creating Europe's greatest humanitarian tragedy since World War II.

This was a war of nationalism. The new frontiers of the nation were to match the frontiers of the new state. Extreme nationalists in advancing militias therefore sought to "cleanse" their captured territories of people from "other nations." They also targeted co-ethnics who refused to contribute.

On the battlefield, nationalism involved plunder and deliberate terror. Captives were often beaten, robbed, or sexually assaulted. Many of the newly created "foreigners" were displaced to makeshift concentration camps. In some places, soldiers trafficked captured women and children in brothels behind the front lines. As the war progressed, foreign observers reported, Serbian forces released women from captivity in late-stage pregnancy. Messages on the sides of the busses made it clear that at least some Serbian soldiers believed the women of the enemy nation would now give birth to "Serbian" children. They apparently conceptualized procreative assault as part of the "ethnic cleansing" of the newly captured territories.[18]

This is shocking, but feminist scholar and care provider Vesna Nikolić-Ristanović asserts that there was nothing terribly exceptional about the soldiers involved. Rather, she argues, patterns of sexual assault often follow power imbalances on the battlefield. As Serbian forces in Bosnia were doing most of the advancing in the early stages of the war, criminal elements in their forces committed most of the atrocities. Yet, the resulting headlines were typically some version of "Serbians Rape Thousands of Croatian and Muslim Women in Bosnia." This was problematic. It implied a collective Serb assault on a collective Croatian or Muslim victim.[19]

The reality was much more complex. Indeed, as V. P. Gagnon has demonstrated, even in the face of relentless nationalist propaganda, Serbs were not unified in their support for Milošević or for the Bosnian Serb politicians and military officials who directed the war locally. As the Bosnian war loomed in early spring 1992, for example, many Serbs opposed nationalism and refused to contribute.[20] It may be a small example, but I am reminded of a small troop of Serbian women from Dah Teatar who, as war broke out, dressed as dark angels and performed antiwar poetry from Bertolt Brecht in the streets of Belgrade. Behind their audience, armed men marched quietly on their way to the new front lines that vivisected Yugoslavia. Yet, at the same time, many more draft-age men avoided military service by booking tickets for foreign vacations from which they did not return. Against all this chaotic movement, Dah's prophetic angels intoned a mashup of Brecht's antiwar poems as they moved across a defunct fountain in the city's main pedestrian mall.[21]

Far from enthusiastically enlisting to "protect" their nation, tens of thousands of young Serbian men wanted no part of Milošević's wars.[22] Meanwhile, militaries on all sides had to scramble to extract enough conscripts to fill their ranks—even to the point of filling combat units with hardened criminals, gangsters, and football hooligans.[23] There was nothing like a national Serbian mobilization to fight the war. Quite the opposite.

So, quite clearly, there was a problem with the "nations as perpetrators and victims" narrative. This became apparent to Nikolić-Ristanović as she provided counseling and protection to victims of sexual assault and domestic abuse on the outskirts of Belgrade. When she reported to the press the growing number of sexually assaulted women escaping the Bosnian war zone to her care, foreign reporters often treated her with indifference. Most of the victims she took in identified as Serbian. But when she reported the Serbian ethnicity of her victims to outsiders, she was often confronted with a sarcastic and angry response, which, to paraphrase, went, "Oh really? So few Serbian victims? Don't you know how many rapes *your* Serbian forces have committed?" Sexual assaults of Bosnian, Muslim, and Croatian women were news, while the assaults of Serbian women were not. From the perspective of Nikolić-Ristanović, this made no sense. Like Bracewell, she wondered how the ethnicity of the victims could possibly contextualize or diminish the suffering they had gone through.[24]

Vesna Kesić, a service provider in Croatia, was no less amazed: nationalists had "turned women into metaphors," she later wrote in a reference to work by Susan Brownmiller, whereby, "a raped Croat or Bosniak woman stands for a raped Croatia or Bosnia."[25] Women had become "symbolic battlegrounds" in the struggle between male nationalists. "Women are bodies in pain," Kesić felt compelled to affirm, "regardless of which ethnic group is at some point recognized as aggressor and which as victim. Croatian women, Bosnian women, Muslim women, Serbian women, Albanian women."[26]

Kesić was one of a group of five prominent women writers in Croatia whose refusal to speak the language of the nationalist political imaginary angered nationalist officials. Labeled the "five witches" by the nationalist press, Kesić and her fellow authors had failed to "report for ideological duty," wrote American journalist Meredith Tax. In the nationalist imaginary, the "witches" cast a spell of critical inquiry over the nation's patriotic leaders, producing self-doubt that would weaken the nation in its existential struggle for survival. Their feminist perspective thus aided the enemy camp. Accordingly, Tuđman's party, the HDZ, denied them access to state-controlled and allied media and subjected them to a campaign of harassment and slander. Tabloids dug deeply into their backgrounds in search of motives for their "anti-Croatian" behavior. The ensuing campaign thus "expatriated" their identities, breathlessly "exposing" the former "communists" in each writer's family and "uncovering" her "foreign ties," such as an ethnic Serb husband or a home in Western Europe.[27]

Such women, the tabloids shouted, were national traitors, not "real" Croatians. They should be silent. What they did not say, however, was that the silencing of the five witches and other critics as "hostile to the nation" stifled critical inquiry that was essential to a functioning democracy. The resulting information vacuum permitted Tuđman's patriotic associates to control state-owned enterprises, secure state contracts, invalidate municipal elections, contextualize their own war crimes, and distort the rule of law, among many, many other things.

୨୦ ଦ୍ଧ

The Bosnian war continued until fall 1995. For much of the war, Bosnian Croats and Bosnian government forces coordinated in their defense against the well-armed Serbian army. But there were also Muslim-Croat clashes as early as late 1992. In 1993, the international community proposed a peace deal, the Vance-Owen Plan, that would divide Bosnia into ethnically separate cantons. When the deal fell apart, Bosnian Croats tied to Tuđman's HDZ concluded that aggression would be rewarded. In the ensuing months, they moved against the Bosnian government side in force—imprisoning "Bosniak" soldiers who had only recently fought in their units, attacking Muslim villages and neighborhoods, and expelling Muslim families from the communities that came under their control.

In 1994, US diplomatic efforts brought the Croats and the Bosnian government back into a common federation. In late summer 1995, Serbian forces led by General Ratko Mladić marched into a UN-maintained "safe haven" in Srebrenica, expelled its sheltering female population, and massacred around 8,000 men and boys. A month later, a Serbian artillery shell killed and wounded scores of shoppers in an outdoor market in besieged Sarajevo. Only then did the US lead NATO and the UN in an extended bombing campaign in support of Bosnian and Croatian forces.[28] As ethnic Serb soldiers were forced into a rapid retreat from positions in Bosnia and Croatia, Tuđman and Milošević agreed to a ceasefire and peace talks.

The wars of Yugoslav dissolution ended, for a while, with the Dayton

Accords—a US-brokered agreement signed in Ohio in November 1995.[29] Dayton restored Croatian borders to their prewar lines, guaranteed refugees the right to return, and created an impossibly complex new map and governance structure for Bosnia and Herzegovina. Bosnian Serbs lost a lot of their captured and cleansed territory in the agreement, but many non-Serbs complained that the new boundary lines still rewarded the aggressors with control over far too many of the villages and towns that they had ethnically reorganized at the point of a gun. As a treaty, Dayton accomplished its main objective to secure the peace.[30] Except for those who were later prosecuted for documentable war crimes, it left most of those who had profited from the war in place with their riches.

Meanwhile, journalists and aid workers had gathered data that would later be used in the International Criminal Tribunal for the Former Yugoslavia (ICTY) against a small handful of the soldiers and their enablers. Thanks to the brave testimony of the victims, to the vital efforts to gather it and take it seriously, and to the work of feminist legal scholars and activists, sexual assault can today be prosecuted in international courts as a crime against humanity. It was a drop of justice in the bucket of crimes that soldiers and politicians had filled during the war, but an important change, nonetheless.

CHAPTER 6

"Transitology"

How I Joined the Global Conspiracy
against Slovakia

I get schooled by a Eurocrat . . . Vaclav Havel, elitist? . . . Liberal
transitology . . . Teaching dos and don'ts . . . Copenhagen
dreaming . . . The democratic peace . . . Civil society takes charge in
Slovakia . . . The Bratislava process . . . 31 chapters nobody read . . .
NATO learns Czech and Hungarian . . .
Liberalism's untested legitimacy.

PREFACE: The corpus of European law, rules, and regulations, or the *Acquis Communautaire*, as they call it, was constantly growing. In the mid-1990s, I heard European Commission officials referring to a 40,000-page document. Yet, within a few years, these same officials were talking about 80,000 and then 100,000 pages. In 1999, the rapid doubling prompted me to ask a Commission bureaucrat whether someone had simply printed up a double-spaced copy of the existing document.

It was supposed to be a joke.

"No," the haughty and *humorless* response came, the Commission is diligent in assuring the "apolitical, *technocratic* harmonization of Europe's single market," and that requires a *growing* body of regulations.

"Where is democracy in all of this?" came my follow-up question.

"I believe in technocratic democracy. Voters elect their politicians, the politicians appoint the commissioners, and the commission makes the rules free from the political interference of local governments."

I was appalled by this Eurocrat's conception of democracy. But, in hindsight, Commission arrogance was merely symptomatic of the distrust many liberals in the West had for the democratic choices of peoples in the

East. It's not that they didn't necessarily want democratic governments to flourish there. They did! But they didn't want to have a democratic debate over the *necessity* of democracy, human rights, and many aspects of the functioning market. There was an assumption that these were desirable outcomes for people whether they wanted them or not.

More broadly, Western liberals simply assumed that their ideas about democracy, society, markets, and, yes, the Commission's technocratic harmonization of the EU's expanding Single European Market should be nonnegotiable. From 1990 through 2004, they expected nothing less than ideological hegemony in Central Europe. This led to countless discussions, in which any "yes, but . . ." argument against convergence with the West was assumed to be either the obfuscation of someone getting rich at everyone else's expense or the bleating of the ignorant. We saw no *legitimate* reasons to resist Western policies. By our logic, opponents were either venal or stupid.

This kind of condescension can get tiring. Yet, we should not forget that the return to liberalism in Central Europe was both highly popular and, as we saw in chapter 4, rooted in regional historical experience. This produced a confluence of interests: a powerful joint venture between Western governments, Western foundations, and liberal Central European elites. They had in common a belief that liberalism would be the natural choice for postcommunist peoples, if only they were given a fair chance to choose it. But they were also willing to encourage this choice when necessary. Occasionally, where illiberal postcommunist political elites were in danger of prevailing over their domestic opponents through undemocratic means, they pushed forcefully back. We now look at five characteristics of this joint venture to build liberalism in Central Europe: elitism, a "transitological" mindset, market integration, EU leverage, and strong Western support for liberal civil society. Combined, these characteristics ensured that Central Europe's local project to embrace liberalism had a distinctly Western imprimatur.

ELITISM: How can anyone be against economic freedom, democracy, and human rights, you might ask? Certainly, that was my view in the 1990s. As a naive graduate student, I didn't understand. Yet, I came across many people who fully bought into illiberal narratives resisting the adoption of human rights, democracy, private property, and integration into a competitive global market. How could they fail to see, I wondered, that these counternarratives were just a cover story to distract people while ruling elites dismantled a fledgling democracy and cornered the (re-)creation of private property and markets? I, too, mentally divided these people into two groups: opportunists who were "on the make" and those who objectively found themselves on the losing side of economic reform. I could not understand why many of the average people I met could not get behind their liberal, pro-European elites.

Recent work from Professor David Ost helps explain at least one vector of this disconnect by revisiting the legacy of Charter '77 cofounder Václav Havel.[1] Havel's classic essay "The Power of the Powerless" exposes how the average citizen's habitual repetition of the communist regime's slogans provides the regime its legitimacy and power. Havel gives us the parable of a man running a vegetable market, a "greengrocer," who posts a slogan from Marx's *Communist Manifesto* in his store each year—thereby performing the Communist Party's legitimacy story. Havel questions the grocer and so many others for being "unquestionably obedient." He asks, What would happen if the greengrocer simply refused to hang the sign?

Havel's answer: "The bill is not long in coming. He will be relieved of his post as manager of the shop and transferred to the warehouse. His pay will be reduced. His hopes for a holiday in Bulgaria will evaporate. His children's access to higher education will be threatened"[2]—clear and valuable incentives, in short, to perform the state's degrading, low-cost ritual of obedience. Havel's response to this was to encourage readers to "live in truth," to never be afraid to speak truth, even when power demands otherwise.

Citing the dangers of rebellion to the average citizen, Ost argues that Havel unfairly blames citizens for allowing the regime to persist. This, Ost points out, is elitist. Havel was hardly an average Czech. He came from a wealthy family whose properties once lined Prague's famous Wenceslas Square. After the communist coup in 1948, however, the state expropriated his family's wealth. Coming of age in the 1950s, Havel would assuredly have had limited opportunities for advancement through a traditional career within the communist system had he tried to make a go of it. Instead, Havel emerged as a brilliant young satirist and playwright in the early to mid-1960s at a time when engaging in the critical arts carried milder sanctions.

Yet, in 1968, the communist world pulled a "bait and switch" on him. Warsaw Pact troops occupied the country and restored a hard-line communist regime. Thereafter, Havel's sharp and witty, anti-bureaucratic opus guaranteed him both additional fame and dissident status. When he copenned the anti-communist "Charter" in 1977, he already had an international reputation, a prison record, and a robust support network. Brilliant and brave as Havel was, Charter '77 was simply another step in an established dissident life—a unique story, written by Havel himself!

Havel served a four-year prison sentence in the early 1980s and another shorter term just before the fall of communism. He used his privilege to help others and fully deserves his position as one of the great heroes of history.[3] Yet, as Ost points out, his greengrocer story had limitations as a counternarrative of power.

Take Simona's dad, for example. Ferko hated communism. But he also reserved disdain for Havel. How? Well, Ferko was well aware of the ability of the state to deprive him and Božena of their livelihood and his children of their education. As you'll recall from chapter 2, he and his brother had personally paid a traumatic price for his father's resistance to communist collectivization policy in the 1950s. He had also observed his father struggling with the "collective action problem" firsthand. Ferko knew, for example, that no one would follow him if he took a rebellious stance in his work at the National Opera and that his children would suffer. He also knew that even if all musicians in the country rebelled, the foreign Warsaw Pact troops stationed on Czechoslovak soil since 1968 would prevent any real change from happening. And then there were the party members—tens of thousands, really—who had no issues with getting ahead by enthusiastically imposing the party's rules. "They legitimized the Communist Party in everything they said," Ferko recently told me, "and then they turned around and terrorized us."

In reality, until conditions changed during the "revolutionary bandwagon" of November 1989, Ferko and his handful of like-minded musician friends in the opera could only dream of saying publicly what they thought privately. The choice to challenge the system was materially irrational to the average citizen. Not surprisingly, when Czechoslovakia's dissidents called on Ferko to act heroically, he responded with a mixture of skepticism and distrust.

"Live in truth?" Ferko may have wondered. "Are you kidding!?"

Havel really didn't get it.

TRANSITOLOGY: A second characteristic of the liberal project emerged soon after the Velvet Revolution. While Ferko really wanted markets and especially democracy for Slovakia, a growing number of experts were eager to explain to him exactly *how* he should want them. In the 1990s, Western embassies and foundations established dozens of organizations and programs to help build liberal democracy, to create functioning market economies, and to develop the human capital necessary to integrate into

Western institutions and markets. The reasoning was benign. Postcommunist European elites wanted to adopt Western-style institutions, but they lacked the expertise, funding, and blueprints. Western organizations tried to help local liberals by providing all three.

Yet, tensions soon emerged. Within just a few months of the revolution, foreign advisers began to corner the emerging market in luxury apartments and to renovate the choicest office spaces in the region's capitals. They often did not know much about the countries they were helping, but they had a lot of very strong opinions about how to build political and economic liberalism, complete with uncontested borders, civil and political rights, free and fair elections, an independent judiciary, business-friendly commercial law, independent and objective journalism, Western language education, and—this is where I came in—critical pedagogy in higher education and secondary schools. All of these, and much more, *"needed to be"* built from scratch.

I write "needed to be" because this is what "we" thought was best for Central Europe. Central Europeans wanted political freedom. Of this there is no doubt. Yet, from the start, many Western advisers and business actors seemed convinced that their role was to give "the locals" knowledge and expertise that they lacked. Most of this first generation of Western experts in the region were appropriately referred to as "transitologists." As David Stark argued, transitologists discounted local experiences and traditions, talents, advice, objections, and institutions. Rather, they compared postcommunist Central Europe with their own idealized Western version of free markets, democracy, and civil society. They then mapped out in detail the steps that postcommunist societies *needed to undertake* to get there and chartered each state's progress on well-publicized scales designed by Western financial and democracy assistance institutions.[4] Transitologists didn't want much debate about the measures themselves. When problems arose, it was far easier to blame "the locals" and their lack of "skill" and "will" to do the "obviously correct" thing.

Moreover, by dominating the organization of civil society in the 1990s, Western funders arguably created the false impression that socially and politically liberal NGOs were purely foreign imports or, to paraphrase an implicit logic, that liberalism is what *"they"* want for *"us."* Even today, authoritarians and nationalists use this counternarrative to assault the legitimacy of liberal NGOs throughout the region.

I personally made many of the mistakes of transitology. On a snowy day in early January 1996, I fled a mind-numbing, library-based dissertation project at Columbia University in New York to join the Civic Education Project (CEP) in Bratislava. CEP had its origins in a George Soros/ Open Society Fund grant to introduce US curriculum and pedagogy to Central Europe's universities. My assignment was to teach a liberal arts-style introductory course in international politics to graduate and undergraduate students at Comenius University.

The graduate program gave MAs in diplomacy and international relations. I thus designed one of my classes for "future diplomats" with the "pedagogical goal" of *"encouraging critical inquiry into the key concepts of international relations theory as demonstrated by students' enhanced ability to express complex analytical arguments in English, both verbally and in writing."*

I failed in my mission.

It started with the room. There were eight rows of desks in a narrow hall, each bolted into the floor—64 places for only 16 students, to be exact. On the first day, all 16 sat in the last three rows. Undaunted, I walked to "their end" of the long, narrow classroom and asked a question. I was into Machiavelli at the time, so after a brief introductory lecture, it was probably something like:

"Should our political leaders be judged according to a different moral standard when they make life-and-death international decisions?" The students shyly looked at each other, but no one raised a hand. So, I asked the question again. Again, no answer.

"Am I being clear—does everyone understand my English?"

Even the crickets were snoring.

Finally, one of the older students in the back row raised his hand and asked, quite triumphantly, in excellent BBC English,

"Oh, we understand you perfectly, but why are you asking us this question? Don't you *know* the answer?"

That course did not go well. The students never got over my reluctance to lecture and were offended by my insistence that they risk thinking publicly about an answer rather than just memorizing and regurgitating the one that I refused to give them in a lecture. Many of these students came from STEM backgrounds and had *never* been asked to express or defend what *they* thought about politics in a classroom.

Worse, I had another 16 students who could not come to class because they had full-time jobs. I did not know it at the time, but they had spontaneously organized a pre-internet version of an online course in which one classmate was tasked to copy down my "lectures" word for word for the working students who could not make it.

My attempts at a seminar-style classroom completely screwed up this strategy. The note taker did not know how to notate the sparse conversations we had, and her working classmates were soon furious with her and then with me. Remarkably, I didn't even know that I had 32 students until I received a surprisingly large number of take-home midterm exams in my inbox. As I began to grade, it immediately became clear that my pedagogy had inflicted catastrophic damage on their attempt at asynchronous learning. Most of them did not have time to do the difficult graduate-level readings I assigned. Several, aided by the library's copy of *Encyclopedia Britannica*, confused realism in international relations with realist art.

"You are so naive!" an Italian colleague later told me. Prior to communism, he told me, higher education in the law and the social sciences had been little more than a training school for bureaucrats in Austria-Hungary and the first Czechoslovak Republic. Processing information had been rewarded while questioning the process had been punished. Marxist education under communism introduced some critical frames and new forms of analysis, but, again, critically challenging the received frameworks of the party was risky and rarely valued.

Survival under conditions of Lockean liberalism often requires the ability to think critically and rapidly solve problems. That's how I've been trained. My new students probably had no problem thinking critically, but they also knew from experience that the key to success in a bureaucracy was not to do it publicly. What if a student took a daring stance in class and a potential employer in the Ministry of Foreign Affairs heard about it? Naively, I *was* asking them to engage in self-destructive behavior!

On a much brighter note, I also had a class of younger undergraduate students in the Department of Politics at Comenius University's Philosophy Faculty. The department was run by the former Charter '77 dissident and prisoner of conscience Miroslav Kusý. Professor Kusý knew the value of critical thought in the classroom and rewarded professors who experimented pedagogically. With Kusý's encouragement and leadership, the department's professors had long since abandoned communist-era dogma, and most were moving beyond the strict lecture/regurgitate pedagogy. Many, like my future coauthors Sona Szomolányi and Darina Malová, were well read in literature from the region as well as from Western Europe, Latin America, and the United States. As soon as they had the opportunity, they situated their own scholarship in a broader range of literature, attended conferences in Vienna, Florence, Berlin, and Boston, and built international reputations.

My undergraduate students were also fantastic. They took risks and were engaged and informed in class. We had daily, spirited debates, and most were full-time students with time to really do the readings. They loved being asked what they thought. This talented group has flourished since graduation, and I see them all the time, on visits to Slovak universities, at diplomatic gatherings, at academic conferences, and on Slovak television where they routinely pop up as political commentators.

MARKET INTEGRATION: As the 1990s progressed, liberalism's joint venture was shaped by the opportunities and challenges that arose from exposure to the global economy. Again, I had a front-row seat for some of this. From 1996 to 1997, I supplemented my graduate student and CEP fellowship income by locating and prescreening local candidates for top positions in Central European subsidiaries of Fortune 500 companies. Traveling between Prague, Bratislava, and Budapest, I conducted dozens of interviews and saw hundreds of résumés. Over time, I became fluent in the disconnection between Western corporate expectations and Central European "business as usual." It was a painful and occasionally humiliating language to learn.

My American employer asked me to set up a team of local researchers in Budapest who would locate and screen the top executives of Hungarian state-owned companies. We based our research methodology on techniques I had learned over the previous three years working part-time for the New York firm that contracted me. Initially, we did everything according to the book, albeit one written in Manhattan, and identified about 10 leading candidates for further interviews. This American methodology led us to 40- to 60-year-old men who had risen through the ranks of communist-era state-owned enterprises and industrial "branch" ministries in the 1980s. They could use the right terminology, but in practice most cared little about the American-style marketing and sales practices that our Fortune 500 client valued. What the executives offered, by contrast, were yellowing Rolodexes filled with the phone numbers of the upper-midlevel state officials who had once made their lives easier in the state-run economy. I expect a few also had a remarkably up-to-date list of friends with a fantastic knowledge of vampire trading companies, transfer pricing, and offshore shell companies.

These gentlemen were superb executives in a mixed state-private economy, but neither their training nor their experience went over well with the US corporate-level executive who flew to Budapest to do the final round of interviews. To take the most awkward example, one gentleman I loved over the phone came to the interview in a bright purple three-piece suit and interrupted *his own* 60-minute interview *twice* to take a phone call. He was then furious when we ended the interview as scheduled to bring in the next candidate. He was proud of his state company's large share of the domestic market but simply could not explain why it had not posted a larger profit despite having products on shelves all over Hungary. I had no idea then, but I suspect now that he or some associates probably had a few vampire companies of their own that were bleeding his state company of cash. He was a postcommunist success story—admired by local employees in the office I set up—but the US executives were appalled.

After a stern dressing down from my client, we stopped presenting these experienced upper-level executives. Instead, we drew heavily from the under-40 generation, those with two to three years of marketing experience getting a company's products onto as many village store shelves as possible in a prominent and attractive display. These younger men *and* women understood the mechanics of retail marketing and sales in a way that pleased our US client.

Integration into Western markets, the result of the policy of trade liberalization, was one of the most important sources of fundamental change in postcommunist Europe. It was deeply resented by many. Yet, wherever foreign capital and products were allowed into a country, they had the irresistible force of gravity. The best and brightest flocked to work for foreign companies. If given the choice and the right price, customers would often choose imports over the familiar, drab local products. Local production and marketing thus improved or died. Many Western companies helped by buying local firms and forging them into important links of their global production chains. As local companies and subsidiaries integrated into larger ventures, their markets grew. Rather than being laid off as they had feared when the firm was privatized to a Western company, many employees got promotions, bigger salaries, and new staff to train. Workers everywhere reoriented their career planning and training toward succeeding in competitive European and global markets. As we shall see in chapter 10, however, many also had difficulty making the transition.

EUROPEAN UNION LEVERAGE: Another vital characteristic of the liberal joint venture was the growing leverage of the **European Union** over Central European politics. The EU was established on January 1, 1993, as a more deeply integrated version of the old European Community that it replaced. Arguably, the EU's defining new feature was the **Single European Market**, in which the states of the EU dropped their internal economic borders. Suddenly, Europeans could buy products from any European country without meeting a single customs official. Although the bureaucratic requirements were greater, Europeans could also work and live most anywhere they wanted within the Union.

The prospect of joining the EU was politically galvanizing in Central Europe. Central Europeans associated the EU with health, prosperity, and freedom. Most, and especially the young, desperately wanted to join. Local excitement put the EU in a position of power over applicant countries. This was quickly incorporated into local elite political strategies.

Professor Milada Vachudova divides this EU leverage into two forms. The first was "active leverage"—or the ability of the EU to offer or withhold specific rewards in exchange for changed behavior. The second form was "passive leverage," a combination of the EU's seductive attraction, the general costs of being excluded, and a desire for social equality in the hierarchy of European peoples. Empowered by these rich forms of leverage, local liberal politicians could pressure their governments toward substantive democratic and market reforms.[5]

Vachudova shows how, early in the decade, the EC/EU relied heavily on passive leverage and, accordingly, exercised less leverage than it could have on the democratic and market performance of postcommunist states. Yet, in 1993, the EU boosted its leverage with the Copenhagen criteria. Set by the EU's collective of top governmental executives at a European Council meeting in Copenhagen, Denmark, the criteria expected applicant states to establish

1. *stable institutions* "guaranteeing democracy, the rule of law, human rights and respect for and protection of minorities";
2. a *"functioning market economy"* and the capacity to cope with the disruptions of competition; and
3. "the ability to take on the *obligations of [EU] membership*" as specified in the accumulated body of EU laws and rulings known as the *Acquis Communautaire*.[6]

Top ministers of the EU countries were initially reluctant to establish a specific process to push applicant countries toward these general goals or even to evaluate whether they had achieved them. There was some fear that postcommunist countries would sap EU resources and flood Western Europe with desperate job seekers. Could Western Europe really handle the addition of 10, mostly poorer new members into the EU? What if plumbers in Poland came to Paris to look for work, one French anti-enlargement campaign later asked? What would happen to French plumbers? How could the EU afford to give Hungarian cows the same rich support currently given French cows? Anxieties among the "EU 15" ran high.

On the other hand, the promise of integrating the economic resources of Central Europe into this borderless new market turned many of Europe's business leaders into big supporters of "European enlargement." They argued that European consumers would benefit from enlarging the EU's single market. Access to cheaper products produced in the East would leave more money in consumers' pockets to buy things they had not even dreamed of—a process called "trade creation." Meanwhile, Eastern labor would free Western Europe's highly skilled workforce from producing old things the old way using old technology. They would now move into the highly productive new sectors of the 21st-century economy where they had an advantage. Enlargement would make Europe richer and more dynamic.

Advocates of enlargement also argued that EU membership would widen Europe's "zone of peace" by stabilizing Central Europe's new democracies. In the 1990s, my field of political science was buzzing with something called democratic peace theory. Proponent Michael Doyle provided empirical evidence to demonstrate that no two democracies had fought a major war with each other, ever. Doyle argued that democratic electorates constrained their leaders, were reluctant to impose their will on other democratic peoples, and had influential commercial classes that preferred trading for things over simply taking them.[7] War, Doyle's theory implied, could be reduced by populating the world with democratic countries connected via trading networks across open markets—a zone of peace. Doyle's basic insights informed the foreign policies of the United States and the EU in the 1990s. President Bill Clinton even integrated them into his major statements on national security.[8]

Arguments for and against the democratic peace theory consumed much of the energy of political scientists in the 1990s. For example, democratic relations might explain why Germany was no longer antagonistic toward its historical rival, France. Yet it was also possible that West Germany and France could be more democratic because they no longer had to wage constant war with each other.

Which is right? I tend to side with a more complex view: that both are correct—democracy and peace are recursively related, that is, the causality runs in both directions. From Milošević in the Balkans to Mečiar in Slovakia, we have already seen why this is. Would-be autocrats are not above making things up, but they thrive when there is a concrete external threat that they can incorporate into their political imaginaries. The presence of threats at the border justifies all sorts of sacrifices at home, including domestic monopolies for patriotic businesses and the expansion of executive power necessary to fight war at the expense of democratic elections, civil liberties, and checks and balances. By this logic, international peace paves the way for democracy by reducing the need for extraordinary executive power. In addition, the more peaceful the international setting is, the more strained, tedious, and even laughable the autocrat's attempt to manufacture an existential threat and demand greater power will be. Peace helps protect democracy and competitive markets.[9]

Nevertheless, I do find a lot worth considering in the democratic peace theory. Political scientists Jack Snyder and Karen Ballentine argue that the competitive intellectual climate of liberal democratic countries is a potential bulwark of peace. Robust democratic scrutiny can undermine the fear-mongering imaginaries of potential autocrats. Where independent oppositional voices and a free press are present, citizens can hear alternative interpretations of the "threat" at the frontier. These alternative voices may also prove to be skeptical about the security justifications for exercising more executive power and keeping foreigners out of the economy. Liberal democratic institutions may therefore help put a brake on the rush to war—especially in cases where the other country is also a liberal democracy.[10]

So, an EU policy that seeks to populate Europe with democracies is not wrong-headed but rather just incomplete. It may be the quality of a democracy that is crucial. Edward Mansfield and Jack Snyder, for example, are skeptical that merely holding elections is enough to undermine the fear-mongering strategies of politicians. Look at what happened in Yugoslavia in 1990! They argue that liberal international peace requires a full domestic commitment and realization of the institutions of a modern Lockean state: civic and political freedoms, the broad horizontal distribution of power across institutions, and the impartial application of the rule of law.[11]

If this is the case, then the answer to failing liberalism is more liberalism, which implies that the EU and the United States were right to condition the expansion of the EU and NATO upon meeting the standards of a liberal democracy. Ideally, it would repeat the miracle of the Franco-German rapprochement with the equally miraculous rapprochements of Hungarians and Slovaks, Poles and Germans, and Serbs and Croats.

WESTERN SUPPORT FOR CIVIL SOCIETY: The final characteristic of the East-West, liberal joint venture was the active support the West gave to liberal political forces in Central Europe to meet its liberal conditions for membership. By the mid- to late 1990s, Brussels was becoming alarmed by democracy's weak foothold in Slovakia, Bulgaria, and Romania. In 1997, the European Commission established some clear consequences for being an applicant laggard in an ambitious set of Agenda 2000 reports on the membership application process. It was a promising strategy.

In 1997, Slovak desire to join the EU was about as close to a consensus as any issue could get. Even Prime Minister Vladimír Mečiar spoke positively about joining as he weakened democracy and let insiders rig state economic policy. This bold contradiction presented him with a problem, however. In July 1997, the Agenda 2000 report on Slovakia made it clear that Mečiar's illiberal-leaning policies were irreconcilable with membership in the EU.[12] The Commission sent Slovakia to the back of the application line. Worse, it gave the Czechs the green light for membership negotiations.

"This is the last straw," one Slovak friend only half-joked at the time. Only weeks earlier, the Czech men's hockey team had humiliated the Slovak team in group play at the World Cup. Now the European Commission had cordially invited the Czechs to interview at the world's most prestigious club and told the Slovaks to wait outside. Unacceptable!

It was a jest, but the frustration was real. In the realm of reforms, as measured by the transitologists, Poland, Hungary, and the Czechs had left Slovakia behind. US Secretary of State Madeline Albright even weighed in, worrying that Mečiar's Slovakia risked becoming "a hole in the map of Europe."[13]

In addition to the EU setback, NATO also chose this time to exclude Slovakia from its expansion process. Slovakia had been vying for NATO membership since 1991, when Czechoslovakia, Poland, and Hungary joined forces to press collectively for NATO membership. This group was known as the Visegrad Group, or the V4 after the Czechoslovakia split, and NATO demanded democratic governance and civilian control over the military as prerequisites for their membership. Citing the quality of Slovak democracy, NATO excluded Slovakia while inviting Czechia, Poland, and Hungary to join in 1999.

The NATO and EU rejections of 1997 made it difficult for Mečiar to justify his contradictory actions at home. He tried to pretend that Slovakia's "enemies" were trying to keep the nation down, but this did not appeal beyond Mečiar's elderly and rural base. Most voters no longer gave Mečiar's friend/enemy imaginary much real credence. In a way, he was the victim of his own prior success. He had secured independence for the country, and now he was "messing it up." Slovaks began to argue that they had only themselves to blame for putting him in power.

Between 1994 and 1998, citizens, local politicians, Western embassies, and a Western-supported network of nongovernmental organizations (NGOs) worked to rescue Slovakia's democracy and the country's European future. While we know that NGOs can be illiberal and occasionally work to erode Lockean checks on concentrated political power, scholars also consider a vibrant NGO sector to be an important sign of a healthy democracy.[14] Usually, citizens express their political preferences in elections. Between elections, however, NGOs can represent the interests of societal groups, often referred to as civil society, to the people in power. NGOs can also express and organize resistance if the people in power encroach upon civil society's essential interests. NGOs are thus the formal organizational representatives of civil society.

In the mid-1990s in Slovakia, liberals looked to NGOs to act against Mečiar's creeping authoritarianism. In 1994, Slovak NGOs began to coordinate their efforts to protect and strengthen civil society. Named the **Third Sector Gremium** (after the Bratislava restaurant where the group met), the group set about protecting an independent civil space that the government could not dominate. This produced a growing conflict with Mečiar's government.[15]

In 1996, a new law forced Slovakia's NGOs to reregister with the government. If they could not meet government requirements, they had to either disband or operate illegally.[16] The Gremium responded with a "Third Sector SOS" campaign to help rescue hundreds of NGOs that risked elimination.[17]

International foundations and foreign embassies played a crucial support role. Sharon Fisher has documented how, in 1995, the **United States Agency for International Development (USAID)** and the US State Department ramped up their assistance to civil society through the Democracy Network. The network diverted assistance from US consultants to local NGOs. Fisher and a detailed post-1998 report from Slovak activist Martin Bútora help fill in the details of what followed. In 1996, 11 donors, including the US-based Charles Stewart Mott Foundation, German Marshall Foundation, and the Open Society Foundation, formed the Slovak Donors' Forum to provide services to help NGOs survive in a hostile political environment. They coordinated grants aimed at promoting democracy and social welfare and gave NGOs the legal and technical support they needed to navigate the government's burdensome new registration requirements.[18]

The result was a remarkable flourishing of civic activity across the country. By February 1998, over 14,000 civic organizations were legally registered in Slovakia—up from around 1,000 after the first application of the restrictive registration law. The organizations focused on an enormous range of issues—from blocking a controversial new dam in Eastern Slovakia to fighting drug addiction. Most of these had little to do with opposing the Mečiar government in the election.

As the 1998 election approached, however, Slovaks formed a growing number of organizations to encourage fellow Slovaks to vote, inform the public about the issues, and ensure that the elections would be free and fair. These efforts culminated in March 1998 with the OK '98 campaign, the brainchild of Pavol Demeš, among others.[19] Named after the acronym for Občianska kampaň ("Citizens Campaign"), OK '98 reassured activists that their efforts could work.

"If we go for it," Demeš wanted people to understand, "it will be OK."[20]

Between March 1998 and the election in September, OK '98 coordinated and helped find funding for over 60 voter information, "get out the vote," and poll monitoring efforts. A small group called GEMMA 93 organized 350 young people carrying Slovak, EU, and NATO flags to march from village to village in an extensive effort that involved door-to-door campaigning and local theater. They handed out brochures and spoke to thousands of potential voters about the principles of parliamentary democracy and why it was important to vote. Another campaign, Rock the Vote, explicitly targeted first-time voters with a series of rock concerts across the country. Again, on the insistence of US funders, the emphasis was on the importance of voting rather than supporting any particular candidate.[21]

There were also efforts to ensure the elections would be free and fair. By 1998, state-run television news served as a political arm of the ruling coalition. To make this monopoly perfectly clear, the National Democratic Institute (NDI), an NGO set up by the Democratic Party of the United States, funded a group of young university graduates to establish MEMO '98. MEMO '98 monitored the difference in news coverage between Mečiar's coalition members and his opposition. They proved that Mečiar's political opposition was barely covered by the evening news, and, then, only negatively.[22]

While the government permitted international observers to observe polling places, it banned Slovak citizens from monitoring the voting or the vote-counting process. In response, an NGO called the Association for Fair Elections set up Civic Eye '98 (Občianske oko '98) to recruit and train election observers. On election day, they monitored polling stations and conducted a parallel vote count based on exit interviews to reveal disparities between the government's count and the probable vote.[23]

Opposition parties had plenty of Western support and advice they could tap into if they wanted. Like the Democrats, the US Republican Party had an organization working outside of the country called the International Republican Institute (IRI). The IRI and the NDI aspired to help post-communist parties build representative parties that would link the Slovak people to their political elites. They were relatively technocratic in their approach, and their party development programs really *were* open to everyone and politically neutral in content. The NDI and the IRI did not support programs that endorsed candidates. They were only *partisan* insofar as Prime Minister Mečiar's already well-organized, well-connected party, Movement for a Democratic Slovakia (HZDS), rarely attended their programs or accepted their advice. So the expertise the US NGOs provided disproportionately benefited the opposition.

In 1997, Mečiar's parliamentary majority passed a law raising the threshold of votes that a party needed to pass to get seats in parliament from 5 percent to 7 percent of the vote. The law threatened to eliminate small parties from parliament and gave Mečiar's large party, HZDS, an advantage by depriving its mid-sized rivals of potential small-party coalition partners. With no small-party partners to join them, the mid-sized parties would be less likely to build a coalition that would achieve a 50 percent majority coalition after the next election.

This backfired. At the urging of US NGOs and Western embassies, a coalition of small and medium-sized center-right parties unified into a single party, named the Slovak Democratic Coalition (SDK). The SDK pulled together an ideologically incoherent range of politicians who papered over their differences and centered their message on the unifying goals of defeating Mečiar and getting back into the good graces of the EU and NATO.[24] This process of centering allowed SDK to reach out across many voters. The SDK coalition rallied behind Mikuláš Dzurinda, a seemingly incorruptible, center-right Christian democrat who campaigned vigorously from village to village by bicycle. Meanwhile, a coalition of three ethnic Hungarian parties also united to ensure parliamentary entry, establishing the Party of the Hungarian Coalition (or SMK).

The combination of civic organization, voter mobilization, opposition unification, and ideological centering produced a spectacular victory for the Slovak opposition in the 1998 elections. A remarkable 84.4 percent of the electorate turned up at the polls, including over 80 percent of the possible pool of first-time voters. While Mečiar's party still had enough support from his base to win a slight plurality, he could no longer form a ruling coalition in parliament.[25] Arguably, Mečiar had put into place an apparatus that would have allowed a bid to steal the election, had he wanted to do this. But as my colleague Kevin Deegan-Krause speculated to me at the time, the mobilization of Slovak society and opposition of the West had been so decisive that Mečiar may have feared the consequences of setting it in motion.

Western embassies were impressed as well. Over the next few years, I would hear embassy and NGO workers refer to the Slovak Model or the Bratislava Process.[26] In reality, Slovakia's loosely coordinated civic and political campaigns learned directly from the recent experiences of Western-backed Bulgarian and Romanian NGOs and had many precedents in US and European Community foreign policy—dating back to Western support for the independent Polish trade union, Solidarity, in the 1980s. Indeed, the US ambassador to Slovakia in 1998 was Ralph Johnson, a talented career diplomat who could draw on his formative experiences in Poland in the 1980s.

The "Bratislava Process" sounded neutral, but it referred to a form of weaponization of liberal Western support for democratic politics. The lesson of the Bratislava Process was that the EU was a valuable electoral magnet. If one could level the political playing field by neutralizing authoritarian advantages, voters would naturally choose the EU, markets, and democracy. In practice, this meant that foreign and local NGOs worked overtime to mobilize civil society, get out the vote in large numbers, and unite the opposition around a centered, pro-EU, and market economy frame.

The election of 1998 was most of all an important milestone for the development of liberalism and Slovakia's EU and NATO membership prospects. After the election, the new Dzurinda government worked hard to get back into the EU membership process. In 1999, Slovakia caught a break when the European Council decided on a new track. Ten applicant countries, including Slovakia, were now invited to begin adopting the *Acquis Communautaire*, conveniently divided into 31 chapters (there are now 35), in preparation for a single "big bang" enlargement of 10 new members in 2004. Only when an applicant had adopted, or "closed," all 31 chapters would it be ready for membership. "Closing" all chapters was a "nonnegotiable" prerequisite.

It was an audacious exertion of the EU's active leverage—a take-it-or-leave-it offer that required applicant countries to pass tens of thousands of pages of EU laws and regulations into their domestic frameworks without much public comment or even scrutiny. "Negotiations" were usually not opportunities to bargain but rather brief windows of opportunity for local officials to demonstrate genuine compliance with EU expectations

to the European Commission. As local officials made progress, European Commission official Heather Grabbe observed, they became increasingly vested in the process—unwilling to unravel the whole package over new sticking points. They began to identify with the accession project.[27]

In Slovakia, in particular, the EU leverage was compelling. The new coalition government of Prime Minister Mikuláš Dzurinda absorbed the lessons from Mečiar's defeat in 1998: resisting the EU would be punished severely at the polling place.[28] The country thus made a particularly willing applicant. As my occasional coauthors Darina Malová and Tim Haughton later observed, Slovakia acted like "an obedient dog faithfully following its master's instructions."[29] Slovakia's negotiators adopted the new EU obligations with little initial complaint.

$$\wp \, \varpi$$

In May 2004, the EU took a gigantic step eastward. Poland, Slovakia, Hungary, Czechia, Slovenia, Latvia, Lithuania, and Estonia, plus Malta and Cyprus, became members in the "big bang" enlargement. Slovakia also finally joined NATO, along with the Baltic countries, Romania, Bulgaria and Slovenia. For most observers, it seemed as if Europe had successfully expanded its "zone of peace" from the Atlantic to the Western fringe of Eurasia in Ukraine, Belarus, and Russia.

The process also looked set to continue. Romania and Bulgaria were well on their way to joining in 2007, and Croatia and Turkey were sending all the right signals. Visionaries were already talking about democratizing the **Western Balkans** (the former Yugoslavia and Albania) through the EU accession process—essentially extending a block of market democracies unified by a single market and protected by the powerful US-backed NATO alliance to well over 30 countries and most of the European continent.

Despite Western elitism, the West's transitological mindset, and the disruptions of market integration, the gains appeared permanent at the time. For the time being, no major political force with realistic aspirations to power could be anti-European or against the single market, liberal democracy, or even NATO. Scholars of the EU began to write about the successful process of EU "socialization" and of "top-down Europeanization."[30] The EU, apparently, had established hegemony.

CHAPTER 7

Intervention

Liberalism Weaponized in the
Western Balkans

OTI uncorks a bottle of civil society in Croatia . . . The EU's Croatian success . . . Dayton's Kosovo problem . . . Albanians raid an armory . . . NATO bombs for peace? . . . Slobo and Srdja join the revolution.

PREFACE: The Bratislava Process was an important force for liberalism in Slovakia, but it became controversial—its results increasingly questionable—as it was resurrected in the Western Balkans and former Soviet Union republics like Ukraine, Georgia, Kyrgyzstan, and Russia. Against a threatening background of greater unilateral US assertiveness, NATO enlargement, and EU expansion, regional leaders equated Western efforts to support democracy with a partisan external intervention to replace them with more subservient, pro-Western governments. As we shall see in the next chapter, this exacerbated tensions between Russia and the West and served as a major concern in Putin's reactions to the West and in his authoritarian turn at home.

There was a lot to recommend the Bratislava Process. Authoritarian leaders like Mečiar in Slovakia, Tuđman in Croatia, and Milošević in Serbia aspired to permanent hegemony over political, social, and economic life in their countries. They limited the independence of the independent media, constrained the ability of the opposition to contest for power, and provided allied businesses with advantages in domestic markets and public procurement. Perhaps worst of all, they justified their control through ethno-national imaginaries that exacerbated international conflict and pitted their citizens against each other. Authoritarians thus mobilized anti-Semitism to attack philanthropists, misogyny to discredit feminists, homophobia to marginalize LGBTQ+ activists, and patriotism to repress liberals. The Bratislava Process strengthened the ability of liberals within societies to resist this authoritarian project.

Moreover, most Western-supported NGOs were officially registered with governments and thus not technically a violation of sovereignty. It was also rhetorically hard for governments to object publicly to Western assistance for the independent media, the rule of law, a balanced parliamentary-executive relationship, free and fair elections, and civil and political rights. Indeed, the very existence of these programs posed governments with a dilemma action. They could allow the assistance in and permit their opponents to gain in strength or block it and admit that they really had no interest in making their democracies work.

Yet, all claims to political neutrality aside, it was clear to all that the Bratislava Process was a regime-challenging intervention, nothing less than a liberal gauntlet thrown at the feet of authoritarian leaders. Put simply, the process aspired to build liberal democratic institutions that would prevent authoritarian politics as usual.

The authoritarian counterattack built seamlessly onto the rhetorical strategies of the nationalist political imaginary: Local opposition and civil society actors were "foreign mercenaries," the "paid agents" of Western governments and (often "Jewish") foundations bent on corrupting and dominating the nation. By 2012-13 in Russia, this narrative became a pretext for a full authoritarian culling of civil and political society, with some of the hardest axes falling on LGBTQ+ citizens, political opponents, ethno-national minorities, and independent journalists.

The West was not prepared for this counterattack. So, while I was a big admirer of the Bratislava Process, at a certain point it became counterproductive—complicating the relationship of postcommunist citizens with their governments and eventually putting the liberal political aspirations of many local democracy activists further out of reach.

It is also important to realize that the project of nonviolent liberalization of authoritarian postcommunist regimes was not the only Western interventionist policy. In 1999, the United States and NATO ignored Russian objections and bombed Serbia until President Milošević agreed to turn administration of Kosovo over to the international community. And, as we'll see in chapter 8, four years later, the United States unilaterally decided to invade Iraq as the head of an ad hoc coalition of states. Meanwhile NATO expanded its membership up to the borders of the former Soviet Union in Central Europe, into the formerly Soviet Baltic states of

Latvia, Lithuania, and Estonia, and threatened Russia with talk of additional enlargements into former Soviet space. These and other policies helped erode Russian relations with the West. Arguably, this tragedy did not need to happen.

This chapter examines Western and local attempts to build liberalism in the Western Balkans at the end of the century. Chapter 8 then examines Russia's deteriorating relations with the West, the United States' Iraq War, and Russia's response to local and international efforts to promote liberalism and security in former Soviet space.

CROATIA'S LIBERAL TURN: Croatia's nationalist president, Franjo Tuđman, died in December 1999. The following month, his party, the HDZ, lost both the presidential and the parliamentary elections. That the year was reminiscent of Slovakia's 1998 electoral breakthrough is not coincidental. Civil society, the political opposition, Western embassies, and the donor community all followed a general script written in Slovakia, but it had a distinctly Croatian story line.

By the late 1990s, Croatia's third-sector NGOs were more controversial than their Slovak counterparts. Croatian civil society was divided between relatively nationalist but sometimes critical NGOs and liberal organizations pushing for human rights, the rule of law, democratic institutions, and postwar reconciliation and justice. While the nationalist NGOs fiercely defended HDZ narratives about Croatia's "homeland war," the more liberal group included many organizations that were critical of the Croatian policies that formed part of the nationalist narrative. The Croatian Helsinki Committee for Human Rights, for example, fought for the rights of Serbian Croats who had been forcibly displaced from their homes. This made its leader something of a hate figure in the nationalist press, which still held Croatia's Serbs responsible for the war.

Liberal NGO leaders more broadly, the tabloids implied, were opportunistic careerists who had sold out the homeland for the foreign interests that were critical of the Croat nation and the patriotic "Homeland War." Meanwhile, many NGOs fought for patriotic or conservative causes, like the rights and benefits of veterans or restrictions on women's reproductive choices. Some NGOs were directly tied to the HDZ or the Tuđman family. They had little sympathy for the HDZ's liberal NGO critics. Unsurprisingly, the NGO sector was divided in its critique of the government, and its leaders regarded each other with skepticism and distrust.[1]

The international community nevertheless focused on building a robust civic check on HDZ power in preparation for the parliamentary elections in 2000. On the surface, steps taken in Croatia resembled those in Slovakia in 1998. In 1997, the United States Agency for International Development (USAID) again set up the Democracy Network, which permitted more direct support to local NGOs. USAID hosted the Office for Transition Initiatives (OTI), which one observer compared to a democracy assistance SWAT team. Like it did in Slovakia, USAID/OTI coordinated with other funders to support a nonpartisan, NGO-led campaign for a large voter turnout and free and fair elections. The international assistance community also encouraged opposition political parties to unify and "center" their messages.[2]

The international community clearly wanted Croatian voters to follow the Slovak voters' lead by voting the incumbent party, the HDZ, out of office. In 1999, the Open Society Institute (OSI) and Freedom House took activists to Bratislava to meet with veterans of OK '98 and learn from the Slovak experience. While the activists were inspired by the successful Slovak example, they felt that closely mimicking the Slovak experience was both impossible and unlikely to work. Nevertheless, OTI and OSI provided institutional support for two umbrella organizations that resembled Slovakia's OK '98 and Civic Eye campaigns. GLAS 99 (Civic Coalition for Free and Fair Elections) focused on voter education and the get out the vote (GOTV) campaign. Meanwhile, GONG (Citizens Organized to Monitor Elections) organized nonpartisan election observers and educated voters on the election process.[3]

GONG received a significant portion of its funding from OTI while its poll watchers were trained in NDI workshops. Its organizers sought distance from the more chaotic and politicized GLAS and soon established the reputation of being strictly nonpartisan and highly professional. GLAS, by contrast, served as an umbrella organization for several coalitions of activists with different donor contacts who occasionally disagreed on priorities. Initially, 35 organizations joined in, rising to 145 by the day of the election.[4]

The international donors insisted that GLAS and GONG remain strictly within a nonpartisan, democracy-promotion framework. Political parties were not directly endorsed, nor were policies advocated.[5] Yet, even more than in Slovakia, just the process of laying out facts could be partisan. The emphasis on a free vote was a clear reminder that earlier elections had not been so fair. People recalled, for example, the 1996 municipal election in Zagreb that President Tuđman invalidated after his HDZ candidate lost. Similarly, media monitors showed that while the state television did a relatively good job of giving political parties equal time on the news, coverage of the government was glowing while coverage of the opposition was negative.[6] OTI-funded "town criers" and other performers simply read the news objectively in public, revealing facts one did not often hear on the HDZ-controlled state television.[7] Perhaps most threatening of all to the government were the GLAS-sponsored rock concerts, wittily repackaged pop songs delivered in MTV-style videos, and funny information campaigns that informed younger voters about the stakes of the election and their power to change the country's direction. These younger voters were never told how to vote, only to do so. But everyone knew that they were unlikely to vote for the HDZ.

Indeed, in a country where the ruling party rigged the rules of the political game, any steps toward a level, democratic playing field would look partisan. The donors knew that if the opposition was well organized and stayed on a pro-European, pro-EU message, if information about regime self-dealing reached voters free of nationalist distortions, if people voted in large numbers, and if the vote was counted fairly, then the late President Tuđman's party would lose. As one international official told me, "We knew who we were fighting for."

Although the HDZ had leading politicians who genuinely wished to make Croatia a normal European democracy, too many of its tycoon supporters were compromised by their past dealings to really trust the democratic process. HDZ ideologues thus doubled down on the nationalist binary of patriots and traitors in the campaign.[8] Media loyal to the HDZ began to warn about a fictional US-funded "Operation Chameleon" pulling the strings of the puppet opposition. Driven by the rumor, police raided GLAS offices and confiscated several computers but found nothing compromising.[9] HDZ's media warned Croatians that the international community, not the Croatian voters, would dictate the results of the election. Mečiar even made an appearance to warn that this was how the United States decided elections.[10]

Meanwhile, the government pulled some tricks from Mečiar's playbook. In 1997, a new law forced NGOs to reregister with the state. As in Slovakia, a few could not meet the stringent new requirements. A year later, and again echoing Mečiar's efforts, the government pushed a new electoral systems law allegedly intended to give the HDZ an advantage. Croatia's normally fractious opposition united in resisting the legislation. When the law passed over their objections, two coalitions of parties came together to compete in the elections as blocks with a greater chance of meeting the electoral thresholds.[11]

In the end, however, voter resentment of HDZ economic mismanagement and self-dealing carried the day. The parliamentary elections brought out 71 percent of Croatia's electorate to vote. The HDZ fared poorly in the election and went into parliamentary opposition. A few weeks later, opposition representative Stjepan Mesić defeated HDZ's candidate for president.

The elections of 2000 sent a message to Croatian nationalist elites that they must either reconcile their own rhetoric with a pro-EU trajectory or risk slipping into political irrelevance. According to Jelena Subotić, HDZ and other politicians thereafter strategically reconfigured Croatian nationalism to be more congruent with EU membership. The HDZ moved to the liberal center, and when they later returned to power, they worked to ensure that the substance of democratic politics and the rule of law prevailed, as demanded by the EU.[12] As Milada Vachudova has pointed out, this shift ironically empowered the newly independent courts to arrest these same HDZ politicians on past corruption charges and sentence them to long jail terms.[13] Nationalist civil society organizations and politicians have not disappeared, and Croatia still wrestles with the issue of how to handle its wartime independence struggle. Still, Croatia eventually met the EU's expectations for membership and joined in 2013.

NATO'S WAR IN SERBIA: Serbia also had a pivotal election in 2000 in which the Bratislava Process played a perhaps decisive role. Yet, three things were different. First, Serbia had one of the most developed oppositional civil societies in the postcommunist world. Serbs had been in the streets in large numbers protesting Milošević for much of the previous decade—and almost constantly since 1996, when President Milošević, like Tuđman, invalidated a municipal election that he lost in the capital city of Belgrade. In 1998, a group of students formed a new group called Otpor ("Resistance"). Working from years of experience and using locally devised forms of nonviolent guerilla tactics, many of which presented the government with hilariously funny dilemma actions, they took opposition to a whole new level. Otpor was one of 30 organizations that helped found IZLAZ 2000 (Exit 2000), a coordinating umbrella group set up to get out the vote. While Otpor's charisma, assertiveness, and energy tended to grab the headlines both before and especially after the 2000 election, over 150 NGOs participated in IZLAZ 2000's campaign to get out the vote, monitor the polls, and ensure a fair election, including women's and Roma groups as well as regional and municipal organizations across Serbia.[14]

Second, the regime was behaving in a decidedly more authoritarian manner than in Slovakia or Croatia. In August 2000, for example, former Serbian Republic president Ivan Stambolić—a potential Milošević rival—

was jogging near his home when he was allegedly rushed into the back of a van, driven to a forest, and executed with two shots to the head. Day-to-day harassment of opposition protesters was also a reality and much riskier than elsewhere. Most of my friends and interviewees who helped organize the opposition to Milošević in 2000 endured some combination of state violence—including beatings, arrests, interrogations, threats, and blackmail. Despite the murder of Robert Remiaš and petty harassment that extended even to my research in Slovakia, civic action was decidedly more dangerous in Serbia than in Croatia or Slovakia.

Third, Serbian politics had been complicated by a US-led **NATO** bombing campaign on Serbia and Montenegro in 1999. Many of my students are unaware of President Bill Clinton's little "war of choice" against the Serbs, but it was a major moment in post-Cold War history—one that essentially put to rest the idealistic notion that the UN Security Council would be the authorizing body legitimizing state-on-state violence after the Cold War.

The backstory to the 78-day bombing campaign is worth noting in some detail. The immediate path to war began with the conclusion of the previous war at Dayton, Ohio, in late November 1995. The Dayton Accords officially ended the Bosnian and Croatian wars but made no effort to deal with Belgrade's repressive administrative rule in Kosovo.

Ethnic Albanian Kosovars were dismayed. As you will recall from chapter 5, Milošević had ordered his forces to occupy Kosovo in 1989. Since then, Ibrahim Rugova had led a mostly nonviolent resistance to Serbian authoritarian control.

The Kosovar Albanians believed that through their bravery, resourcefulness, and restraint from violence, they had demonstrated their right to be a sovereign self-governing nation. The Dayton Accords discredited this choice by ignoring it entirely. Kosovar Albanians observed that the accords rewarded the perpetrators of aggression and ethnic cleansing by giving Bosnian Serbs land and properties that they had seized from Bosniak and Croat communities. Indeed, it created a unified Bosnian federation of two provinces (officially called "entities") loosely based on the conflict lines at the end of the war. The Serbians had to give up much of what they had seized by force, but they could now claim their "own entity," known as the Serbian Republic. The other entity, called the Federation of Bosnia and Herzegovina, reflected the lines held by the alliance between Bosniaks and Croats.[15]

Throughout the new country, Bosnians who had fled or been violently expelled during the war had a "right to return," but most had no wish to risk going back to their prewar homes. Years after the end of the war, I drove from Sarajevo to the Serbian border, and I could see why. Few houses alongside the route had escaped destruction or damage. In one town, the entire Muslim quarter had been razed. A Serbian friend told me that the homes that still stood were often "occupied" by Serbian refugees from other communities. A return to these unrecognizable and unwelcoming communities was complex, dangerous, and traumatic.

Nevertheless, Kosovar Albanians observed that the international community had granted a form of territorial sovereignty to a Serb nation made ethnically homogenous via armed conquest. Younger Kosovars increasingly abandoned Rugova's nonviolent resistance strategy in favor of armed alternatives. The most notable of these was a loosely structured armed movement called the Kosovo Liberation Army (KLA).

According to journalist Tim Judah, the KLA would not have amounted to much due to a lack of weapons. However, in 1997, a classic postcommunist Ponzi scheme collapsed in neighboring Albania—taking the savings of thousands of Albanians with it. Violent demonstrations erupted across the country and forced the police to retreat to their barracks. Protestors took possession of unguarded military and police armories. Kalashnikovs and heavier weaponry slipped into Kosovo through the black market and resistance networks.

Previously limited to a trickle of weapons smuggled in by diaspora groups, KLA formations now found a large supply readily available. Uncoordinated attacks followed—including acts of terrorism that targeted Serbian security forces. The Belgrade-controlled police and military responded with additional military force, killing and displacing civilians, forcing many into the mountains, and radicalizing others. Sexual assault undoubtedly played a role.[16] The violence was most likely underreported. Still 20 years later, one of my Kosovar students reports, the legacy of deaths and sexual assault still lingers traumatically within her small community.

In fall 1998, US Ambassador Richard Holbrook, the architect of the Dayton Accords, brokered a ceasefire agreement for Kosovo. Milošević withdrew 6,000 police officers, and a team of international monitors came in. Some evidence has emerged, however, that a few of these monitors were CIA agents who may have provided logistical support and training to KLA units—although it is not clear if this was significant in its quality and quantity. Regardless, according to the US head of the international monitoring group, KLA units quickly broke or were goaded by Serbs into breaking the ceasefire. Milošević reinserted the police, and Serb retaliations occurred, including many additional attacks on civilians.[17]

The kind explanation for what followed is that the Clinton administration feared the Serbs would launch a systematic campaign of ethnic cleansing in Kosovo. Indeed, astute observer Samantha Power writes as if subsequent action prevented genocide.[18] President Bill Clinton and his Secretary of State, Madeline Albright, recalled the UN's failure to stop Bosnian Serb forces from executing 8,000 Bosnian Muslim men and boys in the Srebrenica massacre of July 1995. Clinton also regretted his role in preventing a more robust UN response to the Rwandan genocide of 1994, in which 800,000 Tutsis were killed by Hutu nationalists. And the administration drew courage from its memories of the quick collapse of Bosnian Serb forces in late summer 1995. They expected Milošević forces to act with greater brutality if not stopped and to capitulate after a brief show of NATO air power.

But such concerns are hard to reconcile with the uncompromising stand the United States took in negotiations at Rambouillet, France. Technically, diplomats from the United Kingdom and France led the talks, but behind the scenes Albright and her envoy, Christopher Hill, issued a firm US ultimatum: unless Milošević turned control over security in the province to NATO, Clinton would order air strikes. An annex, however, also demanded the free movement of NATO forces throughout Serbia and Montenegro (which was all that was left of Yugoslavia). This would have given NATO the right to occupy Serbia militarily and was a nonstarter.

The annex may have simply been a mistake or bad diplomacy, but combined with the documented allegations of CIA support for KLA units, it has provided fuel for the argument that the Clinton administration preferred an armed conflict with Serbia over the negotiated peaceful surrender of Kosovo to the international community. If this is true, then the failed negotiations were a Clinton "success." Milošević refused to sign.[19]

Russia proved good on its promise to veto a UN Security Council-sanctioned military action against Serbia. So, President Clinton controversially turned to NATO to legitimate multinational military intervention. This violated the UN charter.

NATO forces began to bomb Serbia on March 24, 1999. Russia's prime minister, Yevgeny Primakov, was furious but could do little to stop the attacks. The 78-day air assault compelled Serbian forces to leave Kosovo—but not before Serbian military and police forces had forcibly driven 90 percent of the country's Albanian population into flight. As many as 800,000—approximately half the population—are reported to have been forced into neighboring countries at the point of a gun. Here was the genocide the Clinton administration had been fearing, but was it *despite* the war or a Serbian response to it? The answer remains unclear.

Serbian forces stripped the Kosovars of their identifying documents as they left. It was a clear warning that, should Serbia retain possession of Kosovo after the war, ethnic Albanians would not be welcomed back. Hundreds of Serbians and as many as 10,000 Kosovar Albanians died.[20]

This was a tough time to be an anti-Milošević politician or activist in Serbia. Prodemocracy opposition parties and activists were ideologically aligned with Western liberals, and many already depended on Western assistance and advice in their struggles with Milošević. NATO bombs did not help them. They made the regime's political imaginary quite concrete. Activists went into hiding to avoid being beaten, arrested, or conscripted. Political opposition came to a halt.

Instead, there was a quite predictable "rally around the flag" effect as young people put their sardonic humor to work against NATO. With their already well-honed talent for dilemma actions and strong tradition of nationalist civic society organization,[21] many now donned white T-shirts with a red target on the back and occupied bridges and buildings that NATO had not already destroyed. To the surprise of everyone, Serbian defense forces successfully shot down a F-117 "stealth" bomber. A group of students celebrated in front of cameras with a poster taunting, "Sorry, we didn't know it was invisible."

Yet, the NATO assault was relentless and, in the end, compelling. On June 10, 1999, Milošević reluctantly agreed to allow the UN Monitoring Mission in Kosovo to administer Kosovo and withdrew his troops, police, and administrators. The following week, the Red Cross observers reported several tens of thousands of Serbian Kosovars leaving with the Serbian troops and police. KLA reprisals against Albanians, Serbs, and Roma followed.[22] Licking his wounds, Milošević began to prepare for the presidential election in 2000.

SERBIA'S OCTOBER REVOLUTION: The subsequent September 2000 election proved to be the high point for the West's Bratislava Process. It helped that Serbia's opposition and civil society were already well formed and experienced from past battles with the state. Out of a combination of common sense and Otpor urging, Milošević's usually fractured opposition adopted the strategies of centering and opposition unity. A range of 17 vastly disparate political parties formed an anti-Milošević coalition called DOS-17 and selected Vojislav Koštunica, a "moderate" nationalist, to oppose Milošević. Koštunica, it was hoped, could signal a reconciliation of Serbia's national interest with robust democratic competition and Serbian cooperation with the EU. The message was not that Serbian nationalism was bad, only that it was poorly served by Milošević and his cronies. Real

Serbian interests lay with democracy, economic reform, and the possibility of Western integration.

As they did in Croatia and Slovakia, Western NGOs and embassies stepped in with financial support and expertise. In fall 1999, the East-West Institute hosted a conference that brought together NGOs leaders, trade unions, and opposition politicians. Veterans of the Slovak campaign against Mečiar shared their experience, but according to several attendees I spoke to, as in Croatia, the Slovaks' inspiring example was as important as their technical advice. Above all, Miljenko Dereta later told me, they learned that "active citizens *can* play a role in changing politics."[23]

In October 1998, my friends and co-teachers Srdja Popović and Slobodan Đinović joined other veteran student activists to form Otpor, which proved fantastically adept at centering. They had a creative team of colleagues and an army of teens and university students whose visuals and dilemma actions helped turn Milošević's imaginary into the laughing stock of the nation. In the documentary *Bringing Down a Dictator* (the Steven York film that helped propel Srdja and Otpor into the activist version of stardom), there is footage of an Otpor activist demonstrating how a geeky teenager in an Otpor T-shirt must indeed be one of the Otpor "terrorists" that the regime was warning people about. The joke was on the regime, as the kid couldn't have been any less threatening—unless, of course, he decided to vote.[24]

It was all part of what Srdja would later call "laughtivism"—the use of humor to decimate the legitimacy narrative of the powerful. Otpor's laughtivism helped destroy the regime's pernicious political imaginary of enemies and traitors and redraw it to make opposition a patriotic act. This was a hard trick to pull off, as Otpor and Serbia's democratic political opposition were indeed drawing financial and technical support from the very countries that had just bombed them.[25]

As previously noted, Otpor was part of the internationally supported umbrella group IZLAZ 2000, which oversaw GOTV, media monitoring, poll observations, parallel vote tabulation, and much more. The international community was deeply supportive. NDI helped train poll watchers organized by the Center for Free Elections and Democracy (CeSID), for example, which prepared a parallel vote tabulation designed to reveal any government efforts to manipulate electoral results.[26] When police confiscated CeSID computers several days before the elections, their international sponsors quickly replaced them.

Centering attempted to destroy Milošević's political imaginary by publicly reimagining what it meant to be a Serb. This required gaining at least an approving nod and often from the national civil society that had supported the wars—such as the Serbian Orthodox Church, veterans of the previous decade's many battles, football hooligans, miners, and anti-Milošević nationalists.

A typical Otpor dilemma action was to organize anti-Milošević military veterans to gather outside a prison where protestors were being held. The police could release the detainees or risk offending the patriotic veterans who had fought for the nation. Either way, the police lost.

Gender identities played a role too. In one march, women activists from Otpor stood in the front ranks with male activists in the back. The willingness of Otpor activists to take risks was not differentially gendered, but the organizers knew that society was, and they used this knowledge tactically. When the police decided to attack the women in front, photos and videos spread across the country in the independent media—further discrediting the regime by showing how the police had violated Serbian norms of masculinity. Real men do not beat women, the patriarchal trope went.

In late September 2000, Milošević used party control over the polling process to falsify the presidential vote count. The opposition, however, was prepared with a Western-funded parallel vote tabulation from CeSID in which volunteers' records of how people exiting the polls had voted helped reveal that the government's official count was most likely a fraud. In the ensuing days, Otpor and other IZLAZ 2000 organizations, trade unions, and opposition parties created a broad-based uprising that gradually shut down the country. On October 5, 2000, hundreds of thousands of Serbs took control of the streets of Belgrade and stormed the parliament building. Meanwhile, presidential candidate Koštunica and the mayor of Belgrade, Zoran Đinđić, pulled the country's security forces over to their side with promises that security and military interests would be protected in the new era. Bereft of police and military support, the discredited Milošević had no choice but to step down.[27]

It was an exciting time. Yet, with so many of the beneficiaries of the Milošević era still in place and fiercely defending their positions, the euphoria would be short-lived. We will return to this situation in chapter 9. Yet, first, we need to put the struggle for liberalism in Central and Eastern Europe in a broader international context. The West's efforts to expand and consolidate a liberal post-Cold War order were beginning to run into some significant resistance.

CHAPTER 8

International Relations

The West Gets Cocky

*A new dataset . . . Responsibility to protect? . . . 9/11 and
unilateralism . . . Bombs and boots in Afghanistan . . . Powell tells the
UN some whoppers . . . Bombs and boots in Iraq . . . I offend a four-
star general . . . Taking a moment to remember Ben and Nicole . . .
Getting my picture taken in Kyiv . . . Orange aid . . . Russia strikes
back . . . The Euromaidan . . . Vladimir Putin, uber-Grinch*

THE RISE AND FALL OF LIBERAL INTERVENTION: Western-backed
opposition success in Serbia called attention to the differences between
armed uprisings and the nonviolent civil capacity-building strategies of
the Bratislava Process. Which is better at effecting regime change *and*
building democracy? The important work by Maria Stephan and Erica
Chenoweth that I mentioned in chapter 1 provides strong evidence in favor
of strategic nonviolent conflict of the sort that Otpor so effectively waged.[1]

The authors met at Colorado College at a conference that we hosted
with the International Center for Nonviolent Conflict (ICNC), called "People's Power and Pedagogy." Dr. Chenoweth at the time was a brilliant PhD
student at the University of Colorado, Boulder, who was skeptical about
the transformative potential of strategic nonviolent conflict. Dr. Stephan,
the daughter of Catholic peace activists from the Vietnam era, had recently
finished her own doctorate on strategic nonviolent resistance movements
at the Fletcher School of Law and Diplomacy. Dr. Chenoweth suspected
that the literature supporting nonviolence was based on cherry-picked
examples of success. She had a counterexample or explanation for every
feel-good story about nonviolence that Dr. Stephan and her ICNC co-
presenters could offer. Their argument raged on over the next two days, but

as the conference ended something remarkable happened—they agreed to find the data that would resolve their disagreement.

The result was the NAVCO dataset, the first database that takes large-scale violent and nonviolent conflict equally seriously.[2] Drs. Chenoweth and Stephan then crunched the numbers, and to their pleasant surprise, Dr. Stephan had been right. Nonviolent movements were not only superior to violent movements in winning conflicts, but when they did win, they were hands down more likely to produce more democratic outcomes.[3]

Yet there was still the nagging concern that nonviolent uprisings were becoming a Western policy instrument, wielded to challenge unfriendly authoritarian governments. So, despite its success and my own desire to see liberal regimes emerge through nonviolent means, the Bratislava Process of Western intervention in Serbian politics raised some concern.

The West was not entirely out of line to offer nurturing support. From the perspective of prodemocracy NGOs, to do nothing—to be neutral—was to leave the country in the hands of the venal cadres of crony capitalists around Mečiar, Tuđman, and Milošević, who showed no qualms about enriching themselves, even if it meant impoverishing, isolating, and dividing their own people and provoking armed conflict between nations. Moreover, as most of the foreign-supported NGOs usually had the state's legal permission to operate, it was not a violation of sovereignty.

At the time, moreover, much of the debate among liberals was not about whether to take action but *how* to do it. Many of my academic friends became proponents of internationally sanctioned, *armed* intervention in the internal affairs of states when their government neglected or abused their citizens. By the early 2000s, these friends were supporting a new multilateral norm in international relations called Responsibility to Protect (R2P). Since 2005, R2P has empowered the UN Security Council (UNSC) to authorize both violent and nonviolent intervention in cases where states are inflicting or failing to prevent grievous harm to their people.[4]

But international intervention in the domestic affairs of a sovereign state—in its both violent and nonviolent guises—has proven to be an unruly and incompetent genie, one difficult to stuff back into the bottle once uncorked. Intervening is always risky. At the broadest level, it cheapens the international norm of nonintervention in the domestic affairs of other nations—a norm already reeling from US and Soviet Cold War interventions—that is enshrined in the charter of the UN. UN members pledge to respect the sovereignty of other nations. War is only legitimate in self-defense and then only when none of the permanent members of the UNSC—France, China, the United Kingdom, Russia, or the United States—veto it.

The threat of intervention, armed or otherwise, triggers something called the security dilemma. The security dilemma occurs when one's effort to make oneself safer makes others feel more at risk.[5] You may have experienced the security dilemma in some form. As a teenager, my siblings, friends, and I would randomly slug each other in the thick of the muscle on our shoulders. It was a bit of a game, but experience had taught us that the punch hurt less when the arm was flexed. So, for a few awkward years, we came to have perfectly normal conversations with our arms bent and ready to take or deliver a surprise punch. We wouldn't think about it much, and it's certainly not what we wanted. Flexing was just what I did to keep from getting caught unawares, and it invariably led my siblings and friends to flex too.

This is the security dilemma in action, a concept we usually associate with the realist tradition of international relations. The realist starting point is that many aspects of the international system are organized according to the principle of anarchy. Anarchy means that there is no overarching power to protect one's agreements with others from being broken, to stop one's land from being invaded and occupied, or to save one's people from being destroyed or enslaved. It is the driving assumption of what realist theorist Kenneth Waltz famously called the "self-help international system" in his classic work, *Theory of International Politics*. Under anarchy, a parent is not in the room to stop you from getting hit—so you learn to fend for yourself.[6]

If a statesperson is doing their job correctly, according to realism, they must always be concerned about what others might do to their country in the future. Others may simply be trying to protect themselves, but the statesperson can't always assume this, and they often react with precautionary measures—like tightening one's shoulder muscle in the presence of a sibling. There are many ways that a state may help itself, and the appropriate choice depends on its capabilities and those of others.

Central Europe's self-help strategy is typical of small and middle-sized states. Militarily, they are weak, and by comparison their larger sibling, Russia, remains a threat. After the withdrawal of Soviet troops from the region in the early 1990s, Central European states sought additional security by applying to join NATO. The 1999 and 2004 expansions successfully completed the process of reorienting Central Europe's strategic alignment from Moscow to Brussels and Washington.

Given the weakness of Russia at the time, realists like the American diplomat George Kennan protested that NATO enlargement would be needlessly antagonistic. The West and Russia were at ease. Why raise the arm into an offensive-defensive fist? Wouldn't Russia eventually respond in kind? Wouldn't the reemergence of a Western threat give Russian leaders an excuse to brush off nationalist imaginary as a prelude to becoming more authoritarian at home? It made no sense to Kennan.[7]

Clinton's predecessor, President George H. W. Bush, had helped bring the Cold War to an end by embracing these realist principles. At the Malta Conference of December 2-3, 1989, he promised Soviet premier Gorbachev that the United States would not use the Soviet withdrawal from Central Europe to gain a unilateral advantage. It was sound, realist logic then, and it went a long way toward helping ease the Soviets' security concerns. But on December 8, 1991, the Soviet Union imploded, and soon after, the US foreign policy establishment was confronted with horrific humanitarian catastrophes in Somalia, Bosnia, Rwanda, and Kosovo. Russia bungled its turn to markets and turned out to be a weak state that no longer commanded the level of US attention that it once did. Many liberals in the West also bet that a rich ecosystem of market democracies and coordinating international organizations promoting liberal values could transform great power competitors into a more amicable community committed to peacefully tackling collective challenges.[8] Anarchy did not need to resemble an endless boys' game of threatening and defending against sucker punches. It could be mitigated.

By bombing Kosovo without UNSC approval and by expanding NATO to the former borders of the Soviet Union, however, Clinton alerted Russia to its diminished power status. Worse, the use of the Bratislava Process to assist Milošević's domestic opposition made it clear that the West would deliberately target illiberal, anti-Western leaders—even if they were friends of Russia. Russians could not help but note that there were quite a few illiberal leaders in allied countries closer to home who were vulnerable to Western intervention. As in Serbia, these allies were collecting a robust assortment of Western NGOs, located in the capitals, that were offering assistance in the effort to build democracy. The Clinton administration thus made it clear that the UNSC norms of multilateral decision-making and nonintervention provided poor checks on the use of US power, in both its violent and its nonviolent forms. Russians found this new state of affairs to be both humiliating and threatening, but reeling from a decade of catastrophic economic mismanagement and military decline, they could do little about it.

Then came the new administration of President George W. Bush and

September 11, 2001. On "9/11," 19 men, armed with no more than box cutters, commandeered four jet airliners and flew them into the twin towers of the World Trade Center, the Pentagon, and, after its passengers stormed the cockpit, a field in Pennsylvania. The attack propelled the United States further down the road of international intervention than it had been since the Vietnam War. At first, US leaders legitimately argued that the United States had been attacked and, under both the UN and NATO charters, had a right to defend itself. Russia—which was facing internal security issues of its own—obligingly backed UNSC approval for a NATO-led, multinational effort to invade Afghanistan, the country where Osama bin Laden had organized the 9/11 attack.

Despite this, President George W. Bush and Vice President Dick Cheney used 9/11 to openly reject the multilateralism of the UNSC in favor of US unilateralism. Under multilateralism, the US respects the collective decisions of its partners in the UNSC. Under unilateralism, by contrast, the US determines the rules governing the use of its military force. Others can join if they want, giving it the veneer of multinational support, but the US president is really calling the shots.

Unilateralism had some significant bipartisan backing. American journalist Charles Krauthammer notably called the post-Cold War period a "unipolar moment."[9] With the collapse of the Soviet Union and China only beginning to rise, the United States was left standing as the world's preeminent power, able to project force anywhere on the planet and fight two major wars simultaneously. Such a turn in the balance of power, unilateralists like Krauthammer argued, gave the United States extraordinary global responsibilities and special rights. Was this moral, they asked? Krauthammer and others argued that it was. Since the United States was providing security to its allies, it should have disproportionate and final say into how it would do it.[10] Moreover, Krauthammer observed with a surprising lack of skepticism, US values were liberal, hence "benign," and certainly superior to UNSC realpolitik.[11]

President George W. Bush summarized a shift to unapologetic unilateralism in his June 2002 speech at the West Point Academy.[12] He revealed a new political imaginary—a dangerous post-Cold War world in which our biggest adversary was no longer a conventional power that could be contained or deterred, like Russia or China. The new threat was from non-state militant organizations, like bin Laden's group, Al-Qaeda, which could hide and organize on the territory of failed states that could not police their own affairs. Bush also called out a category of rogue states, like North Korea, Iraq, and Iran—his famed "axis of evil"—which failed to play by the global rules of the game, sponsored nonstate militant groups abroad, and supposedly sought biological, chemical, or nuclear weapons, also known colloquially as **weapons of mass destruction (WMDs)**. The leaders of rogue states were led by unstable, irrational, or ideological dictators, Bush added. Containment and deterrence would not work on them.

The conclusion of these propositions became known as the **Bush Doctrine**. Since rogue states and nonstate militants could not be deterred by traditional military and diplomatic means, and since they could at least theoretically acquire and use WMDs against targets in the West, the Bush administration had to be militarily proactive. Bush thus claimed the right to bomb, invade, or pressure potential threats *before* they could become a clear and present danger to the American people. He would also encourage international stability by aggressively promoting democracy where he could.

President Bush, who identified as a Texan and liked a macho cowboy swagger, used his new imaginary to cock the rifle of America's military and diplomatic might and level it in the direction of states that refused to play by "America's rules." Altogether, Bush demanded that over 60 states make adjustments to ensure that the United States and its allies feel adequately secure.

In reality, Bush only partially called the shots. Vice President Dick Cheney, Secretary of Defense Donald Rumsfeld, and a team of cabinet members and advisers known as neoconservatives shaped foreign policy in Bush's first four years. The primary target of the "neocons" was Iraq, a large multiethnic, Middle Eastern oil producer led by a genuine tyrant, President Saddam Hussein. I could spill a lot of ink on how Hussein developed from being a US-supported tyrant in the 1980s into an enemy tyrant and a threat to regional security in 1990, but that would take too long. Suffice it to say that Hussein ran afoul of the international community when his troops invaded and occupied Kuwait in August 1990. In the Gulf War of March 1991, President George H. W. Bush built a UNSC-approved multinational coalition led by the United States and the United Kingdom that pushed Hussein's troops out of Kuwait. Hussein remained in power, but over the next decade, the international community hobbled his economy with international sanctions and occupied his air space with airborne warning and control systems and fully armed F-16s.

Iraq was not really a major threat to the United States or even its major allies after that, in my opinion. In September 2001, President Hussein's police were arresting rather than supporting nonstate militants. Nor was Iraq capable of building biological or nuclear weapons without being observed. Despite some resistance from the Iraqis, UN inspectors believed they had confirmed that Iraq had no real WMD capacity. Thousands of chemical artillery shells from earlier wars still had to be found. Yet, these aging tactical frontline weapons were not a strategic threat much beyond Iraqi borders. The Iraqi army did not use them in the 1991 Gulf War, nor were any units equipped to use them in 2003 when the regime was threatened by US invasion.

Regardless, select United States intelligence actors cooked up some reasonable doubt about Iraqi compliance, which Secretary of State Colin Powell presented to the UN on February 5, 2002. Powell, a career military officer, was the perfect choice for this speech. As a top defense official in the Bush Sr. and Clinton administrations, he had insisted that military force should be used only when US lives and property were at risk. In the early 1990s, this proviso became part of what is known as the Powell Doctrine.[13]

Working with the younger President Bush in 2003, however, Powell now made the case for invading Iraq. Many experts (including himself apparently) felt that his evidence was flimsy and stretched.[14] None of the realist thinkers that I knew were even remotely convinced that he had built a successful case for invasion rooted in the realist principle of US national security. Yet, the decision to invade had already been made. Powell's job was to justify it.

US allies in NATO split over the issue. In Central Europe, Poland, Czechia, and Hungary all backed the US administration's case by signing a letter of support for the action, along with Britain, Portugal, and Denmark. A few days later, most of the rest of Central Europe signed on too. As NATO members or NATO aspirants nestled between Germany and Russia, Central Europeans valued a powerful US-led NATO alliance to counter their large neighbors' dominance. NATO was, a British diplomat once famously quipped, designed to "keep the Russians out, the Americans in, and the Germans down."[15] Central Europeans took this to heart. They were afraid of Russia, and they needed the United States in the alliance to provide a check on Germany. Yet, German and especially French leaders were furious with the Central Europeans' deference to what they saw as US recklessness in the Middle East. "They've missed a good chance to keep quiet," lectured French president Jacques Chirac.[16]

Central European backing for a US war in the Middle East was quite disturbing to me as well at the time. I wondered how a Czech government of former nonviolent resisters could now support what I believed would be a gratuitous and ill-advised armed invasion. From chapter 1, you may recall Martin Palouš, the nonviolent Charter '77 activist who served me stale beer after his release from prison in late October 1989. In 2003, his studies in international law and diplomacy and his friendship with President Havel had led to his appointment as the Czech ambassador to the United States. We had kept in touch since 1989, and in 2004 he graciously accepted my invitation to come to Colorado Springs to give a talk on campus and to the local community. I asked him to speak, in between these talks, to our students of nonviolence on his Charter '77 experience.

I tried to be polite about Czech support for the Iraq invasion, but fortunately one of my students bravely asked, "How do you reconcile your nonviolent Charter '77 background with your government's support for the Iraq invasion?" I did not write down Palouš's response, but to paraphrase, he said something like, "We were not *for* nonviolence. We were against tyranny. If we could have used weapons to beat the communists, we would have gladly done so." For Ambassador Palouš, and indeed for a few of my Serbian Otpor friends, nonviolence was a *tactical* choice, not a personal principle. Weapons would have been useless against the well-armed state, so they used what was available.

On a fun sidenote, Ambassador Palouš capped off his visit to Colorado Springs by accepting a VIP tour of the North American Aerospace Defense Command (NORAD), the military base overseeing North American airspace. NORAD is notable for the Christmas Santa Tracker (Google it!) and was then located in a cave a mile inside Cheyenne Mountain on the southwestern side of Colorado Springs. I asked Ambassador Palouš if I could tag along, and to our mutual surprise, the military agreed.

Back when I was learning Slovak in 1996, I studied by memorizing random sentences. My favorite sentence—"What would happen if I pushed *this* red button?"—had so far gone unused in real life. Fortunately, one of the rooms in NORAD's interior complex had a big red button. Turning to Palouš, I asked my long-rehearsed question in accented Slovak. Not missing a beat, he responded in Czech, "I don't know, John. Try!" This got a short giggle from both of us. Yet, before I could explain the joke to the soldiers around us, our four-star host and his assistants stiffened and escorted us to the next room in the complex.

In addition to stressing NATO, the Iraq invasion proved to be an irritant to Russian-US relations. In 2003, President Vladimir Putin's inhumane pacification of a rebellion in the Russian republic of Chechnya was coming to a close. Putin was sympathetic and even supportive of Bush's war against the Taliban in Afghanistan and terrorism more broadly. But he wanted reciprocal support in his own brutal fight against Chechen separatists at home. He did not get it. Instead, the United States lectured him on the need to uphold human rights and build democracy. I agreed with this sentiment but coming from a US government whose officials justified internationally illegal occupation, torture, abduction, and incarceration without due process, it was blatantly hypocritical. The United States could not speak with much moral force.

So, Russian foreign policy leaders did not object to the United States' use of force per se, but they found the aggressive unilateral extension of US power into Iraq to be unwarranted, threatening to unaligned countries everywhere, and, well, stupid—even from the perspective of US national interest. Russian president Vladimir Putin likely watched the Iraq invasion the way a Formula 1 driver watches a bitter rival crash into a wall. He might have even laughed aloud when, not finding any WMDs, Bush officials said that the invasion was still valuable because it would bring democracy, respect for human rights, improved status for women, and private enterprise and markets to Iraq. By 2006, these efforts, too, had failed, while occupying forces and administrators embarrassed the United States with documented human rights abuses, allegations of corruption, and incompetence.[17]

With five military institutions located in Colorado Springs, local residents perhaps felt the wars more directly than those living in most other parts of the United States. The parents of our children's friends kept getting deployed for months at a time. One barbeque turned sour as a recently returned US Army officer used racist terms to describe the probably illegal interrogation techniques he used on Iraqi prisoners. The patio quickly divided between those who were sympathetic and a few who were who were horrified. This was about the time when an "improvised explosive device" killed my coteacher, Nicole Suveges, while she worked for a private contractor in Iraq. She had been studying for her PhD at Johns Hopkins University when she took the job to supplement her meager salary as an adjunct lecturer. *Five* years later (George W. Bush's wars remain the longest military conflicts outside of North America in US history), a US Marine corporal pointed a loaded gun at the head of my former student and friend Ben and pulled the trigger. Ben and his unit had recently returned from their third combat deployment and were only hours from an honorable discharge from service. I had the good fortune to reminisce with Ben's mother, who contrasted his tough-guy soldier persona at school with the thoughtful and loving son she had sent to fight Bush's costly wars.

Bush's 2003 choice to invade Iraq smashed a small portion of humanity's admittedly flawed and unjust stained-glass window into millions of shards—each a painful personal memory. By 2019, a conservative estimate of the direct death toll from Bush's war in Iraq was around 300,000, including approximately 9,000 official US military and US contractor deaths. Insurgent leaders and Iraqi weakness also played a significant role in the subsequent rise of the Islamic State of Iraq and Syria (ISIS). The Afghan conflict continues today, but in late 2019, the conservative estimated death toll was around 160,000, with well over 3,000 coalition deaths. At least 200,000 have died in related conflicts in Pakistan, Syria, and Yemen. The real cost has been much greater—both in the United States and in the conflict regions. Neither Ben nor any of the tens of thousands of soldiers and civilians who have died from suicide, addiction, homelessness, or non-combat violence are included in these official tallies.[18]

THE KREMLIN MAKES A POINT: Russia's ruling elite since the 1999 Kosovo bombing include some of the most distasteful people in this brief post-Cold War history. They should not get a pass in this chapter. They often outclass the US foreign policy establishment in inhumanity, venality, cynicism, and willingness to employ realpolitik at an enormous human cost. Still, they *are* the leaders of a sovereign state with legitimate security concerns. Kosovo, Iraq, and NATO expansion right up to the borders of the former Soviet Union seemed almost designed to make Russia flinch and flex. To add to the insult, in 2001, President Bush abolished the Cold War-era, Anti-Ballistic Missile Treaty and planned to spread an anti-ballistic missile complex between Poland and Czechia, the Soviet Union's former Warsaw Pact "allies." Many of these efforts have done nothing to improve US or Central European security and have spurred Russia into developing costly and recklessly dangerous nuclear cruise missiles, a new submarine that threatens coastal cities with tidal annihilation, and other alt-tech countermeasures.

Russian president Putin has never subscribed to liberal, "end-of-history" universalism. Rather, his grand strategy has over time fallen into the political tradition of a great authoritarian power. In practice, this requires steady discipline emanating from the Kremlin horizontally across Russia's regions and vertically through society. Civil society is allowed to exist, but it must be aligned (or *alignable* in a crisis) with Kremlin goals. From this core of strength, the Kremlin protects itself by the limited projection of power in the near abroad and more recently in areas of strategic interest, like Syria.

Putin is also convinced, I've been told, that US and Western-backed NGOs are the primary driving force for the revolutions against pro-Russian authoritarians in the former Soviet space.[19] It is true, of course,

that these NGOs played a role in the dismissal of pro-Russian governments in Serbia in 2000, Georgia in 2003, and Ukraine in 2004-5.[20] Still,
we should not discount the agency and legitimacy of literally hundreds of
thousands of post-Soviet citizens demanding change. Would these protests have taken to the streets were the United States *not* supportive? I
believe so. The history of people rising up against *US-backed* authoritarian regimes and against regimes where the United States or EU were not
even on the radar indicates that there are times when states become so
venal and abusive that a portion of their citizens take action—regardless
of whether NDI, IRI, or OTI and associated democracy-promoting NGOs
are providing assistance. Nor was US backing a direct factor in the onset of
the Arab Spring uprisings of 2011. I think it is overly simplistic to reduce
anti-regime protests to a simple act of US statecraft. But this is apparently
how Putin saw it.

Still, it is equally indisputable that authoritarian regimes, globally,
face significant challenges from their citizens and that the EU and West
Europe have *selectively* been materially supportive. Just over a year before
the Ukrainian uprising known as the **Orange Revolution**, I visited Ukraine
to do some research on the property-transformation process. While there,
I also met with US and NGO officials to see if there was anything like the
Bratislava Process being put in place. I found that there was, and to a larger
extent than I had expected. When I arrived, the government had failed to
renew the registration for NDI and IRI and had recently kicked out an official from the Washington, DC-based prodemocracy NGO called Freedom
House.[21] With IRI and NDI lacking the permission to be there, their ongoing operations were potentially a violation of sovereignty.[22]

It was quickly made clear to me that the Western-backed NGO sector
was under close watch by, well, someone. Both of my outdoor interviews
with officials from the US congressional NGOs were openly recorded, and
in one, my NDI host and I were photographed.[23] A man in an unmissable
orange jumpsuit interrupted my IRI interview in a café when he placed a
briefcase next to us on the table. It might have had a recording device in
it, but the real purpose was simply to harass my IRI host. It had little to
do with me. I had just naively stumbled into a zone already under surveillance.[24] We called for the check and finished the discussion in the IRI
offices. Later, I heard that they too were quite likely bugged.

After the interview, the man in the orange jumpsuit was waiting outside and followed me for about 15 minutes as I walked up the hill. The
brightly colored jumpsuit freaked me out, of course, but it also made me
laugh. "They" obviously—and quite correctly—had very little faith in my

ability to know if I was being followed! My IRI contact was knowledge-able and provided an excellent explanation—rooted in domestic political jockeying—for why Ukrainian security was being *so open* about its sur-veillance at that time, but his reasons are less important here than the reasons for the surveillance in the first place.

There was indeed a concerted effort on the part of Western embassies to resurrect the Bratislava Process in Ukraine. As in Slovakia, Croatia, and Serbia, Western-backed NGOs were openly contributing expertise and funding to help citizens and opposition parties negate some of the admin-istrative advantages of the party in power. Among many other things, the NGOs strengthened political parties, monitored state television, assisted the independent media, helped get out the youth vote through an Otpor-like (and advised) group called Pora ("Enough"), observed polling stations for irregularities, and compiled parallel estimates of the vote.[25]

A few Western embassy people I spoke to nevertheless doubted the Ukrainians' ability to rise up, Serbian style, if the government tried to cheat—especially the youth. The Ukrainians quickly proved them wrong. In fall 2004, the Party of Regions candidate for president, Viktor Yanu-kovych, tried to win a presidential runoff through fraud. Over the ensu-ing six weeks, hundreds of thousands of citizens from Kyiv and elsewhere seized control of Independence Square (the Maidan) and refused to leave until the fraud was addressed. Finally, the Supreme Court issued an order to hold a free and fair presidential runoff election. It is, in my view, simply inaccurate to write off this prolonged burst of mass, civic resistance as the simple product of Western interference.

Russia, it should be remembered, also intervened, although it is less clearly documented. Moscow countered Western NGOs with their own party advisers, known as "political technologists," who were trained in the burgeoning new competitive authoritarian art of "managed democracy." They reportedly provided significant funding for the incumbent party and pro-regime media. Russia may have also played a role in a nearly successful attempt to kill opposition candidate Viktor Yushchenko with a disfiguring dose of dioxin. The leading suspect in the poisoning later fled to Russia, where his Russian citizenship protected him from extradition. Despite this intervention, Yushchenko, the Western-backed candidate, prevailed in 2005. This infuriated Putin.

In 2007, in speech to world leaders in Munich, Putin openly called for a return to multipolarity. Henceforth, he hinted, Russia would confront US initiatives more directly. The first tests of the new policy came within a few months. In February 2008, the United States gave backing to Kosovo's unilateral declaration of independence from Serbia. Then, in April, Bush insisted at a NATO summit in Bucharest, Romania, that the former Soviet Republics of Ukraine and Georgia should have the right to join NATO. In August, Russia used a Georgian decision to secure sovereignty over secessionist South Ossetia by force of arms to justify invading Georgia.

The Russian point was twofold. First, if Kosovar Albanians could unilaterally detach themselves from Serbia, why couldn't South Ossetians leave Georgia?[26] Second, the invasion made it clear that Georgia would be a liability to NATO. Georgia would be more likely to draw the alliance into war with Russia than to strengthen its members' collective security. The Russians quickly withdrew after making rapid gains, but they did so voluntarily from a position of local dominance. Most importantly, Bush's aspiration for expanding NATO further into former Soviet space had suffered a clear setback.[27]

President Putin's second term ended in 2008—even before the Georgian invasion. Rather than stepping into retirement, however, he engineered an exchange of offices with his pragmatic prime minister, Dimitry Medvedev. From 2009 to 2011, President Barack Obama and President Medvedev refocused bilateral relations around mutual interests rather than an idealistic project of convergence with Western ideals. In 2011, among other things, the "reset" policy culminated in START, the Strategic Arms Reduction Treaty that reduced nuclear arsenals by 30 percent. Obama's former ambassador to Russia, Michael McFaul, points to this era to demonstrate that the previous eight years of US sovereign encroachment had not destined the two countries to hostility.[28]

Yet, US unilateralism and the Bratislava Process were legacies that lurked in the background when Putin returned to the presidency. In Russia's fall 2011 parliamentary election, Prime Minister Putin's main backing party, United Russia, fared less well than expected—perhaps the predictable result of being the party in power during the 2008-10 Great Recession. At the last minute, media officials who allegedly feared Putin's anger appear to have panicked and tacked double-digit increases onto the United Russia tally in their news broadcast. The problem was that in their haste, they forgot to compensate by reducing the other parties' shares of the vote. The evening news featured the loyal media guilelessly presenting the "final" results. Added up, the column revealed that 147 percent of the people had voted to extend United Russia's parliamentary dominance!

"We are the 146 percent!" read one of the cleverest posters in the ensuing demonstrations. Over the next months, citizens of Moscow and St. Petersburg took to the streets in an ongoing dance of anti- and pro-government demonstrations, known as the Snow Revolution. Each side attributed the enthusiasm of the other to the incentives offered by behind-the-scenes actors, Western-based NGOs on one side and the regime on the other.

Putin decisively won a March 2012 presidential election that he might have won fairly if it had been allowed. Soon after, the executive-parliamentary majority got serious about demobilizing Russia's oppositional civil society. They used arrests, a concerted anti-protest media effort, growing restrictions on public gatherings, support for nationalist civil society, and new restrictions on any organization that accepted foreign funding to slowly raise the cost of opposition. Someone gunned down leading opposition activist Boris Nemtsov on a bridge overlooking the Kremlin. Observers could not help but comment on the symbolism of the location.

Putin and his propaganda apparatus made full use of the nationalist political imaginary. A coordinated media campaign identified civil resisters and associated protest with national betrayal, corruption, and European decadence and indecency. LGBTQ+ activists took the brunt of the identity offensive.[29] The Orthodox Church, pro-Putin civil activists, and parliamentary officials accused LGBTQ+ groups of being US and European agents, religious apostates, a threat to children, and a danger to the reproduction of the nation. Restrictive laws curtailing the LGBTQ+ community's right to assembly and expression followed. Worse, in the now-pacified Russian republic of Chechnya, the pro-Putin government abducted, tortured, and killed dozens to hundreds of men suspected of having sex with other men.[30]

Russian efforts now seek to ensure that any gains the West makes in other areas of the former Soviet Union are pyrrhic at best. In 2010, the Great Recession and elite infighting among the winners of the Orange Revolution helped the previously defeated pro-Russian leader Viktor Yanukovych to win the Ukrainian presidency. He quickly settled accounts by imprisoning one of his chief rivals, Yulia Tymoshenko, on controversial charges of abuse of power while she was prime minister.[31] Over the next few years, he eroded democratic checks on his power and allegedly allowed the country to return to levels of corruption considered high by Ukrainian standards. In late fall 2013, Yanukovych made a controversial decision to tie Ukraine more tightly into the Russian economic and political orbit. The choice was actually defensible on a number of counts, but it also voided a deal to deepen ties with the EU. Citizens of Kyiv, backed by Ukrainians across the country but particularly those in the nationalistic west, objected and, for the second time, seized control over Independence Square.

Once again, it is hard to explain the size, duration, and socio-regional depth and breadth of the uprising by referring solely to Western influence, but this is how it was portrayed from Moscow. From the start, pro-Russian politicians in Ukraine and abroad associated the Euromaidan uprising of 2013–14 with the democracy promotion efforts of the EU and the United States. The United States badly misplayed its cards. Senator John McCain appeared on the square to hand out doughnuts. Unfortunately, he posed for a photograph with some extreme anti-Russian nationalists. Even worse, foreign security agents recorded a top US State Department official in a conversation with the US ambassador to Ukraine discussing who should lead the new government once the sitting elected president was removed by yet another Western-backed people's power movement.

I had sympathies with the liberal students and other citizens in the square. Yanukovych had subverted the rules of the democratic game to a degree that called into question the country's democratic credentials. Ukraine risked becoming another Russian-style managed democracy in Putin's orbit. Ukrainians had every right to challenge the increasingly illiberal acts of their government.

Yet, the Maidan resistance provided some terrible "optics." I was particularly disquieted by the participation of a right-wing block of Russophobe nationalists called the Right Sector and the political party Freedom, which made no apologies for its controversial roots in the World War II era. Yet, their efforts appeared to have been crucial in the final days' defense of the square from security forces. It was also concerning that the opposition appeared to violate a last-minute deal brokered by the international community in which Yanukovych was to keep his position. As the action in and around the square became increasingly violent, however, Yanukovych fled. The United States and the EU quickly endorsed the interim regime and a call for new presidential elections.[32]

Putin was not long in responding. For once, my crystal ball was accurate. At the time, my colleague and I were preparing to take Colorado College students to study regional literature, history, and politics in a small village near Sudak on the Ukrainian peninsula of Crimea. I held off on buying the plane tickets. It seemed unlikely that Putin would allow Yanukovych's departure to go unanswered.

The last time we taught the study-abroad class, in summer 2012, billboards across the peninsula celebrated Crimea's Russian culture and friendship. We were hosted by a family of indigenous Krymi (often referred to as Crimean Tartars), but most everyone else we spoke to identified as Russo-Ukrainian or Russian. Many had settler-colonial roots dating as far back as the conquest of the region in 1783 by Catherine the Great. Other Russian settlers came in after Stalin deported the entire population of Krymi to Central Asia in 1944. These ethnic Russians had strong pro-Russian feelings and often (our hosts said "unfairly") considered the returning indigenous Muslim Krymi to have betrayed the Soviet Union during World War II. A free and fair referendum would have quite likely produced a narrow vote for Crimean secession to the Russian Federation.

After Kosovo, however, Russia could defend annexing the peninsula on the grounds of national self-determination.[33] On the day I faced either buying or losing our low-priced flights, irregular Russian military forces, dubbed "little green men" for their lack of identifying national insignia, forcibly occupied the peninsula. A hasty local referendum produced an overwhelming but hardly free or fair vote in favor of succession, and Russia annexed Crimea.

At the same time, Russia encouraged and supported a militarized separatist conflict in the industrially developed Donbass region of eastern Ukraine. The rebels' pretext was again the self-determination and safety of the ethnic Russian people who lived there. The conflict continued to simmer, enabling Putin to accomplish a strategic victory. Ukraine's European future and its NATO hopes receded to distant concerns. Its politics became distorted by the rise of Ukrainian nationalists, whose pernicious, anti-Russian political imaginary now found a concrete reference point in the shattered villages and towns of the Donbas and the Russian flags flying in Crimea. Yes, you can join the Western orbit if you want, Putin essentially said, but you will do so bereft of many of your valuable coal and steel industries, most of your coastline, maritime access to your eastern coastal cities, your naval base, and any sense of lasting protection from additional conflict and annexation should you really misbehave.

EPILOGUE: Russian president Putin has fully "securitized" and nationalized civil society—putting an end to the liberal wager that Russian interests could converge with liberalism.[34] He began early by tethering the media, herding oligarchs into the Kremlin pen, and constitutionally centralizing power. Since 2013, he has redoubled his efforts by terrorizing LGBTQ+ activist groups, expelling or suppressing NGOs with foreign connections, and partially criminalizing autonomous, democratic activity. Nevertheless, citizens have repeatedly taken to the streets of Moscow and St. Petersburg and other cities. It is unclear where this will lead. The urban middle-class protestors of the big cities have often failed to connect with people in the regions. Moreover, Putin remains very popular everywhere.

Still, it is interesting to watch the confusion of Russia's political elites. They genuinely seem to accept the thesis that protest really is just the product of Western meddling. Yet, the American and European NGOs have left the country, sexual minorities are back in the closet, and George Soros is enemy number 1, whose friendship everyone denies. Meanwhile, Russians routinely take to the streets for their basic political rights. Like the Grinch who cannot stop Christmas from coming, Putin cannot stop protest.

Western democracy aid to Russia has long passed the point where it could be of much use to Russia's embattled liberals. Moreover, the unmentioned pachyderm tiptoeing throughout this chapter is that states have interests, not friends. When those interests clash with liberal ideals, state interests usually prevail. Postcommunist Europe has been lucky in this respect—Western interests and liberal ideals have overlapped significantly. But it did not have to be that way.

I am reminded of Azerbaijan in 2003, where the oil-drunk dictatorship of the Aliyev clan stole the presidential election and crushed its US-advised opposition and civil society. Admittedly, the opposition included a number of nationalists who had promised to reignite a destructive conflict with neighboring Armenia over the disputed territory of Nagorno-Karabakh. Still, IRI, NDI, and a range of US-backed, democracy-enhancing NGOs could only stand back dutifully as Secretary of Defense Donald Rumsfeld appeared in Baku. Enough of these silly democracy games, Rumsfeld said, as Ilham Aliyev donned his bloodied crown. Azerbaijan is an important US friend in the war in Afghanistan and a vital alternative to Russia as a supplier of oil and gas to Europe. Let's get back to the nation's business.[35]

I hope this is not a surprise to any of my readers, but the United States is a fickle ally to liberals abroad. It is a great power like most in history—one that can fight the good fight for human rights and accountable government on the one hand and literally bless a violent dictator on the other. It is also a reminder to citizens everywhere to be careful about foreign assistance when it is offered. Allies can be extraordinarily helpful, but one also risks playing into authoritarian narratives about one's patriotic credentials. And when the police batons start to fly, even the most liberal of foreign friends are unlikely to be near at hand.

CHAPTER 9

Homophobia

The Political Uses of Fear

A somber vigil . . . The Western origins of LGBTQ+ identities . . .
A hierarchy of human rights in Serbia . . . An intersectional paradox . . .
Bombs over Belgrade, redux . . . Otpor mocks a dictator . . . The
Massacre Pride Parade . . . Meanwhile in Slovakia . . . EU ex machina.

PREFACE: It was a warm June afternoon in front of the US Embassy in Bratislava's Hviezdoslav Square. Under the branches of a large chestnut tree, American and Slovak flags draped over a rainbow flag. Small groups of queer, lesbian, gay, bisexual, transgender, and allied people arrived from all over the city. Each of us knelt in front of the flags to light a candle in remembrance of the victims of the Pulse nightclub massacre in Orlando, Florida, just a few days earlier.

A semicircle of people thickened around a growing carpet of wax and flame. The numbers were heartening, but not a single news crew, not one mainstream journalist, not even a Slovak politician attended to remark on the events. The only public authorities I saw were the two top officials from the US Embassy. Somberly, they paid their respects to the organizers, lit their candles, and joined us in quiet mourning.

Hana Fábry, Slovakia's veteran lesbian activist, broke the silence. Her speech was brief, one sentence really, but she said the perfect thing:

"I really don't have much to say except, don't be afraid!"

One can speculate about the Florida shooter's motives, but Fábry revealed how personally the Slovak activists in the square took the Pulse tragedy. It credibly could have been them. In the political imaginaries of Slovakia's most conservative religious leaders and most extreme nationalists, sexual minorities have a place among the community's enemies. From Russia to Serbia to Slovakia, conservative political and religious authorities have warned of the LGBTQ+ menace—treacherous citizens under the influence of a Western ideology who are bent on the corruption and demographic extinction of nations through the conversion of children to decadent behavior and nonreproductive sex.

LGBTQ+ citizens of the former Czechoslovakia, and most everywhere else in postcommunist Europe, have not found much safety with democratization.[1] Mainstream democracy movements have fought authoritarianism through policies of centering—a rhetorical and symbolic effort to seize the symbols of patriotism from the autocrats. In so doing, they have often ignored the needs of ethnic, sexual, and gender minorities. Worse, as a strategy, centering often wraps the prodemocracy fold in the warm embrace of social and religious conservatives while ignoring their homophobia. LGBTQ+ communities have largely had to fend for themselves.

This chapter examines the political emergence of LGBTQ+ communities in Slovakia and Serbia since the fall of communism. During communism and in the first decade after its fall, sexual and gender communities were too small to even merit a mention in the fearmongering imaginations of the region's would-be authoritarians. One could insult or threaten an individual by questioning their assumed heterosexuality, but a significant, self-identified LGBTQ+ community remained hidden on the margins of mainstream politics.

This changed as LGBTQ+ activists organized in the late 1990s and early 2000s to protect and advocate for themselves. Ethnographer Viera Lorencová has demonstrated how, as they "became visible," they were incorporated into the political imaginaries of conservative politicians and religious leaders.[2]

The EU and liberal Western community have been an important activist resource throughout. EU leverage has been instrumental in securing the extension of nondiscrimination legislation to sexual minorities. But this assistance has come at a cost. In Serbia, nationalist actors used the LGBTQ+ community's association with the West to "expatriate" their identities—to insinuate that the LGBTQ+ community is not truly of Serbia but rather part of a foreign-led assault on the nation and on Serbian Orthodoxy. In Slovakia, conservative Christian politicians partially employed this strategy during the EU accession process, but their effectiveness was constrained by the uncompromising language of the EU's Treaty of Amsterdam, which explicitly demanded that member states protect sexual and gender minorities from discrimination. As we'll see in the next chapter, however, this did not stop a combination of Catholic conservatives and Evangelical Christians from resurrecting the imaginary a decade later.

❦ ❧

Sex between consenting men was legalized as early as 1961 in Czechoslovakia following a recommendation from the medical community citing a decade of research that proved homosexuality was a normal part of human sexuality.[3] The Communist Party quietly changed the law but failed to engage the public in a discussion about the reason for the change.[4] Culture and policy continued to tolerate open homophobia. Nor was there increased protection from homophobic acts, including dismissal from one's job, physical assault, and exclusion from family and community circles. Many LGBTQ+ people grew up believing that their own sexual or gender orientation was a form of disease or, worse, an immoral depravity.

None of this changed with the fall of communism. Activists in the 1990s thus focused on creating community networks and places for lesbians and gays to meet and learn to live in safety and without shame. Trans activists fought for a more trans-appropriate medical regime. Activists also networked internationally and began to adopt the growing Western LGBTQ+ spectrum of labels as signs of pride and normalcy. They won small victories by queering hetero-centric spaces through public hand-holding, challenges to heteronormative forms of dress, gay and lesbian film festivals, queer parties, vigils, and publications. Gradually they built networks of activists and allies ready to advocate for the community politically.[5]

Still, public knowledge of the LGBTQ+ community—its experiences and needs—was nonexistent. If you had asked a Central European in the 1990s or even the early 2000s whether their country hosted a significant population of gay men or lesbian women, most would probably have said no. Many would have added that widespread, open homosexuality was a "Western" phenomenon. Pressed, however, they might also have admitted to knowing someone, perhaps an unmarried uncle or a female colleague, who they suspected liked to sleep with their own gender.

The terms of pride that make up the LGBTQ+ acronym—lesbian, gay, bisexual, transgender, and queer—came late to postcommunist Europe. In everyday language, it was (and still is) common and unremarked for otherwise intelligent and educated people to use homophobic slurs without embarrassment or apology. LGBTQ+ terminology and the very concept of a LGBTQ+ community are from the West. The activist choice to use these terms helped associate them with Western Europe and the United States.[6]

Despite these issues with authenticity, the West was a vital resource to the nascent LGBTQ+ community throughout Central Europe and the Balkans. Early victories—such as the equalization of the age of heterosexual and homosexual consent in 1990 in Czechoslovakia or the legalization of sex between men in Serbia in 1994—were achieved due largely to the activism of Western embassies and elite attraction to EU norms of nondiscrimination. LGBTQ+ organizations played a role but remained weak. To the extent that they had any funding at all, they were largely reliant on small grants from international networks of activists.

It took a long time for the liberal, prodemocracy community to begin to actively focus on the needs of LGBTQ+ persons. Lepa Mladenović, a groundbreaking activist in Serbia, personally encountered what she called a "hierarchy of human rights" within the pro-Western human rights community. To take only one example, at the height of the Bosnian war in 1994, she was attacked while putting up posters for a lesbian event in Belgrade. Yet when she reported the homophobic assault to a local human rights official in Belgrade, the organization had no category for homophobic acts on its list of human rights violations. From the official's perspective, the homophobic violence was not a human rights issue.[7]

Nor were Serbian opposition parties and movements of much help— despite their deep concern with human rights and democracy. Authoritarian president Slobodan Milošević used speeches and the state-controlled media to locate his opposition among "the enemies of the people." This imaginary frequently had hints of homophobia.[8] During antigovernment protests in 1996, for example, state propagandists created a flyer from a fictitious gay organization that declared gay and lesbian solidarity with Milošević's opponents. The idea was to discredit activists by associating opposition to the government with LGBTQ+ support. The pamphlet was clearly faked, so no one took it seriously. Yet opposition politicians did nothing to counter the gist of government propaganda—that gays and lesbians were "deviant" and "anti-Serb."[9]

LGBTQ+ activists soon got used to being ignored by liberal democracy activists. Centering meant that the opposition had to be careful that its symbolism was not socially "controversial." The Serbian Orthodox Church was homophobic but quite popular among Milošević's older and rural supporters, for whom orthodoxy was an important aspect of Serbian national identity. Had the women in the front lines of Otpor marches been waving the rainbow flag, many observers might have contextualized the regime's violence as duly provoked. Indeed, as we shall see, such justifications for violence later become commonplace.

These dynamics put LGBTQ+ activists in a classic double-bind.[10] They faced an intersectionality paradox in which the choice to fight for one's rights as a sexual or gender minority would have meant being marginalized within the broader prodemocracy movement. One could not easily fight both forms of oppression at the same time. The gay and lesbian Otpor veterans whom I spoke with recognized the paradox and pragmatically chose a "democracy first, LGBTQ+ rights next" approach. They proudly contributed to the student opposition to President Milošević in the second half of the 1990s, but they usually did so in full heteronormative regalia, that is to say, closeted.[11]

However, they quickly add, this was problematic. Centering retained a mainstream nationalism at the heart of the anti-Milošević movement that complicated the post-revolution politics. The victors of the October 5, 2000 revolution, President Koštunica and Prime Minister Đinđić, gave informal guarantees of impunity to people in the security forces and military who were directly involved in war crimes, including ethnically driven murder, beatings, and sexual assault of civilians, looting, and smuggling. These promises may have made the virtually bloodless overthrow of Milošević possible. Yet, they also allowed the security forces to become part of the new democratic Serbia without becoming democrats.[12] For obvious reasons, the security forces feared an honest accounting of how they got where they were and fought hard against the post-Milošević liberalization of Serbia.

Similarly, many leaders of the Serbian business class had established their wealth by doing business with Milošević's allegedly corrupt rule. Milošević's departure did not change their preference for privileged access to government contracts, licenses, and socially owned enterprises. Like crony capitalists all over postcommunist Europe, they were suspicious of a truly independent and inquisitive media. They also did not want the vigorous competition that would come with liberal market reform and government transparency and accountability. Rather than starting to compete in a more globally integrated market for a living, they sought to co-opt the new government into doing business their way. This meant retaining privileged access to state policies that controlled economic activity and asserting a high degree of control over the state and independent media.[13]

In short, after the revolution, a significant part of the Milošević-era political and economic elite remained as committed as ever to maintaining the nationalist narratives of power that had justified their rise into positions of wealth and influence.[14] They doubled down on the myth that they had done their patriotic part in the war against "fascist" Croats and "jihadist" Muslims. They also resisted Western demands for economic and political reforms emanating from the EU and Western embassies. Tragically, homophobia soon became an important rhetorical asset in this effort and made life even more difficult for LGBTQ+ activists.

The first democratically chosen prime minister, Zoran Đinđić, had to balance the guarantees given to the military and other security forces with intense pressure coming from the EU and Western embassies to extradite Milošević and others to The Hague, where they could be tried by the International Criminal Tribunal for the Former Yugoslavia (ICTY). Security officials saw extradition as a threat. They likely worried, "If Milošević goes, who is next?" Nationalists thus intensified their attacks on the ICTY and the Western governments that supported it.[15] The tabloid and conservative media made it an article of faith—even among many otherwise liberal veterans of Otpor—that the ICTY's chief prosecutor, Carla Del Ponte, was anti-Serbian.

On the other hand, Prime Minister Zoran Đinđić was under enormous pressure from the West. In 2001, he bravely agreed to extradite Milošević to the ICTY prison in The Hague. This was a disaster for Đinđić. Within two years, he would be assassinated in an organized crime/security force operation that its conspirators called "Stop The Hague."[16]

Yet, LGBTQ+ activists suffered too. On the day Milošević was extradited, the lesbian and gay groups Labris and Gayten staged Belgrade's first pride parade. The awkward timing allowed Serb nationalists to link Milošević's extradition and the parade as symbols of "what the West wants." Taking the homophobia of officials and the general population as a given, nationalist thugs and football hooligans attacked the parade in force. The assailants easily outnumbered the few police officers present (many of whom stood aside). Dozens of activists were injured and hospitalized. Activists would later refer to the events of the day as "The Massacre Pride Parade."[17]

In the aftermath of the assault, officials *excused* the attackers for their actions: the parade of "immorality" on the streets of Belgrade was a natural and predictable "provocation." Apparently, they *expected* "normal" Serbian men to be driven to violence by the sight of homosexuals in public! Đinđić blamed LGBTQ+ organizers for pushing for their rights "too early." President Koštunica was silent about the use of organized violence against citizens exercising their right to peaceable assembly. Overall, the liberal community blamed the victims.[18]

Such denials and obfuscations were part of a broader pattern. LGBTQ+ activists, as well as one EU official whom coauthor Edward Moe and I spoke to, speculated with reasonable confidence that individuals in the security forces had encouraged and perhaps organized the attack as a way of lowering the legitimacy (and raising the cost) of cooperation with the ICTY and EU officials demanding political and economic reform.[19] Violence was a way of conflating the West's demands for reform and accountability with a "homosexual agenda" that would not be tolerated at home. According to Daša Duhaček, it also demonstrated the cost that could be paid by those who would question Serbia's nationalist self-convictions.[20]

The silencing of critical voices ensured that a majority of Serbian citizens had no opportunity to unravel the self-serving myths proffered by the nationalist elite. As of 2005, 81 percent of Serbian citizens polled still believed that *Serbs* had been the greatest victims of the wars of the 1990s.[21] Once again, this myth served to protect the reputations, wealth, and power of powerful people who claimed legitimacy from their role in the wars. Scholar Christian Axboe Nielsen adds that Serbian politicians could also point to the risk of violence to argue that society was not yet ready to meet stringent demands for reform from the West, all the while maintaining the official appearance of attempting to comply.[22]

MEANWHILE IN SLOVAKIA: Slovak LGBTQ+ activists faced stresses that, while not identical, at least echoed the Serb experience. They did not have to contend with the war or with the brutality of an authoritarian Milošević regime, but they too faced an intersectionality paradox under the illiberal rule of Prime Minister Vladimir Mečiar and had an unpleasant political "coming out" afterward. Thanks to the recollections of, among others, veteran activist Hana Fábry, and to the pioneering work of Viera Lorencová, an ethnographer who chronicled and analyzed activist efforts in person, we have detailed firsthand accounts of this period.

Under communism, Slovakia's anti-regime resistance had been led by Catholic activists, including the jailed dissident Ján Čarnogurský. While Čarnogurský and others had struggled bravely for freedom of conscience under communism, they were also social conservatives. Now part of a democracy, conservatives were free to assert openly their belief that homosexuality was either a sinful personal choice or a curable disease. Many even believed that the right to freedom of conscience gave Christians the right to discriminate against those who they felt lived sinfully.

By the mid-1990s, Čarnogurský and other former activists had become key players in Slovakia's major opposition parties and a crucial part of the Bratislava Process. To recap, the Bratislava Process was the coordinated, Western-supported campaign to defeat Prime Minister Mečiar, in which "centering" and "opposition unity" played a major role in opposition strategy. The result was lowest common denominator politics in which the unifying frames of opposition excluded the concerns of LGBTQ+ activists.

LGBTQ+ groups joined the Western-supported forum for civic activists known as the Third Sector Gremium but felt unwelcome. As Fábry recalls, "Others looked at us as if we were a monkey in the zoo."[23] Concurrently, pioneer LGBTQ+ organizers Ivan Požgai and Marián Vojtek of Gayten submitted draft legislation to parliament that would put same-sex legal unions on the same footing as heterosexual unions. Most anti-Mečiar groups paid no attention. No party in parliament, including the liberal opposition, even acknowledged the initiative.[24]

Lorencová traces in detail how, following the defeat of Mečiar in 1998, conservative coalition members blocked socially progressive initiatives and actively engaged in excluding LGBTQ+ voices in parliament. Things only became more explicit as LGBTQ+ activists, now unified in a political umbrella organization called Inciatíva Inakosť ("Otherness Initiative"), pushed more forcefully for legal recognition of same-sex partnerships and nondiscrimination.[25]

In 2001, Inakost' prevailed upon the social democrats in the governing coalition to begin discussions about legalizing registered partnerships. After sitting on the initiative for several months, the leadership of the Christian Democratic Movement (KDH), tried to use the proposal to their advantage in upcoming elections. At a memorable press conference, the KDH's leader and minister of justice, Ján Čarnogurský, publicly blocked the initiative, declaring, "While I am Minister of Justice, the registered partnership of homosexuals will not exist in Slovakia." Same-sex registration, he explained in a trope that has since become a common part of the conservative argument, would lead to more homosexuals, fewer children, and an exacerbation of Slovakia's long-term demographic problems. "[As] there will be not enough work force [*sic*] ... for retirement funds, the weakening of family through registered partnerships of homosexuals would ... speed up a collapse of our social system."[26] KDH member of parliament (MP) Alojz Rakús, a former minister of health, followed, asserting that homosexuality was an affliction that could be cured. A gay- and lesbian-tolerant society, he reiterated, would promote more homosexuality and devalue the traditional family with a focus on raising children.[27]

Hana Fábry joked to me (and others) that Čarnogurský was the "biggest activist" for Inakosť because his public comments often included a remark that would send journalists to the organization for a response.[28] The KDH's efforts to define itself as the protector of "traditional values" gave the LGBTQ+ activist community unprecedented visibility in the media. After years of marginalization, gay and lesbian activists were interviewed for the evening news or quoted in the newspapers. This was the first time that many citizens encountered openly "out" Slovaks. Yet, as Lorencová argues, thanks to the efforts of Čarnogurský, the community stepped under the political spotlight on a homophobic stage.[29] Over the next 10 years, public hostility toward sexual minorities grew.

Slovakia's 2002 election produced a right-leaning government in which the KDH played a major part. The social democratic allies of Inakosť failed to pass the threshold to get into parliament. Over the next four years, the KDH promoted a political imaginary that cast itself as the nation's defense against the "indecency" of sexual and gender minorities. Yet unlike in the more nationalist Serbia, according to Conor O'Dwyer, "conservative politicians did not attempt to link homosexuality to the EU."[30]

Shut out of parliament and demonized in public, as Lorencová documents, LGBTQ+ activists turned to the EU, and particularly the European Commission, for support. In 1999, the EU Treaty of Amsterdam added sexual minorities to the list of groups to be protected from discrimination. European Commission Directive 2000/78/EC then made compliant domestic protection the legal obligation of all EU states.[31] After 2000, no applicant country could enter the EU without clear laws protecting sexual minorities.

Slovakia's leading Catholic party, the KDH, nevertheless fought hard to exclude LGBTQ+ persons from the country's new treaty compliant nondiscrimination legislation.[32] To justify Slovak exceptionalism, the party even formed a brief majority with Mečiar—now in the opposition—to assert the right to declare state sovereignty over the EU on "Cultural and Ethical Issues." This was umbrella language that KDH members hoped would allow Slovaks to fire LGBTQ+ people from jobs, secure limitations on abortion, limit sex education in schools, and reduce access to contraception.[33] The EU simply ignored the nonbinding declaration.

Meanwhile, the KDH and nationalist politicians demonstrated quite effectively why sexual minorities needed protection. In parliamentary discussion, nationalist politicians openly referred to sexual minorities using the language's most pejorative term, while KDH MPs spoke of the need to ban gays and lesbians from teaching. Other KDH MPs promised, as if it were a good thing, that the deliberate omission of LGBTQ+ persons from the antidiscrimination measures would *permit* their dismissal from their jobs.[34]

According to Lorencová, the response by Inakosť to these and other snubs was to rally in front of parliament to remind the country that "without us, you will never make it into the EU!"[35] The European Commission then backed the activists and threatened to exclude Slovakia from the EU expansion of 2004. Politically, that would have been an existential catastrophe for any party. Under intense EU pressure, an overwhelming parliamentary majority finally passed an LGBTQ+-inclusive nondiscrimination protection law in May 2004.

THE EU QUEERS SERBIA: Serbia's LGBTQ+ community also benefited from EU leverage, after a delay. With the assassination of Zoran Đinđić, Serbia's leading pro-European politician, in 2003, Serbian nationalist politicians gained control over Serbian politics. There was a lot to replenish their imaginary of enemies. Memories of the NATO bombing were still fresh. The UN now occupied Serbian sovereign territory in Kosovo, and the international community continued to insist that Serbian politicians and officials were largely responsible for the wars of the 1990s. EU commissioners wanted an apology from the state for supporting the Bosnian Serb forces that slaughtered 8,000 men and boys at Srebrenica in 1995. Meanwhile, the ICTY expected Serb help to apprehend and extradite the massacre's architect, General Ratko Mladić, and his political patron, the Bosnian Serb wartime political leader Radovan Karadžić. The EU and the United States also wanted a less confrontational stance on Kosovo and a greater willingness to undertake domestic political and economic reforms.

This was a long list, but it turned out that the EU's leverage in Serbia was quite strong. In 2008, over 70 percent of Serbs supported joining the EU. Most families had at least one member who had emigrated after 1980. Despite the nationalist tabloid narrative of "fraternal love" between Russia and Serbia, these emigrants invariably looked for new homes in Western Europe, Canada, Australia, and the United States. At a minimum, Serbs wanted the benefits that most other postcommunist Europeans had, particularly visa-free travel in Europe. Serbians hoped to have the right to work and settle anywhere in Europe's single market. They also resented Croatia's head start on membership. Thanks to the reform initiatives of HDZ politicians after returning to power in 2003, Croatia was now on track to join the EU in 2013.[36]

Such leverage had the potential to give the EU an important role in Serbian politics. In early 2008, however, Serbia's relations with the West reached a nadir. On February 17, 2008, Kosovo declared independence from Serbia with US backing.[37] Kosovo's assertion of ethnic Albanian sovereignty over culturally significant Serbian lands with a sizable Serbian minority created an uproar in Serbian politics. Anger within the cabinet led to a collapse of the ruling coalition and a call for new elections. By April 2008, the extreme nationalist Serbian Radical Party was polling around 50 percent. Its leader, Vojislav Šešelj, however, had led one of Serbia's most notorious Serbian militias in the early 1990s and was accordingly in The Hague, indicted for war crimes. Its new leader, Tomislav Nikolić, spoke of his aspiration to make Serbia a "Russian province."[38]

The EU used this moment to offer a Stabilization and Association Agreement (SAA) to the caretaker Serbian government. The SAA was a first concrete step toward closer association with the EU, including potential visa-free travel and eventual membership. This opportunity dramatically changed the frame of the election.

Elite responses really said it all. Nikolić traveled to Moscow to discuss bringing Serbia into a Russian-Belarussian association that would fight the hegemony of the EU and the United States. By contrast, the successor to Zoran Đinđic, Boris Tadić, formed a multiparty coalition that campaigned under the name "For a European Serbia" and promised liberal economic and democratic reforms. Tadić rode the wave of pro-EU enthusiasm to an easy plurality of the 2008 vote. Yet to form a government, the party was compelled into coalition with Milošević's former party, the SPS. Following the lead of Mečiar's HZDS and Tuđman's HDZ, the SPS now situated itself as a center-left, pro-EU party and welcomed Boris Milićević, an openly gay activist from the Gay Straight Alliance, into the party.[39]

The nationalist right collapse in April-May 2008 demonstrated the potent leverage of the EU. Nationalists suddenly had to accommodate their message to EU demands or face political irrelevance. Coincidence or not, the Bosnian Serb war criminal Radovan Karadžić was quickly discovered in Belgrade and arrested in summer 2008. General Ratko Mladić, the man most responsible for the Srebrenica massacre and the shelling of Sarajevo, was apprehended several years later.

As in Slovakia, elite commitment in Serbia to the EU gave LGBTQ+ activists leverage, but it also made them a target among the nationalist opposition. Again, the EU made a nonnegotiable demand that nondiscrimination protection be extended to sexual and gender minorities. Nevertheless, in 2009 a bishop of the Serbian Orthodox Church pushed parliamentarians into excluding LGBTQ+ persons from a new antidiscrimination law only hours before it was to go to a parliamentary vote. EU officials and LGBTQ+ activists quickly convinced parliamentary leaders to suspend the vote and launched an intensive information and lobbying campaign. Within a month, the law passed with original inclusive language.

Although parliament made steps toward EU norms, homophobic nationalists and religious conservatives remained active, often violently so. In 2010, the EU pressured Belgrade to "permit" a pride parade downtown. In response, nationalist groups engaged in a well-organized, citywide campaign of intimidation, blanketing Belgrade with graffiti and posters that threatened, "We Are Waiting for You." Per the usual script, extremists advocated homophobic violence as a "patriotic" defense against anti-Serbian "traitors." Extremist homophobe Miša Vacić explained the campaign's position by stating that LGBTQ+ people incited the violence "by bringing . . . their Satanic rituals into the streets of Belgrade." Blame for the promised violence thus lay with LGBTQ+ activists. This frame had the apparent backing of the Serbian Orthodox Church, whose leader later described the planned parade as an act of violence against the Serbian people.[40] The tabloid media wholeheartedly embraced the idea that LGBTQ+ persons' immorality and lack of patriotism invited, and even demanded, a violent response.[41]

The city provided heavy and effective police protection this time, but football hooligans, extreme nationalists, and reportedly some Orthodox priests showed up in large numbers, attacked and injured many police, and caused widespread damage to downtown streets and stores. Nationalists and pro-EU liberals predictably contextualized the violence—again blaming the marchers for provoking Serbian men to outrage. Many concluded that the best way to stop the violence was to avoid future "provocations," like a repeat of the parade. Some LGBTQ+ activists agreed, deepening divisions within the LGBTQ+ community over an appropriate strategy.[42]

∽ ∾

Serbia has since made strides in making and enforcing a legal rights framework for sexual and gender minorities, but homophobia remains strongly entrenched in the nationalist political imaginary—a ready-made argument for avoiding liberal reform. That is perhaps to be expected, but, sadly, liberals continue to be uncertain allies. In April 2017, a group of my students and I were treated in Belgrade to several consecutive days of large-scale student-led marches protesting irregularities in the presidential election. As thousands of students marched by, occasional hateful signs linking President Alexander Vučić with homosexuality marred the otherwise nonviolent march.

The older generation of anti-Milošević activist veterans whom I hung out with were thrilled with the students' organization and the size of the turnout. Many marched alongside their children in support. However, my friends were disgusted to see the tradition of homophobic opposition resurrected in a new generation. A few urgent conversations were held with the student organizers, and homophobic messaging disappeared from the remainder of the marches. Yet, this did not stop several mainstream opposition political leaders from marching side by side with extreme nationalist homophobes in later demonstrations.

At the end of 2019, Serbia had postcommunist Europe's first openly lesbian prime minister. Yet her association with the populist and increasingly authoritarian politics of President Alexander Vučić and her refusal to address issues of importance to the LGBTQ+ communities led these same friends to accuse the regime of "pink washing" its obligations as an EU aspirant with respect to sexual and gender minorities.

Meanwhile, in Slovakia, after the Great Financial Crisis of 2008-2010, homophobia reemerged as an organizing logic for the socially conservative right. This is wrapped up in the emergence of populist politics in Slovakia and the democratic weakening in the region more generally. I thus address it in the next chapter.

CHAPTER 10

Populism

Austerity, Fear, and Loathing on Central Europe's Periphery

Was it all just schnitzel and beer? . . . Granny democrats . . . Cooking up some populism . . . Eurozone blues . . . Why you should avoid doing shots with the landlord . . . Arson and old race . . . The "culture of death" . . . . Fantasies about genocide . . . Migrants and white supremacy('s) rules . . . Fascists in parliament . . . Tom blows my mind . . . Marching for Ján and Martina.

PREFACE: Božena recently told us a story about why her mother, Štefania, used to go to the communist May Day festivities. As you may remember from chapter 2, communism worked for Štefania. She was born in 1923 to a land-poor family in rural Slovakia with few prospects of advancing beyond her parents' work as rural day laborers on larger farms. Under communism, however, these farms became the property of a state-directed cooperative. Štefania's family gladly turned over their three hectares of land to the co-op in order to be part of a much larger venture.

The co-op put Štefania to work in dairy production, where the state's investment in industrial milking technology made her much more productive than ever before. In the 1960s and 1970s, she would arrive at the farm's mechanized dairy at 4:00 a.m., clean the stalls, wash and disinfect the udders, and attach automated milking equipment. She would arrive home just before noon each day, exhausted. Then began her second unpaid job of tending to her private garden and livestock and keeping a household for her five children and husband. Štefania's grueling routine would extend into the evening when she would finally fall asleep at 8:30 p.m.

Štefania never joined the Communist Party. Still, she loved the communist May Day celebration. It was more than a welcome break. It gave her an escape from her daily routine in a way that was valued by the state. In the morning, she and her comrades from the farm would take several buses to the capital for a parade and other festivities. Štefania's collective farm was one of the best in Czechoslovakia and would receive due recognition in the ceremonies. There would also be socializing, free *gulaš*, beer, and a 100-crown payment for attending.

Štefania's feelings of validation extended well beyond the parade. In recognition of the five children she bore to help build socialism, she was permitted to retire with a pension at the age of 54. Yet, her skills were in such demand that she continued laboring at the dairy as a substitute— often working full-time for months. Bonuses came in the form of live-stock, grain, and vegetables. She earned enough cash to install running water in the kitchen of her ancient mudbrick home, although the lack of a village sewer forced her to keep the outhouse. In the back, she had a little lot and a barn where she kept chickens, geese, rabbits, and as many as two pigs. She fed them with grain she received for free from the co-op. Štefania often marveled at communism's ability to provide ample food for her family and livestock.

It's perhaps easy to scoff at this simple countryside existence. Liberal reformers would note that Štefania's generation had very little personal wealth to show for all their effort. Between 2001 and 2006, all four of Simona's grandparents passed away in the care of a child. Štefania, Alexander, Františka, and Izidor gifted to their children a legacy of love, hard work, and lessons of resilience during tough times, but little else. I estimate that their *total combined* personal assets (including their homes) were worth less than $40,000 when they passed. That is the lifetime savings acquired by four thrifty, hard-working people over 200 years of labor—a capital accumulation rate of 11 cents for each hour of work in the formal economy!

It's not much to show, they'd think.

But, the point of labor under communism was to build capital *for use by the state*, not the individual. And the point of the state was to share the proceeds of this capital more or less equitably. Regardless of communism's flaws, this is basically what happened in Western Slovakia, and Štefania was deeply grateful. Most in her generation did not become personally rich, but most were not materially impoverished either.

Capitalism thus came as something of a shock to Štefania. The Lockean state ushered in by the Velvet Revolution in 1989 felt no need to validate her life of hard work. In the wave of liberal triumph that followed the uprising, her generation's accomplishments were vilified in the press and despised by government policy. The new state did not feel obliged to care much for the elderly. Rather, governments chose to fight inflation by forbidding pensions to rise in step with prices. Meanwhile, the advanced education, health, and eldercare systems that Štefania's generation had helped build fell into disrepair due to budget cuts and fiscal restraints.

Yet, perhaps the biggest blow was that the Lockean state privatized her generation's capital bequest from communism to a select portion of the younger generation of Slovaks who had played little role in creating it. Štefania's generation was not entirely ignored. Simona's grandparents all acquired privatization vouchers and even a small check from the direct sale of their collective farms to a private owner. Yet, even if they did not get ripped off in the great privatization shark feed described in chapter 3, this payout only amounted to a month's pension check. Much of the real capital of the state was simply expropriated by political insiders through vampire techniques and privatization deals, some of which were quite shady. It was a direct form of "capital accumulation through dispossession." Today, the cubic glass and steel mansions of these entrepreneurs line the heights above Bratislava Castle. Meanwhile, the elderly subsist on their barely adequate pensions and the only partially compensated eldercare provided by their children and grandchildren.

Štefania spent the last decade of her life lamenting the passing of communism. She grew up hungry and impoverished in a democracy, and she spent her final years marginalized in a democracy. In between, things were better for her. With all honesty she could exclaim, as she often did, *"My* life was always best under communism!"

I tell this extended story because it offers a counternarrative rarely taken seriously by liberals in Slovakia and the West. It helps explain one of the most important features of Central European life in the postcommunist era—the reserve of elderly, poorly educated, or less urban voters who are disproportionately willing to support would-be authoritarian populists like Vladimír Mečiar at the polls. Observers in the 1990s liked to call these voters *Babky Demokratky*—"granny democrats." They'd say it condescendingly—with a laugh or a sneer.

But Štefania and others were not idiots. They voted for Mečiar in the 1990s and later for populists like the handsome left-populist prime minister Robert Fico because these men knew how to speak to voters marginalized by liberalism—to address their economic concerns, their anger at being dispossessed by insider privatization, and their conviction that elites had rigged democratic politics and the market economy against them. They hated the liberal lectures they heard from intellectuals on TV and that smirking insinuation that they were too dumb to know what was best for themselves or their country. They were, by contrast, a broadly differentiated group, united by a suspicion that the liberal project of transferring economic risk and responsibility from society to the individual would do little to aid them in their final years.

The great irony, however, was that there was little these populist politicians could do for Štefania and others on the losing side of the transformation. As we saw in chapter 6, EU accession expanded Europe's community of property-protecting, market-oriented states and set the rules as they began to conduct business across Europe's Single European Market. Average Slovaks had no input into these rules. Moreover, as Slovakia and its neighbors integrated into the EU, responsibility for their immediate economic performance shifted to decision-making bodies outside of their governments' direct control. Their countries' growing export orientation made local economies vulnerable to fluctuations in especially German demand. Worse, both the German government and the new European Central Bank (ECB) chose to emphasize price stability in the core over unemployment in the periphery. This policy, in turn, had distinct distributional effects, meaning that it helped some and hurt others, in Central Europe.

Concurrently, integration into European markets for capital limited the choices of Central European governments. The ease of capital flight, the ability of investors simply to cash in their chips and go to another country, meant that if a small country like Slovakia engaged in worrisome debt-driven spending, investors would sell Slovak crowns, the currency would cheapen, and prices and interest rates would go up. Under the rules of the day, the only way to fix this would be to slash government spending, a policy called austerity.[1] So even left-wing politicians learned that running a large annual fiscal deficit was little different than jumping out of an airplane without a parachute; one could feel blissfully light and unburdened for a while, but only until one hit the ground.

Elected representatives could do little to change these structures, no matter how much they promised to improve things. So how did they differentiate themselves in elections? Sheri Berman, Mark Blyth, Abby Innes, and Julia Lynch, among others, argue that they turned to populism,[2] an ideologically fickle, leader-driven popular movement of "the pure people" against "the elite" who abuse them.[3] In Central Europe, populists have found plenty of source material to work with, including the economically impotent political institutions just described; frustration with uneven opportunities and social inequality; suspicion and resentment of foreign elite; anger at local political corruption; easily stoked fears of racial, gender, or sexual difference; and a related 200-year-old Central European anxiety about ethno-national survival.

Central European politicians have incorporated these populist concerns, in varying proportions, into their messages, producing different populist frames. We might even think of a spectrum of populisms or, as Anna Grzymala-Busse writes, a multiplicity of forms.[4] Czechia's populist prime minister, Andrej Babiš, Milada Vachudova argues, is quite different from the region's perennial bad boy, Hungary's Viktor Orbán, or Poland's populist Law and Justice Party.[5] Populisms do share a range of common ingredients, but like a pie, they vary widely depending on the available ingredients and the cook. In Central Europe, it may even make more sense to speak about populist *politics* than populist politicians. Not all politicians fit the definition of a populist all the time, but many adopt some elements of populist appeals and strategies at some point.[6]

This rest of this chapter moves in three related directions. In the first section, and with help from Comenius University professor Darina Malová, I discuss how neoliberalism created a mismatch between the economic needs of a substantial portion of Slovaks and the tools available to address them.[7] In the second section, I look at how politicians and cultural leaders returned to the nationalist political imaginary for legitimacy, pitting the Slovak people against "existential threats" from the LGBTQ+ community, migrants, and EU officials. Finally, I examine Slovakia's liberal countermovement, one rooted in shocking revelations about the very real corruption of the Slovakia political elite.

I. Neoliberalism Triumphant

Grandmother Štefania was always careful to qualify her praise for communism. "*My* life" was better, she'd say, not "*our* life" or even the general "life was better . . ." that so often leads polling questions. Štefania knew that others had suffered from party rule, and she was happy to see how her grandchildren now had a chance to prosper in the global market economy. She also had the fortune of living in Western Slovakia—one of Central Europe's great success stories. All around her, foreign and domestic investment was transforming the local landscape: industrial complexes, single-family housing developments, luxury and middle-class apartments, clean parks, well-equipped playgrounds and schools, restaurants, cafés and bars, revitalized spas, smoothly paved and well-marked roads and bicycle paths, and comfortable, air-conditioned buses and trains. In short, all the hallmarks of middle-class Western European life sprang from the drab cooperative farms and midcentury food production facilities bequeathed by communism.

Her grandchildren would arrive in her village frequently to visit—often in a new VW or even in an Audi—to enjoy the traditional Sunday lunch of chicken soup and schnitzel. Conversation would invariably turn to the communist past, but with the kids there, the conversation always took a pejorative turn. Štefania understood this sentiment, but she probably would have also appreciated at least some recognition of how her generation's hard work took Slovakia from an agricultural backwater to a middle-income country in just thirty years. She was not so much against the change as she was against being undervalued by the present in rhetoric and policy. Her new government, however, focused its attention elsewhere.

All over Central Europe, governments were inventing new ways of rewarding international capitalists for investing their cash there, a process that Hilary Appel and Mitchell Orenstein have called "competitive signaling."[8] Competitive signaling was like an extra helping of whipped cream on the multinational corporations' ridiculously large chocolate sundae. It wasn't really needed to make investments flourish, but corporations lapped it up. Central Europe's talented, low-cost workers and the region's ready interior access to the enormous Single European Market already made it a natural location for all sorts of service, manufacturing, and food-processing operations. By 2006, investment was pouring into the region from all over the world, with the large manufacturing multinationals from Germany, Austria, France, South Korea, and Japan leading the way.

Having lagged in attracting investors in the 1990s, Slovakia now vaulted to the head of the pack by "competitively signaling" its people's willingness to work hard and expect little. In 2002, Slovaks elected a center-right governing coalition headed again by Prime Minister Mikuláš Dzurinda of the Slovak Christian and Democratic Union (SKDÚ). The new coalition empowered a young cadre of US-trained or -inspired bureaucrats who had been versed in a radical version of free market economics called neoliberalism. Neoliberals believe that economies do best when individuals are more fully responsible for brokering their well-being in a market free from undue government interference. Wherever possible, they transfer economic choice to the individual, along with the responsibility for failure. If one fails, for example, by refusing to save in a private pension, displeasing a boss, or not making enough money to pay school or hospital fees, that is one's own fault.[9] Policy makers are to be competent technocrats, the guardians of market forces, not social engineers.[10]

The Dzurinda government (2002-2006) was the regional pioneer in a range of investment-friendly experiments that Appel and Orenstein have called "avant-garde" neoliberalism.[11] This included privatizing public services like airports or freight lines; a flat tax in which everyone except the very poorest paid the same low rate; flexible labor laws that allowed employers to hire and fire workers more easily; and a private pension reform that diverted savings from the pay-as-you-go system to private funds invested on the Bratislava stock exchange.[12]

Yet, the new government's most substantial reform measure was to adopt the "Maastricht convergence criteria," a set of rules that the new ECB expected countries to follow in preparation for adopting a pan-European currency called the euro. Slovakia still had its own currency, the Slovak crown, but to avoid destabilizing short-term runs between the crown and the euro, Slovak policy had to make the crown mimic the euro in all but physical appearance. This removed any advantage to individuals in exchanging one currency for the other in the search for better interest rates or in the expectation that the exchange rates would soon change. It was called limiting the "arbitrage opportunity" for capital.

To accomplish the twinning of the euro and aspirant-member currencies like the crown, the Maastricht criteria expected governments to

(1) keep their inflation level close to the rates of the three lowest-inflation members of the zone;

(2) run a fiscal deficit of no more than 3 percent of GDP; and

(3) maintain an overall ratio between total debt the state owed to others and annual GDP of less than 60 percent (the debt to GDP ratio).

Once these indicators "converged" across countries, policy makers reasoned, applicants could simply, and at no cost to themselves, exchange their crowns for euros and their own national banks could, for the most part, close shop. Slovakia scheduled its swap for January 2009.

The Maastricht criteria were important in another way as well. The ECB was like an orchestra conductor with a single baton. With all member states playing one economic tune in unison, the ECB could choose a single monetary policy that kept them in harmony. Moreover, when the music lagged and unemployment was rising, it could increase the tempo— making money easier to get to stimulate investment and growth. When it was rushed and inflation loomed, it would slow the economic tempo down by making money harder to get. As a member of the orchestra, Slovakia voluntarily gave up its right to choose both the musical score and any discretion over how it would be played.

Yet, the Maastricht criteria ignored the possibility of distributional effects *within* countries. Most Central European countries have wide regional disparities in wealth and levels of development, and the persistence and intensity of this disparity are at least partially to blame for the region's populist turn. Slovakia is one of the most extreme examples. Until recently, its central and eastern regions—areas that Darina Malová and I have called its "internal periphery"—have had Europe's *highest* unemployment rates, topping 20 and even 25 percent. These regions often contain an embattled Roma population entering their *third* decade of post-communist poverty, abetted by state policies of austerity, expropriation, and neglect. The regions are also marked by poor infrastructure, inadequate state services, and fewer local employment opportunities.[13]

Central Europe's internal peripheries desperately needed fiscal transfers, more educational opportunities, less corruption, and heavier public and private investments in the sorts of infrastructure projects that encourage wealth-generating investment and employment. Yet, the Maastricht criteria discouraged the level of deficit spending that would make much of this possible.

People in Slovakia's internal periphery responded through outward migration. For three straight decades, talented, educated, and entrepreneurial youth fled for jobs elsewhere. According to Stephen Holmes and Ivan Krastev, this exacerbated local fears of demographic decline; deprived liberal parties of their natural voter base—the young; and deepened existential ethno-national fears surrounding the influx of nonwhite, non-Christian migrants into the EU.[14]

Ironically, migration also bolstered the neoliberal model of uneven development. Migratory workers escaping Slovakia's underdeveloped areas provided corporations and the public sector with a reserve labor force—helping keep wages and inflation down as the core developed regions benefited from the foreign direct investment boom. It also released some of the unemployment pressures in peripheral areas.

The Maastricht criteria were thus brilliant for Slovakia's western region, the triangle situated around the Vah River that runs between the cities of Bratislava, Žilina, and Nitra. This is where Štefania lived. This region received the lion's share of foreign investment and government spending. The western triangle was often referred to as "Central Europe's Detroit" because Slovakia made more cars per capita than any other country in the world. But the region also produced flatscreen TVs and monitors, auto parts, mobile phones, tires, corporate services, agricultural equipment and products, tourism, media and entertainment, higher education, and national governance. Here, employment was robust, driving Simona's generation of friends and family to two decades of upward mobility.

The Maastricht criteria made workers in the triangle richer in another way. As foreign investors and consumers demanded Slovak land, labor, and products in the 2000-2008 period, they drove up prices. To let off this inflationary pressure, the Slovak National Bank made Slovakia more expensive to foreigners by revaluing the crown against the euro. Whereas it took almost 50 crowns to buy one euro in 2000, by 2009, when the euro replaced the crown, it took only 21 crowns. The rise in the euro value of the crown also meant that Slovak labor became more expensive for foreigners to hire, but thanks to heavy investments in manufacturing technology, infrastructure, organization, and training, individual Slovak workers made more with an hour of labor than ever before. This is another way of saying that productivity gains kept pace with currency appreciation, ensuring that the real wage impact on corporations did not go up. Quite suddenly, many Slovaks became wealthier as the global purchasing power of their Slovak wages grew.

However, none of this applied to the internal periphery, where wages of unskilled labor stagnated and unemployment ran from 10 to 25 percent throughout the eurozone accession period.[15] The EU sought to compensate for Central Europe's regional imbalances somewhat with direct budgetary transfers called EU "cohesion funds." These funds helped, but they did not eliminate the disparities within countries. Often, they went toward infrastructure projects in the boom regions—and, indeed, helped make the "boom" possible. For example, the north-south corridor between Žilina and Bratislava and the east-west corridor between Nitra and Bratislava were unified by modern highways built in the 1990s with EU funds. By contrast, the connecting highway between Slovakia's peripheral eastern steel center of Košice and the capital Bratislava was only reaching completion in 2019. Such facts are hard to explain without at least some reference to administrative incompetence and corruption—something that any observant Central or Eastern Slovakian can tell you about in detail. For 20 years, they would explain, the right to complete an EU-funded project with cost overruns and long delays has been something of a Central European tradition—one of the great perks of having friends in power.

It seems easy to blame Slovakia's finance ministers for adhering to the Maastricht norm of fiscal restraint, but this would be unfair. Fiscal restraint is a Northern European norm rooted in the pragmatic recognition that mobile international capital will quickly punish smaller economies that challenge it. Case in point: in 2006, a young Slovak politician named Robert Fico led his party, Direction-Social Democracy (Smer-SD), to a plurality in parliamentary elections. Fico claimed to be a social democrat with a skilled team of experts backing him, but he was also developing into somewhat of a populist who drew support from the same sorts of voters who had supported Mečiar's HZDS and the Slovak National Party (SNS) in the 1990s.[16] Štefania was a big fan of both and, had she lived a few more months in 2006, would have almost certainly voted for Fico. His campaign benefited from the corruption scandals and infighting that rocked his opponents in the ruling coalition. But he won because he could speak for the concerns of Slovakia's internal periphery and others around the country, like Štefania, who felt stressed by the pressure of rising prices, stagnating fixed incomes, and stories of corruption in the neoliberal, pro-EU Dzurinda government.

Fico made electoral promises in the campaign to undo the Dzurinda-era reforms, and he openly questioned Maastricht's fiscal straitjacket. Meanwhile, he had no allies on the liberal center-right and was thus forced to form a cabinet with Vladimír Mečiar's HZDS and the nationalist party, the SNS. On the surface, this looked like a return to the 1990s era. In July 2006, investors holding crown-based assets became concerned that this new government would run big fiscal deficits. Betting that the crown would soon lose value, they sold their crowns and bought euros.

The Slovak National Bank (NBS) stopped the gambit by using a portion of its euro reserves to repurchase Slovak crowns, but it was quite costly. Had the collective bet against the crown continued, and it nearly did, the NBS would have eventually run out of euros to defend the value of the crown. The result would have been a currency depreciation, a decrease in the number of euros one could buy with the same number of crowns. Slovaks would have become poorer and cheaper overnight, and, ironically, the immediate leap in the prices of imported goods and demand for cheapened Slovak goods would have produced inflation. Under the financial rules of the day, this would have required hobbling cuts in government spending, making people even poorer. Fico, in short, almost created what is known as a depreciation-inflation spiral.[17]

It was enough to get Fico's attention. On July 12, 2006, he met with NBS president Ivan Šramko to discuss the run on the crown and, allegedly, to receive a quick primer on the pitfalls of capital mobility and the benefits of a strengthening currency. Following the meeting, Fico emphasized his government's commitment to the fiscal discipline of the Maastricht criteria, and he promised to meet the January 2009 target for adopting the euro. His government's ensuing budget was notable for its fiscal restraint, further calming the markets. No government since then has challenged the norm of fiscal restraint in any *meaningful* way. Indeed, as Darina Malová and Branislav Dolný have shown, the norm of fiscal restraint is one of the few values that Slovakia's political elite appear to hold in common.[18]

With investors reassured that the new government would not borrow heavily to run a higher fiscal deficit, Slovakia's foreign investment boom continued. In 2006 and 2007, Slovakia ranked among the world's best-performing economies. GDP growth topped *10 percent* in 2007. Between 2000 and the end of 2006, a cumulative total of US$18.6 billion of foreign investment produced the infrastructure for export-led development. Despite unprecedented demand for Slovak products in 2007, inflation only reached 2.8 percent—a level made possible by revaluation of the currency against the euro, technology-enabled workers, and the country's rapidly dropping but still significant 11 percent unemployment rate.[19] This unemployment remained disproportionately heavy in the internal periphery, where youth and Roma unemployment were well over 20 percent.[20]

Fico's government left most of the Dzurinda government's avant-garde reforms intact until well into the next decade. That was not what he had been elected to do, but the logic of financial integration into global markets and the fantastic success of Slovakia's boom regions convinced him otherwise.

Slovakia was not alone in this boom—although it was the star performer. The first decade of the century brought rapid *but uneven* development throughout the region. Poland and Czechia were not making serious efforts to adopt the euro. Yet, there too the threat of capital flight helped encourage fiscal discipline.

Then came the great Global Financial Crisis of 2008-10. It started as a private debt crisis in US real estate markets but quickly spread. Central Europeans experienced it as an export crisis and a halt in foreign investment. Over the previous 20 years, the region had fully integrated into Western European markets. Now, as Germans and the French stopped buying Slovak-made cars and flat-screen TVs, production slumped. Unemployment, which according to Eurostat, had dipped below 10 percent in 2008, shot back up to over 14 percent overall and returned to almost 20 percent in Slovakia's peripheral regions.

Fico's government began to issue unemployment checks, among other efforts, pushing the budget deficit to almost 8 percent of GDP in 2009. This broke the Maastricht rules, but unlike in 2006, the negative impact was minimal. Collectively, *all* the eurozone governments ran large deficits to stimulate their ailing economies and to care for their unemployed. Because Slovakia had been a eurozone member since January 2009, investments were already in euro-denominated assets. Investors did not have to fear that a currency devaluation would reduce the value of their assets. The state could also effectively borrow at lower rates in Euros made even cheaper as the ECB obligingly loosened credit and bought debt to make more borrowing and investment possible.

Slovaks could not borrow and spend all the way to recovery, however. As the primary market for most Central European goods, Germany was the most important player in this. Indeed, German fiscal choices are perhaps as important as ECB policy in determining Central European growth. In 2009-10, like everyone else, the German government borrowed a lot of money, which it pumped into its economy. German citizens then spent a small portion of this on Slovak goods and services, helping drive Slovakia to a robust, export-fueled 5.1 percent bounce in 2010.

But in 2011, something odd happened in Berlin. Rather than continue to run a government deficit and speed the Single European Market to recovery, the government reduced its deficit spending to a mere 1 percent of GDP. Worse, along with the ECB and the European Commission, German chancellor Angela Merkel encouraged everyone else to reduce their deficits as well. After that, Germany insisted on balancing its budget or running a surplus.

This was a form of fiscal realpolitik. German inflation remained low, but Central European growth correspondingly slumped and remained anemic until 2015. From 2011 to 2014, GDP growth in Slovakia did not exceed 3 percent. That is far too low for a country with unemployment rates in the mid-teens. But the government could do little to drive more growth. Thanks to Slovakia's integration into European markets, that responsibility now lay largely with the German government.[21]

The deliberate German decision not to stimulate recovery between 2011 and 2015 generated a lot of criticism from knowledgeable observers. They found the German and eurozone obsession with collective fiscal restraint needlessly destructive.[22] As noted, it makes sense for Slovakia and other small countries to keep their spending restrained. Yet, with Germany as the engine that drives Central European growth, its decision to limit its spending so soon after a major recession hurt its eastern and southern neighbors.[23] The policy was like putting sick patients on a diet and then feigning surprise when they failed to gain weight.

Nowhere was this more obvious than in Greece. In the 2008-10 Great Recession, Greece, a eurozone member, collapsed into recession and found itself unable to meet the payments it owed on its outstanding debt to European banks. As a euro-currency country, it could not devalue the currency and escape the crisis by cheapening itself and exporting more. Instead, the European Commission, the IMF, and the ECB (known collectively as the Troika) prescribed austerity. To secure emergency funding from eurozone partners, Greece was expected to *raise* taxes and divert government from social expenditures to paying off the debts to the banks. These euro-extractive measures threw the economy into an even deeper recession, which deprived the government of funds to meet its obligations.[24] Despite early predictions to the contrary, Greece remained distressed and had to ask repeatedly for emergency funding to keep from defaulting on its obligations to European banks.[25]

Greece was not the only peripheral eurozone country to have debt problems. Portugal, Spain, Ireland, and Iceland were all potentially over-leveraged and, unlike Greece, had enough debt to devastate Europe's banks if they failed to pay. Yet, remarkably, the eurozone did not have a mechanism for emergency funding. Instead, the Troika muddled through with tie-over loans while the EU altered its treaty structure to create the European Stability Mechanism (ESM). The ESM created a system to help troubled eurozone members meet their debt obligations during crises.

Slovakia refused to contribute to an early Greek "bailout" package. Slovaks treated it like a morality play. Politicians resentfully pronounced that while they had been fiscally prudent, the Greeks had been living it up on borrowed money that they could no longer return. Politicians began to think of Germany's anti-inflationary fiscal choices as a virtuous policy to be challenged only in cases of extreme emergency. Indeed, four successive Slovak governments—spanning Slovakia's ideological spectrum—supported collective restraint on spending and borrowing, despite the ongoing crisis in Greece and elsewhere on the EU's periphery.

It is not that the will to innovate was not there. Where Fico's government had greater discretion, it used it to moderate many aspects of Dzurinda-era neoliberalism. For example, after nearly a decade of criticism, the new Smer government amended the flat tax by creating a higher tax rate for the rich, corporations, and, symbolically, politicians. A new law also made contributions to private pension accounts voluntary and gave the elderly some new benefits, like free public transportation.

Yet, when it came to fiscal policy, neoliberals did not have to defeat Fico because he already thought like they did. They had triumphed in the battle of ideas. In the coup de grâce, in early 2012, eurozone members agreed to a fiscal pact in which they passed domestic laws to punish themselves if they accumulated high levels of state debt.[26]

Neoliberalism's victory was not without consequences. Fiscal restraint in Europe's core extended the period of anemic growth in Central Europe.

This long crisis was much more severe in Central Europe's internal peripheries than in places like Bratislava, Prague, or Budapest. Not surprisingly, as the peripheral regions grew more slowly and hemorrhaged their most talented youth to Europe's boom regions, and as the political system proved incapable of doing anything about it, voters turned to populism, extreme nationalism, and a form of cynicism about the value of the EU known as Euroscepticism.

II. Racism, Homophobia, and Slovakia's Conservative Political Imaginaries

This distrust of Brussels would have surprised Slovakia's liberals in 1998. With the defeat of Mečiar, most felt that the era of illiberal politics had been soundly tucked away in the past and that politics had "consolidated" around the rules of the democratic game that the EU demanded. European accession in 2004 helped reinforce this view. Yet, Mečiar's style of politics never sank far from the surface. Two years after accession to the EU, Prime Minister Fico's Smer party won a plurality in parliamentary elections. Fico's campaign emphasized the corruption of the ruling neoliberal coalition, their neglect of the average Slovak, and his party's technocratic skill at managing EU membership more equitably. His populist messages and redistributive economic promises alienated him from the center-right. To govern, therefore, he had to form a nationalist-populist coalition that included not only Mečiar's party, the would-be autocrats of the 1990s, but also Ján Slota of the nationalist SNS. Mečiar and Slota were too toxic for Fico to allow them to take cabinet positions personally, but their parties' participation in the parliamentary majority coalition was nevertheless a scandal.

Slota was openly homophobic. He called gay marriage a perversity and promised to spit on pride parade participants if they dared to take part.[27] He was also a virulent racist who targeted the Roma, a marginalized Central European ethnic minority commonly referred to by the racist term "gypsy." In the 1990s, Slota threatened to "solve" the "gypsy problem" with a "small yard and a long whip."[28]

Liberals condemned Slota's racist and homophobic language, but they rarely, if ever, thought about the role of the liberal transition in contributing to the vote that put a racist, homophobic party in the ruling coalition. Nor was there any real recognition of how, for many among Central Europe's Roma, the liberal, export-led growth model had been little more than a cruel joke—contributing to their marginalization and reinforcing the anti-Roma racism that, quite frankly, many liberals shared. Like others from Central Europe's internal periphery, Roma have migrated to find work. Yet, white racism and the lack of education and skills associated with Roma have reinforced their position on the margins of the European workforce. Where Roma do have formal jobs, these are often the poorest paid and least desirable positions available. Increasingly, competition from white Ukrainian and Balkan migrants has made even these jobs hard to get. Not surprisingly, then, Roma employment is often, but by no means always, on the margins of the European economy—informal, opportunistic, or predatory. This reinforces historical stigmatization and the dynamic of mutual hostility that some white Central Europeans use to justify their toxic mix of racism and often unapologetic applause for the extreme "solutions" offered by national populists like Slota.

Meanwhile, as the core of economic development extends its reach into Central Europe, Roma communities have come under constant pressure from a state apparatus used—both legally and illegally—to control, contain, or displace them. When I arrived in Slovakia for the first time in the mid-1990s, Roma were living in communities in many of the dilapidated historical buildings in the centers of Bratislava, Trnava, and Nitra. They were highly unemployed in the early transformation period, and few paid their bills. By the late 1990s, these families had been evicted from their residences or ordered out under the principle of eminent domain (the state practice of seizing private property when it is in the public interest). The buildings were restored and often incorporated into open-air pedestrian malls consisting of restaurants, hotels, cafés, and shops. Aggressive policing of the remaining Roma often made them de facto non-Roma zones.

Yet the dispossessing process of eviction and exclusion plagued the Roma even in the internal periphery. In summer 2016, Simona and I joined her brother's family and her parents at a renovated cottage on the edge of a small village in Eastern Slovakia. When we told some acquaintances in Bratislava of our plans, they "helpfully" warned, "Be sure the village you go to does not have many gypsies."

The cottage was a three-hour drive from the capital, a cozy, well-kept log cabin with hiking trails right out the back door and national parks only a short drive away. We cooked smoked meats over the firepit each night under the tall pine canopy and drank an abundant amount of Slovakia's fruity-tart white wine. On our final night, the friendly landlord stopped by with a bottle of his homemade *slivovica* to thank us for staying. A couple of shots into a slang-laden conversation that I could barely follow, I stepped out back to join my sons around the fire outside and avoid a plum brandy hangover.

Half an hour later, Simona joined us, outraged. As the shots had continued, the landlord had shared a blow-by-blow account of how he and his fellow villagers had dealt with its "gypsy problem" as part of an effort to make it more attractive to tourists. The stories included unjust imprisonment and intimidation. The final Roma resident, a relatively well-off older woman, departed after her house "accidentally" burned down while she was out of town at a family funeral. Warned of an impending arson attack on the woman's house, the local fire department helped ensure the conflagration would not spread, but nothing more.

That the local instruments of the state had been used to expropriate the property of marginalized citizens should come as no surprise. To return to the discussion started in chapter 2, the origins of the rule of law and representative forms of democracy lay in their value to property owners with the right to vote. Slovakia is more inclusive than the original Lockean state, but as Slovakia's newfound wealth has made the development of new industries possible, capital has seeped into new places and found them, well, inconveniently occupied.

It is the old story of capital accumulation by dispossession playing itself out all over again. And while Slovakia is, by most standards, a liberal democracy, the long history of racialized dispossession has rendered the Roma people nearly voiceless within it. As the land they legally own or "illegally" squat increases in value to the white population, they risk being pushed out—either legally or illegally—with little recourse or redress in local institutions and frequently with inadequate compensation.[29]

Racism has helped ensure that there has been little solidarity between the Roma and whites in the internal periphery, as both have struggled with the challenges of the postcommunist transformation. A disproportionately larger percentage of white voters in these regions support populists on both the left and the right who can voice their personal frustrations, be they with the Roma, the corrupt elites, or the seemingly ungovernable peripheral economy whose most valuable export is its talented youth. Most politicians have been circumspect about making open anti-Roma sentiments. But many also try to make it clear that in the conflict between EU officials or human rights NGOs and the matter-of-fact racism of local white citizens, their sympathies lie with the latter.

Anti-Roma sentiment is simply one part of a broader set of economic, racial, and ethno-national anxieties that have been tightly interwoven in the rise of Central European populism. The unifying glue was—and, yes, you can say it in a deep movie trailer voice—*existential fear*. As Slovakia's talented youth fled their villages, those left behind have been vulnerable to concerns about their own demographic decline.[30] It has contributed to a nationalist discourse that is somewhat similar to the Serbian anti-Albanian sentiment in the late 1980s and even has distant echoes of German and Hungarian fears of Slavic dominance in the mid-1800s.

It is quite common to hear people assert that the Roma enlarge their families simply to access a bigger share of the state's fiscally restrained social services. Meanwhile, Catholic conservatives, evangelicals, the Christian Democratic Movement (KDH), and even Robert Fico himself have helped fashion a populist political imaginary in which the EU, socialists, feminists, and LGBTQ+ activists threaten the well-being and even survival of white, Christian Europe.[31]

One of the first apostles of the new imaginary was German Christian conservative Gabriele Kuby. In November 2012, Kuby toured Slovakia to promote a Slovak translation of her new book. According to a study by Comenius University researcher Petra Ďurinová, after Kuby's visit, the phrase "gender ideology" began to circulate with regular frequency in the mainstream media.[32] In Kuby's world, "gender ideology" encapsulates ideas that portray gender as fluid rather than binary and that consider same-sex relations to be on the spectrum of normal human sexuality. Yet, her analysis is hardly fair to these concepts. Kuby warns of a world in which children change gender and sexuality according to both whim and convenience, where masturbation is taught in kindergarten, and where gays and lesbians recruit children and teens to emulate their chosen lifestyle and live childless lives.

In an interview, Kuby explains that gender ideology is a Brussels-sponsored, left-elite project to throw society into "chaos and anarchy" and introduce a "new totalitarian regime." I presume that her fear of anti-Christian totalitarianism results from her controversial assertion that "97%" of people "instinctively" recoil from homosexuality and therefore will have to be oppressed by the EU to accept it. The key architects of gender ideology span the spectrum of local accomplices among the cultural elite, green and left parties, any government in which the left holds sway, the EU, the UN, Warren Buffett, the Rockefellers, and, of course, the billionaire philanthropist George Soros, whose funding first brought me to teach in Bratislava in 1996. The best mode of counterattack, Kuby argues, is to organize locally to stop gender ideology from being taught in schools and to reverse laws protecting sexual minorities.[33]

Kuby's visit to Slovakia complemented an extended cultural campaign led by the conservative wing of the Catholic Church, whose networks of parish priests and devout activists could be mobilized for collective action. In November 2013, the Slovak government sponsored human rights workshops in Slovakia to gather information on the needs of marginalized communities. The original expectation was that the workshops would give members of marginalized communities—including sexual and gender minorities—an opportunity to suggest steps toward better state policies.

Yet, socially conservative activists were far better organized. They took over the workshops to wage "cultural battle" with the workshop organizers over the very concept of human rights. The *starting point* for discussion for many of the attendees was that homosexuality was both a mental disease and a depravity, that human rights began at conception, and that freedom of conscience gave one the right to actively discriminate against minorities in business, education, and government.

Views expressed at the meetings also reflected the growing influence of the internet trolls and the difficulty people were having recognizing manufactured fictions and conspiracy theories. Russian funding, troll factories, and media support have played a role, but, really, the sources of Slovakia's populist turn seemed so overdetermined by 2016 that one wonders if the Russians even needed to bother nudging it along.[34] Many participants sincerely repeated some of the fears raised in Kuby's work, for example, that the EU promoted masturbation lessons in kindergarten and that left-leaning Western EU member states had policies to separate children from their socially conservative parents. Underlying all of this was an emerging fear that an LGBTQ+-permissive Slovakia would attract children to non-procreative sex and lead to lower birth rates and eventual national "auto-genocide," a concept promoted in a pamphlet distributed by a new NGO called Alliance for Family, headed by founder Anton Chromík.[35]

The link between homosexuality and genocide may seem insane to many, but in late 2013, Catholic Church bishops and priests in Slovakia and Poland indeed linked homosexuality and genocide to press their attack on women's reproductive rights. The unifying concept in the imaginary was a "culture of death." Put simply, a culture of death exists where society permits contraception and abortions, legalizes supposedly childless same-sex marriages, and offers legal protections for LGBTQ+ groups. By reducing births through permissive sexual and reproductive choice, Slovak bishops warned in statements read to parishioners from the pulpit, death culture "genuinely threatens the existence of the nation."[36] Those promoting death culture, the bishops continued, "hide behind grand phrases about freedom and happiness of people about whom they do not care at all."[37]

Some priests gave the campaign a specific homophobic turn. As ultra-conservative Catholic priest Marián Kuffa explained to his parishioners, there are two types of homosexuals, those who cannot help it and those who choose it. The latter group, Kuffa warned, are "not just ordinary murderers but . . . mass murderers; this is a genocide of our nation!"[38]

The conservative bishops' offensive gained some political traction in 2014 when the KDH reached out from the parliamentary opposition to make a deal with the ruling Smer party to change the Slovak constitution. With the KDH on board, Fico could assemble a constitutional majority. Heretofore, a number of Smer politicians had been supportive on the question of registered partnerships for nonbinary couples. Fico, by contrast, had been largely silent. Yet, Smer now backed a KDH-proposed constitutional amendment limiting marriage to the union of a man and a woman. In return, the KDH blessed an amendment allowing the government to investigate and vet sitting Slovak judges—potentially putting them in the pockets of the ruling party.[39]

Not to be outdone, Anton Chromík acquired enough signatures to hold a national referendum on three issues: banning LGBTQ+ marriage, preventing same-sex couples from gaining the right to adopt children, and giving students the right to skip sex education classes and weirdly (because it was not in the curriculum) any classes that discussed euthanasia. Most Slovaks were uninterested. Despite Slovakia's relatively conservative electorate, only 21.4 percent of eligible voters showed up on referendum day—far short of the 50 percent needed for a referendum to be binding.[40]

Many of my liberal Slovak friends documented their day of *not voting* on social media. Jozef, for example, took his children to football practice and then met his wife, Zuzka, for a family walk in the park. This is what families should do, the day's informal campaign illustrated—they don't wallow in hate. Indeed, for mainstream liberals, the referendum was something of a wakeup call. Thanks to Catholic conservatives and Chromík, liberals could now see how LGBTQ+ rights, women's reproductive rights, and political liberalism were jointly vulnerable.

This had an impact among liberals in Bratislava. When I arrived with my family for sabbatical in winter 2016, my colleagues and students at Comenius University were more interested than ever before in the plight of sexual and gender minorities in Central Europe. My department's faculty were aware and welcoming. LGBTQ+ students were now openly out in greater numbers, queering their public appearance, and active politically.

The heartwarming response of liberal allies was limited, however—a drop in the bucket, really. Their lone voices for an inclusive and tolerant

Slovakia were soon drowned out by a new manufactured panic, this time about migrants.

Slovakia was gearing up for a parliamentary election in March 2016—and with the "queer fear" card already played by the KDH and others, Smer leader and Prime Minister Robert Fico seized on the efforts of migrants to escape instability, violence, and poverty in Syria, Iraq, and elsewhere. None of these immigrants—seriously, zero—were seeking refuge in Slovakia. Rather, they were on their way to the wealthier, more multiethnically diverse EU countries like Holland, Germany, France, the United Kingdom, and Sweden. This concentration was taxing these states' capacity—especially Sweden's—to provide humane assistance. In May 2015, the European Commission proposed that the burden of taking in refugees be spread across the member states according to a quota system. The Commission assigned Slovakia only 800 refugees. Yet, Fico promptly joined other Central European EU members in rejecting Brussels's quota.

Over the course of the summer, Fico, who we had presumed to be an atheist, made repeated Christian-chauvinist and xenophobic statements about migrants. He also argued that, although he did not wish to challenge the EU norm of solidarity, he rejected the right of the European Commission to impose migrants on Slovakia. It was an unwarranted intrusion on national sovereignty. The migrants had no desire to come to Slovakia, he correctly pointed out, and would divert scarce resources from needy Slovaks. But then, he added, migrants would raise the risk of "terrorism" in Slovakia, threaten Slovakia's Christian culture, and pose a lasting assimilation problem. Fico used radical militant attacks in Paris and alleged migrant-led sexual assaults in Germany on New Year's Eve to justify a surveillance policy on "every Muslim" in Slovakia.[41] This appeared to strike a chord. Simona and I even heard a racist acquaintance worry aloud that the Muslim men simply wanted to come to Europe to rape Slovak women.

Fico's hostility toward the European Commission and brown, non-Christian immigrants put him rhetorically in league with Slovakia's most extreme politicians, particularly Marián Kotleba, who led a neofascist political party called People's Party-Our Slovakia (ĽSNS). Kotleba got his start in the central Slovak region of Banská Bystrica—the heart of the internal periphery. His party's name deliberately referred to the Hlinka Slovak People's Party—the successful party of the 1930s most remembered for taking political power in Slovakia in 1939 with Hitler's blessing and then delivering Slovak Jews, Roma, and others to the Nazis.[42]

Kotleba's movement unapologetically honored this fascist wartime legacy—its members were known in the recent past to wear the Slovak state's World War II-era uniforms. By 2016, they had ditched the fascist cosplay for suits and Christian lapel pins. The ĽSNS became a leader in the Central European alternative-right movement, embracing a heteronormative, Christian white supremacist doctrine to justify its bid for power. In particular, it drew strength from and nourished "replacement theory," which argues that the "liberal EU policies" of birth restriction and multiculturalism are deliberately intended to replace white, Christian Europeans with brown, black, and/or Muslim immigrants.[43]

Before Europe's migrant crisis, the ĽSNS was a regional central Slovak party, and few saw the potential for its extremist message to carry nationally. However, on June 20, 2015, Kotleba staged a mildly violent demonstration in the capital, Bratislava, under the slogan, "Stop the Islamisation of Europe! Together against the *dictat* of Brussels; Europe for Europeans!" In an incendiary speech, he wished his followers "a beautiful and nice white day."[44]

The anti-migrant revolt against the European Commission was, more broadly, a regional phenomenon and so was the racialized populism that accompanied it. In neighboring Hungary, Prime Minister Viktor Orbán echoed Fico and Kotleba in rejecting refugee resettlement on civilizational grounds, and he built a border fence that redirected migrants traveling from Serbia toward another EU member state, Croatia. Meanwhile, countries began to introduce border checks within the Schengen Area, a European region created by treaty that eliminates border controls.

Arguably, even from his own perspective, Fico may have been too successful in stoking fear.[45] Before the election of 2016, polls indicated that 70 percent of Slovak citizens were against hosting refugees, while 63 percent considered them to be a security threat.[46] Accordingly, otherwise pro-EU parties found it prudent, and easy, to validate Fico's rhetoric—essentially removing his advantage. Smer's campaign pledged, "We will protect you!" but other parties riffed on the same message. In winter 2016, Slovakia's roadside billboards presented a tableau of well-coiffed, white politicians, arms crossed in stern three-quarter poses, pledging to keep the nation, home, and family safe. One friend quipped, "I have never felt so defended in my life!"

With virtually all parties pledging to defend the nation from immigrants and the heavy hand of Brussels, Fico may have gained no voter advantage from the issue. Instead, people appear to have voted with their pocketbooks. A Eurobarometer poll in summer 2016 placed migrants *fifth* on a prioritized list of voter issues. The major concern was unemployment, followed by anxiety about health care and social security. The most mentioned issues related to the economic well-being of those polled.

Fico's Smer still won more votes than its rivals in 2016, but it lost many of its 2012 voters to the resurgent, nationalist right. This forced Fico into coalition with an odd constellation of right-wing conservatives, Slovak nationalists from the SNS, and an unexpectedly opportunistic liberal Slovak-Hungarian party called Most ("Bridge"). Despite the Christian democrats' leadership in stoking homophobia and protecting Slovaks from migrants, their party, the KDH, performed poorly. This was not because Slovaks were sick of the conservative Christian community's warnings about gender ideology but rather, I suspect, because several other major political parties had plenty of opportunity to reassure voters that they were just as homophobic. With nothing really to distinguish itself, an aging electorate, and the Smer and two nationalist parties crowding their social agenda, the KDH did not even clear the 5 percent required to get into parliament in the 2016 elections.

According to scholar Marek Hlavec, Slovakia's three most populist parties (Smer, SNS, and ĽSNS) secured proportionally more support from those areas with lower education rates and higher unemployment, which were, arguably, the best proxies for distressed, peripheral regions in his dataset.[47] Kotleba's ĽSNS goose-stepped into parliament with 8 percent—the third largest tally. Kotleba announced that party members would start patrolling passenger railcars to defend citizens from Roma and migrant riders.

The internal periphery's support for Smer and Slovakia's two nationalist parties did not mean that the unemployed drove the populist vote: Slovakia's underemployed Roma population has historically had low voter turnout and rarely voted for Kotleba. As in other European and US regions where populist electoral uprisings have shaken the established order, much of the populist vote came from the Central European equivalent of blue-collar workers, insecure in their futures, resentful of self-interested elites, and often stressed by the conditions of stagnating purchasing power and competition from technological change and globalized production. It is also notable that about one in five young first-time voters supported the ĽSNS, according to social scientist Olga Gyárfášová. When asked why, few would admit to racism, homophobia, or fear of migrants but instead emphasized their desire to send a clear message to an indifferent, unresponsive political elite.[48]

Arguably, stoking fears provided political parties with less of an advantage than they had hoped because it was so easy for a range of parties to do. Rather, social conservatism, persistent economic distress, low personal advancement opportunities, and frustration with Bratislava's corruption and loss of economic sovereignty also helped drive the populist shift in 2016. Young Slovaks in particular were fed up with the lack of alternatives. For many, voting took on the almost Sampson-like quality of bringing the master's temple down on all heads, regardless of who was crushed.

There is an old lesson to be learned here. Where basic economic questions have been taken off the table, politicians will still look for ways to compete. In Slovakia, they became a bit like rival lifeguards on a turbulent lake. As people wallowed precariously in the water, the guards competed to protect the lake from imagined threats, like marauding bears and incompetent colleagues. No party asked why so many people were on the verge of drowning or how one might make the lake less dangerous to swimmers. Imagination rather than lake engineering and actual lifeguarding was the salient value of politics. Yet, imagining threats is relatively easy to do. No real expertise is required, and one guard is about the same as the others.[49] This is the lesson that Fico and the KDH learned in 2016.

III. Civil Society Fights Back!

In some respects, Slovakia has been lucky. Populist, anti-elite politics has had a significant and quite successful liberal component, one based in civil society. This has served as a "firewall" for democracy.[50] Not only has it punished political elites for corruption, but it has also helped restrain the once dominant party, Smer, in power. Indeed, I would argue that this civic check on Slovakia's political elite has helped prevent Slovakia from following Hungary and Poland further down the path of illiberalism.

Slovakia is fortunate enough to have some superb independent journalists—born in the existential fight for democracy during the Mečiar years and challenged ever since by a cynical elite who see them as a threat to "business as usual." Sometime in spring 2009, I met my old acquaintance Tom Nicholson for a cup of coffee. I knew Tom from the mid-1990s when he was a Canadian reporter helping to build the reputation of the *Slovak Spectator*, one of the best English-language newspapers in Central Europe. By 2009, Tom was a well-known investigative journalist for the leading liberal newspaper, *Sme*. A few minutes into our conversation, he pulled out a thick file that I later learned was given to him by Peter Holúbek, a former agent in the Slovak Information Service.

This is where Slovakia got lucky. The file contained transcripts of alleged recordings initiated in 2005 when Holúbek noticed that an apartment near his was being used for meetings between important politicians and the chief executive of the Penta Group, Jaroslav Haščák. Holúbek became suspicious and began a wiretap operation. The operation produced recordings of Haščák discussing financial kickbacks in apparent exchange for favorable privatization deals and other favors. The immediate culprits were from the neoliberal ruling coalition of Prime Minister Mikuláš Dzurinda. Future prime minister Robert Fico attended one meeting. At others, his party secretary appeared—perhaps as a proxy—where discussions vaguely referred to "dark money" to fund Fico's party, Smer.[51] If Tom's transcripts were real, they implied that in 2005, at the apex of the avant-garde neoliberal era, many in the ruling political elite of Slovakia were "on the take."

I was not much help to Tom. Without the recordings, the transcripts could have been a planted forgery or doctored to make some people look bad. I was more worried about his safety. Tom kept the transcripts secret while he did further investigation for a best-selling book he was writing named *Gorilla*, the code name for the surveillance operation that produced the recordings.[52]

Someone—not Tom—finally leaked the documents online in 2011. The press dubbed it the "Gorilla scandal." Gorilla confirmed what many Slovaks had felt about their political elites: that thieves and politicians were the real sovereign power in their state, not the Slovak voters. Once again, it was politics "*O nás, bez nás!*" Tom's new book helped fill in many of the details.

Blame for the scandal fell largely on Mikulaš Dzurinda, whose party, the SKDÚ, was then enjoying a third term in government under Prime Minister Iveta Radičová. Large public protests followed, and with Dzurinda and other compromised figures still associated with the SKDÚ, its popular support plummeted.

In late 2011, a junior coalition party led by the neoliberal, Eurosceptic economist Robert Sulík unexpectedly withdrew its backing for the Radičová government. Sulík claimed it was because Radičová supported the EU treaty amendment creating the European Stability Mechanism, discussed above, which was needed to provide emergency funding to countries in trouble. Without Slovakia's approval, there would be no security system for the euro and the viability of the eurozone would be in danger. Radičová was under a lot of pressure.

Lacking coalition support, Radičová turned to Fico's Smer, then in the opposition, to pass the bill. Fico exacted a high price. Smer would give her the votes to pass the treaty, but in exchange, she must hold an early election.[53] Radičová knew that because of her party's association with Gorilla, it would fare poorly in the elections. Yet, she agreed.

The SKDÚ did not even win enough votes to return to parliament. Instead, the 2013 election returned Robert Fico and his party, the Smer, to power with an unprecedented absolute majority in parliament. This was a pivotal moment in Slovak politics. Unlike any Slovak prime minister since 1990, Fico could now rule without coalition partners. Similar electoral results in Poland, Serbia, and, as we will see in the next chapter, Hungary have been a prelude to redesigning the political system in a way that gives the ruling party a decided advantage in subsequent elections.

This did not happen in Slovakia. Part of the reason is because Fico lacked a constitutional majority and thus could not easily rewrite the rules of the game, as Orbán had done in Hungary. Yet another possibility is that the country's experience with Mečiar in the 1990s and Gorilla in 2011-12 had trained Slovaks to be skeptical about their politicians. This skepticism may have helped Slovaks prevent politicians from fully colonizing Slovakia's political institutions and civil society.

The depth of Slovakia's political corruption and the resilience of its civil society again became apparent after February 21, 2018. On that night, assassins executed the young journalist Ján Kuciak and his fiancé, Martina Kušnírová, in their home. Kuciak's investigations quickly sprang to the front pages of Slovakia's independent media. The dead journalist, it turned out, was a gifted investigative reporter whose inquiries had uncovered a number of possible economic crimes. A close read revealed a range of characters who might have wanted him dead, including Smer politicians and an Italian Mafioso who may have been swindling the EU's euro funds destined for distressed Slovak communities.[54] The tabloid press, of course, focused on a former model who left her Mafioso boyfriend to work for Smer, where she rose scandalously fast to the position of chief state adviser to Prime Minister Robert Fico. What was the prime minister doing by giving the glamorous ex-girlfriend of a gangster a top political appointment? Rumor had it that he'd fallen in love, which was perhaps endearing but did not help his case.

In the days after the murder, outraged Slovaks staged demonstrations wherever they could gather. Bratislava-based university students harnessed their "moral shock" into a movement they called For a Decent Slovakia (FDS). On March 9, 2018, FDS held the largest Slovak demonstration since the Velvet Revolution. From our living room in Colorado, Simona and

I watched on Facebook as the young crowd pulled out their keys and rang them like bells, just as Simona had done in that very square 29 years before. All 60,000 then sang the Slovak national anthem. Under intense pressure, Prime Minister Fico and his most compromised cabinet members stepped down. Fico handed the premiership to his Smer colleague Peter Pellegrini, who later began to distance himself from Fico's team.

Meanwhile, an intensive and remarkably persistent police action looked into the murders under the anxious gaze of Smer politicians. In September 2018, investigators arrested two gunmen, the gangster-businessman Marián Kočner, and two possible co-conspirators. Before Kuciak was murdered, the young journalist had published an article alleging that Kočner had defrauded the state of tax revenue, among other things.[55] Infuriated, Kočner had called the journalist and made explicit threats against him and his family. Kuciak filed a criminal complaint with a state prosecutor and kept on digging.[56]

Kočner was an obvious suspect, hiding in plain sight. Yet he was confident he would not be arrested. Over more than a decade, he had acquired a trove of compromising documents on the political elite in the form of dozens of recordings and documents readily available in his office, in his home, and on his phone. The Gorilla recordings were there, confirming Tom Nicholson's transcripts word for word.[57] Other recordings were damaging to Smer. Kočner, in his own words, discussed his influence over tax authorities, Slovakia's former attorney general, the prosecutor to whom Kuciak had filed his complaint, and leading businesspersons, as well as Fico and one of his closest colleagues.[58] In one recording, Kočner attempted to reduce his tax bill by claiming to have made a prior arrangement with Fico. Kočner asserted that without his help, Fico would not have been reelected prime minister. Indeed, remember Sulík's defection from the Radičová government and the ensuing elections that brought Fico back into power?[59] Kočner implied that he and Sulík had engineered the fall of the government.[60]

The scandal was devastating to Slovakia's ruling elite. In early 2020, the Smer performed poorly in parliamentary elections. Traditional, pro-EU liberals failed again to make a strong showing. Instead, voters promoted a relatively new party led by a charismatic yet ideologically unanchored populist, Igor Matovič. His new cabinet promised to rule with fiscal rectitude, technical competence, and less corruption, but he made no plans to help the internal periphery cope with the growing economic crisis caused by the Covid-19 pandemic shutdown.

EPILOGUE: I once naively thought that EU membership would permanently consign populism to the fringes of Central European politics. It appeared to me in 2004 that the EU had successfully spliced liberalism into the region's foundational DNA. The years since have proven me wrong. Liberalism has been a fragile dream, partially shattered by a new generation of "granny democrats" and others who have struggled while parts of the region have prospered.

If there is hopeful news, one finds it in liberal civil society and in liberal civic movements around the region.[61] Yet, merely holding corrupt elites accountable for their actions is not enough. If the analysis here is correct, then Slovakia's variant of populist politics has emerged against a common backdrop of conservative social anxieties and resentments activated by the uneven distribution of benefits of market integration and the inability of national elites to do much to address it. Bereft of real economic policy alternatives, politicians have found a resource in the arts of the political imaginary, rooted in fears—both ancient and new.

Štefania passed away in 2006. Had she lived another 15 years, what would she have made of all this? Her husband was a Communist Party member who took up arms against Slovakia's pro-Nazi government in 1944. Štefania had worked hard all her life for her children and her community. If the Communist Party claimed her labor for the "proletariat," so be it; she was proud of her accomplishments. She knew that her exertions made everyone better off, which is about all we can or should really hope to accomplish in our lives.

Simona suspects that her grandmother today would still be a Smer voter. Despite Fico's flaws, he knew how to speak to Štefania and validate her life and concerns. She would, of course, have been disappointed with Fico's government for its corruption, but she would have saved her choicest words for the liberal elite. She would have drilled her laser-sharp humor through their hollow claims about self-reliance and personal responsibility. She was not blind to the insider privileges that put many of them where they are. Most of all, Štefania would have felt a lot more sympathy for those who could not cope.

While liberal civic movements rightly seek to discipline or displace their self-dealing elite and restore healthy competition to political institutions, they need to join Europe in rethinking the EU's economic distributional formulas. Are there ways of preserving the political agency of the individual while ensuring that prosperity is more widely shared? There are no easy solutions, but I think that Štefania and other "granny democrats" would be pleased to join this effort of reimagining.

CHAPTER 11

Illiberal Democracy

The Political Economy of Hungary's
Liberal Unraveling

With Zsolt Gál, Comenius University

*Locke and Smith predict a Hungarian meltdown . . . Kelemen blames
the EU . . . Hungarian socialists make a mess of things . . . Orbán rips
up the liberal democratic playbook . . . Hungary's robust economy . . .
The EU, Orbán's enabler.*

If Slovakia's populist politics has roots in European economic policies and
market integration, then we should not be surprised to find that populism
is a regional trend. After all, Slovakia's neighbors face many of the same
issues. Among these, Hungary's national populist prime minister Viktor
Orbán has travelled furthest down the populist road—creating a model
of political and economic management that is being emulated by Serbia,
echoed in Poland, and threatened in Bulgaria, Romania, Czechia, and elsewhere. In this chapter, Zsolt Gál of Bratislava's Comenius University and
I examine the nexus between Central Europe's illiberal turn and its economic performance, with a particular focus on Hungary.

The Lockean tradition expects that the unraveling of the liberal social
contract will have severe economic and social side effects—including capital flight, suppressed investment, and deteriorating labor and public voice.
In the preface to this book, I discussed two alternatives to the Lockean
state. In the first, the state is too weak to protect property. In the second,
the state is so strong that it becomes a threat to property owners. Both
create a problem in the calculus of investors: "Why," they ask, "should we
invest here if the fruit of our effort will simply be taken away?" Whether

the threat is from bandits or the government, a reduction in the guarantees protecting property and investment is expected to be harmful to the market economy.

In Hungary, we have the second type of unraveling—one in which the populist executive slips the bonds of democratic constraint and becomes, potentially, too strong. While one would expect a less constrained executive to complicate the decision-making calculus of investors, their flight might be mitigated by the possibilities of patronage, the ability of certain actors to secure favors from the executive that guarantee them a profit. In this scenario, politically connected actors find it far easier, more certain, and usually more lucrative to lobby for a profit than to earn one through successful performance on a competitive market. The trick, of course, is for the state to find resources to dispense. In this chapter, we find that many of those resources come freely from the EU in the form of cohesion funds—money supplied to Central European governments to help them "catch up" economically and socially with richer EU members.

Still, many actors will not have this privileged access to patronage favors. For them, the illiberal political turn will be accompanied by greater political and economic risk—from mundane bureaucratic shakedowns to more costly demands for side payments in exchange for permission to keep operating. In the worst-case scenario, best categorized by the Russian word *reiderstvo*, the state forgoes its Lockean role as the protector of property rights and, instead, engages in the "centrally led" confiscation of property.[1]

Labor, too, may feel the effects of the less constrained executive. As noted in chapter 2, labor has not generally been naturally "written in" to the social contract between state power and capital. Historically, it has had to fight its way in through collective political action and even violent revolution. While the liberal reforms of the postcommunist era have been unfriendly to organized labor and collective action, there is little reason for this to change under a *less* liberal government. If anything, labor's concerns might receive even less of a hearing from the collusion of the executive, its pet oligarchs, and multinational companies.

Nowhere in the EU has the illiberal political "turn" been more pronounced in Central Europe than in Hungary. For this reason, Zsolt Gál and I examine this case to see if these expectations hold up. Overall, we do find the distortions that one would expect when the rule of law and legislation are shaped around the prerogatives of the executive—complete with captured EU tenders and alarming reports of *reiderstvo*. Yet, paradoxically, these expected effects appear to be economically sustainable in the medium turn. By many indicators, the country is even flourishing.

Hungary is thus a confounding case. It is like those odd snowflakes that float upward in a storm that I wrote about in this book's preface. Snowflakes flying upward are not what we would expect given our experience with storms and gravity, and we need to discover why.

We share political economist R. Daniel Kelemen's finding that the EU, once a force for liberalism in the Central and Eastern Europe (CEE) region, has played an important role in Hungary's illiberal turn.[2] First, we argue that the eurozone's emphasis on collective fiscal restraint has helped bolster the conditions for national populist politics in Hungary's internal periphery. Hungary has many distressed communities, and these provide a strong bastion of support for populist politicians. Second, the right to freedom of movement within the Single European Market appears to have helped sustain illiberal politicians. Young citizens who cannot earn a living in Hungary often leave, depriving opposition parties of their natural voter base. They then bolster the Hungarian economy by sending part of their paychecks home. Third, the EU budgetary transfers for government contracts (also known as tenders) have provided governments and entrepreneurs alike an important incentive to engage in corrupt dealings. In addition, the need to enable these deals and keep them from the public eye provides an additional incentive to attack the liberal institutions that can expose and punish them. As Professor Kelemen has pointed out, Hungary's political economy is increasingly describable using the model of rents and resource curse rather than the liberal model of specialization, trade, competition, and creative destruction.[3] Finally, perhaps most ominously of all, the EU lacks the institutional apparatus to discipline its first illiberal member state and seems destined to continue in its self-defeating policies.[4]

Hungarian democratic erosion, or "backsliding," is a relatively recent phenomenon—merely a decade old as of this writing. As a prerequisite for entry into the EU in May 2004, Hungary had to prove, under the Copenhagen criteria and EU treaty obligations, that it was democratic in both the form and the operation of its institutions. Originally located on the center-right on the political spectrum, Prime Minister Viktor Orbán's now dominant party, Fidesz, drifted toward the nationalist right toward the end of the 1990s.[5] In the decade following Fidesz's creation in 1988, Orbán attempted to provide a center-right alternative to the center-left Hungarian Socialist Party (MSZP). Yet, as early 1997, he began to add distinct notes of a national-populist political imaginary to his messaging, warning that "foreign minded" elites sought to build an "open society" in which the Hungarian nation became no more than "an investment site. Where no nation, only a population exists."[6]

Fidesz spent eight years in opposition from 2002 to 2010, during which two successive center-left governments dragged the Hungarian economy through successive policies of overspending (2002-6), austerity (2007-8), and deep recession (2008-10).[7] In a key inflection point in 2006, Hungarian Prime Minister Ferenc Gyurcsány (MSZP) garnered votes by committing to what he knew were unsustainable spending promises. In a leaked, closed-door speech after the election, the prime minister revealed that he had been cynically and deliberately lying about the state of the country's finances to get reelected. Since 2002, Fidesz had been building grassroots support through local alternative civic organizations known as "civic circles." Outraged by the lies, these and other groups took to Budapest's streets in actions marked by property destruction and police brutality.[8]

To help its reelection, Gyurcsány's government ran a 9 percent deficit in 2006 and spent freely. Once reelected, however, the government enacted austerity measures. Hungary's export markets then collapsed with the onset of the Global Financial Crisis. In 2008 the country saw a 6.7 percent drop in GDP mitigated by a $25.1 billion bailout from the IMF, EU, and World Bank. The loan allowed the government to meet its high debt bill and write unemployment checks. Still, unemployment rose from 8 percent to close to 11 percent nationally. New IMF conditions arguably restrained the government from borrowing more heavily to relieve the hardship of its citizens. Policy makers then took a deep breath and looked to Germany to stimulate its economy and restore demand for Hungarian exports.[9]

As in Slovakia, Poland, and elsewhere, the unemployment burden was disproportionately concentrated in the distressed rural and smaller urban communities that had not benefited from the decade's boom in foreign investment. In these towns and villages, unemployment often topped 15 percent or even 20 percent. This contributed to the outward migration of the youth to Budapest and other high-employment regions of Europe.

Unlike Slovakia, which adopted the euro in January 2009, Hungary still had its own currency. In early 2009, the value of the forint fell against the euro. This made Hungary's products and labor cheaper to foreigners. Yet, given that these foreigners were also in deep recession, it did not do much to stimulate investment in either Hungary or Hungarian exports. Worse, over the past 10 years, Hungarian citizens had borrowed money in a foreign currency, usually the euro, to buy homes and make other purchases. Foreign currency loans had lower interest rates, but borrowers were also gambling that the rate of exchange between the forint, in which they earned their income, and the euro, in which they borrowed their money, would remain stable. Devaluation exposed this gamble and raised the size of Hungarians' personal debts.[10]

Running against such a dismal record, Fidesz cruised to a victory in the 2010 parliamentary elections. The size of the protest vote gave Fidesz a two-thirds supermajority in parliament and the ability to redesign the Hungarian constitution. Orbán argued that the country's democratic institutions were the vehicles by which his predecessors had robbed the country and sold out its interests.[11] Since people could not trust their politicians or their government bureaucrats, he added, the nation needed a strong leader, like himself, who would rule more directly in the people's interest.[12] Rather than make the institutions function better as a check on the power of the elected elite, Orbán ran them through a constitutional retrofit that gave his party, Fidesz, and its allies an undue advantage in politics and the economy. The changes reduced checks on the power of the parliamentary majority and gave the government greater control over state bureaucrats, who could now be replaced at will.[13] Most of these major changes were passed without consulting other political parties, notifying the public, or asking for comment from civil society organizations.[14]

Had Slovakia's ex-prime minister Vladimír Mečiar succeeded in establishing hegemony over Slovak political life in 1998, chances are that Slovakia's political landscape would have looked much like Hungary's by the end of 2019.[15] Even more than Mečiar's HZDS, however, Orbán eliminated formal and informal political checks on his own power, dominated the media, marginalized civil society, and limited academic freedom.[16]

The first major target for change was the courts. A liberal would have looked for ways to give the legal system greater independence and integrity. Instead, parliament's supermajority enlarged the Constitutional Court to make room for Orbán-friendly appointees. Changes also made it easier for Orbán to replace judges across the country. It then limited the ability of the Constitutional Court to review parliament's new laws for constitutional compatibility, allowing parliament to pass laws with less fear of a domestic judicial rebuke. Henceforth, the courts could only challenge laws on procedural grounds, and they could not rely on earlier decisions in making their decision.[17]

Orbán also addressed ongoing concerns about ethnic Hungarians abroad who, to paraphrase, remained "stranded" by the borders drawn in the 1920 Treaty of Trianon. In 2010, his parliamentary majority offered ethnic Hungarians living in Romania, Slovakia, Serbia, or Ukraine the opportunity to claim dual citizenship.[18] There is, of course, nothing terribly wrong with dual citizenship. In the Central European context, however, Orbán's efforts reinvigorated old Central European anxieties. Critics feared he wanted the Hungarian state to reestablish sovereignty over those places where ethnic Hungarians lived. In Slovakia, Prime Minister Robert Fico secured a law in response—depriving people of their Slovak citizenship if they accepted Orbán's offer.

The ability of most Hungarians to locate alternative, objective sources of Hungarian language information became limited. Orbán's allies made substantial acquisitions in television, online, and print outlets and used them to present overtly pro-government perspectives. The government also used the state media to present a pro-government line and stifle or distort opposition voices. While independent opposition media were still available, particularly online, a constitutional amendment gave the Fidesz-controlled state media preferential rights in covering electoral campaigns. Meanwhile, the Fidesz-controlled Media Oversight Board gained the power to fine media companies to the point of bankruptcy.[19]

The political opposition also faced new challenges at the polls. By extending citizenship to ethnic Hungarians abroad, Hungary gained close to a half million voters—most of whom conveniently voted for Fidesz by mail. Meanwhile, Orbán's failure to poll well among youthful and educated voters was mitigated by the departure of so many of them abroad for work. Unlike Hungary's new dual citizens in Romania, Serbia, and Ukraine, the young migrants had to cast their ballot in person at the country's local consulate. Most responded, predictably, by not voting at all.[20]

Early constitutional changes also manipulated voter districts and parliamentary thresholds in ways that clearly benefited Fidesz over its rivals. The new constitution then locked this advantage in place by requiring a constitutional majority to change the new rules. In the 2018 election, Orbán renewed his constitutional supermajority a third time with just under 50 percent of the popular vote.[21]

The government attacked critical voices, particularly in civil society organizations and the universities. It compromised the academic independence of universities and created a legal and intellectual environment that forced Central European University, a leading graduate program in social sciences, to relocate much of its work to Vienna, Austria.[22] It also passed laws that made it more difficult for foreign-supported NGOs to operate in the country. Raids by financial officials and burdensome new restrictions forced many NGOs to leave. A pejorative image of philanthropist George Soros also figured prominently in Fidesz campaigns, appearing on billboards across the country as the alleged organizer of a broader conspiracy against the Hungarian nation.[23]

Tying these efforts together in the Hungarian imagination was a populist, anti-elite narrative that imagined the nation beset from existential threats from abroad and from elite "traitors" in the opposition. In 2014, Orbán explicitly repositioned Hungary ideologically as a self-proclaimed "illiberal democracy" with the mission of providing for a Hungarian nation reeling economically from the Great Financial Crisis and the corruption of liberalism.[24] This became in part a demographic project—rooted in existential fears for the future biological reproduction of the nation. The government accordingly passed understandably popular measures like tax breaks that support large families. Yet, it also condemned LGBTQ+ citizens, harassed their NGOs, and banned state support for gender studies programs.[25]

Against this broader ideological campaign, the migrant crisis of 2015-16 fit Fidesz's needs well. Orbán joined Fico in rejecting Brussels's quotas and in portraying migrants as an "Islamic invasion force" and a threat to Christian Europe.[26] Unlike Slovakia, however, Hungary was a transit country for migrants trying to get to Western Europe. Rather than coordinate with neighboring EU countries and Serbia to ensure a collective, humane response to a human tragedy, Orbán demonized the migrants and redirected them into other countries by building and patrolling a long fence along the southern border with Serbia.

Reiderstvo: To summarize so far, between 2010 and 2019, Prime Minister Orbán and his top party associates dismantled many serious institutional checks on their authority, reconfigured the rules to give their party, Fisdesz, a significant and perhaps insurmountable electoral advantage, and marginalized critical voices in civil society.[27] It should not be a shocker, therefore, to learn that key businessmen in Orbán's circle played a role in consolidating his power and profiting from it.

Of course, this is not the way Orbán portrayed it. His unifying idea was to avoid falling into the same dependence that his predecessor's government had on foreign banks and the IMF tutelage that followed. Ironically, his emphasis on greater economic sovereignty was consistent with the eurozone's policies of collective fiscal restraint discussed in the last chapter. So, while Slovakia followed the German fiscal lead to bind its economy to the core, anti-inflationary countries of the eurozone, Hungary did it to gain greater domestic financial control.

Fiscal restraint was, therefore, entirely consistent with a policy of state-directed *reiderstvo*. Orbán's goal was to create what he called a "national capitalist class," composed of a group of Fidesz-connected tycoons who would cooperate on state policy and be supportive in political competition. National capitalists cannot reproduce the global production networks that the German engineering and automotive firms provided, so government policy was accommodating to the large manufacturing multinationals that drove Hungary's export sales. Elsewhere, but particularly in banking, media, retail, and energy, Orbán's business allies worked with the state in often aggressive moves to bring companies into his orbit.

One target was banking. By 2010-11, Hungarian banks were already in trouble. The 2009 devaluation of the forint made it much more difficult for Hungarians to repay their loans. By 2011, 15 percent of all outstanding Hungarian loans were nonperforming, meaning that the borrowers (often consisting of newly unemployed home mortgage holders) were not paying back the money they owed. To help indebted households, Orbán's majority passed rules allowing borrowers to fully repay their loans at the 2008 exchange rate, if they could. Only borrowers in good standing could afford it, however, which increased the proportion of bad debt in banks' portfolios. To add to the pain, new policies also subjected banks to costly additional regulations, a series of heavy fines, and a new "crisis tax" on the size of the banks' assets regardless of the local subsidiary's profitability.[28]

These were popular measures and not without some justification. A tax on bank assets, for example, might be a good way of preventing a local subsidiary from overpaying its foreign parent company for goods and services. Companies often use such internal pricing to reduce the taxable profits of the local company while increasing the profits of the parent company. The parent can then declare its profits in a country with lower taxes. This is the practice of transfer pricing. Yet, according to Bálint Madlovics and Bálint Magyar, Orbán's measures were designed less to get banks to pay taxes in Hungary and more to encourage parent owners to sell their operations to Fidesz-connected buyers. In the authors' sample case study of the Bavarian-owned MKB Bank, the German parent company initially replenished the Hungarian subsidiary bank's capital rather than sell it off to local buyers. The Hungarian National Bank nevertheless took over administration of the subsidiary bank, transferred its liabilities to the public ledger, injected new cash, and sold it to political loyalists.[29]

Government-orchestrated takeovers were allegedly common in other sectors as well and remarkably prevalent, according to a survey of business executives.[30] In one case of clear *reiderstvo*, Lajos Simicska, a wealthy oligarch who was—for the moment—an Orbán favorite, tried to purchase ESMA, a billboard company. ESMA was a perfect target for a state-orchestrated raid. With its capital literally planted in the ground in the form of billboards, the owners could not extract their capital and flee the country. When the owners rejected Simicska's low purchase offers, tax officials began to investigate the company. In parliament, meanwhile, a former Simicska employee introduced a new "safety law" banning advertisement along a sidewalk within five meters of a roadway. The law passed.

Unable to rent many of its billboards under the new law, ESMA's revenues plummeted. Ironically, Simicska's own billboard company was also initially hurt by the law, but Fidesz MPs quickly passed an amendment to the law exempting it. After two years of operating at a loss, ESMA's owners sold the company to another oligarch connected to Orbán. Less than four months later, parliament rescinded its "safety measure." ESMA's revenues tripled the following year after securing a five-year contract to become the city of Budapest's primary advertiser. In 2018, ESMA rented billboard space to Fidesz at a 95 percent discount while freezing out the party's political opposition from many of its advertising spaces.[31]

Through similar measures, most Hungarian media and advertising operations are now owned by government-supporting enterprises. Media companies not only reinforce pro-government messaging but also contribute funds to the Central European Press and Media Foundation (KESMA). Established by longtime Orbán loyalist Gábor Liszkay, the foundation is a pro-governmental media coordination site to which various oligarchs and owners of pro-government media "donate" their newspapers, websites, and radio and television channels. According to Atlatszo (a Hungarian anti-corruption NGO) the foundation now controls 476 media outlets. To avoid an investigation by the Hungarian Competition Authority and the Hungarian Media Council, the Orbán government declared KESMA to be of "national importance" and thus exempted from legal restrictions.

With the government leaning heavily on media enterprises to limit their critical content and to coordinate their reporting, media independence slipped. Most educated people in the main cities, with access to the internet, still found alternative perspectives on Hungarian politics and some genuine investigative reporting. Yet outside of Budapest, where people received most of their information from television, the picture was quite different. In 2019, the NGO Reporters without Borders ranked Hungary 87th in the world for its media freedom.[32]

THE EU AS CAUSE AND CATALYST: Hungary's illiberal turn presents us with a puzzle. Despite the significant shift in power to the executive in Hungary, by the middle of the decade the country experienced respectable GDP growth, falling unemployment, increasing real wages, and a restrained annual budget deficit. A glance at Hungarian economic performance after 2010 would not indicate that anything was amiss in the state of the political economy. The government could even claim that it had performed with admirable skill after eight years of economic incompetence under the MSZP and that its turn to an illiberal democracy had produced no ill economic effects. Our answer, shared with R. Daniel Kelemen, is that without the EU, the economic picture by the end of the decade would have been less rosy.[33]

Before we turn to this argument, however, we need to revisit the argument that Europe's financial architecture played a role in the region's populist turn. To summarize an important yet complex point from the last chapter, after the Great Recession of 2008-10, the Troika and the German government called the fiscal shots in Europe. Beginning in 2011-12, their strategy was to reestablish the Maastricht norm of low levels of deficit spending across eurozone members and their major trading partners. Collective fiscal restraint was good for Central Europe's boom regions—the urban centers, like Budapest, Bratislava and Warsaw, and manufacturing regions, like Hungary west of the Danube, Slovakia's western triangle, and Poland's Katowice/Krakow region. Conditions there closely reflected those of the EU core. Yet, the policy did little to aid distressed rural and urban communities that missed the Single European Market's investment boom.

Orbán's predecessor government flouted the Maastricht criteria and paid the price with austerity from 2007 to 2010. It also maneuvered itself into a position of dependence in which Hungary had to weather the Great Recession under IMF tutelage. Orbán took power in 2010 at the height of the Great Recession. After engaging in counter-cyclical deficit spending in conjunction with other Northern and Central European countries, the new government became a solid contributor to collective fiscal restraint and did not allow spending to exceed 3 percent of GDP for the rest of the decade.

To pay for this, however, the government tapped into citizens' benefits and savings. The most notable measure was to raise the value-added tax on all purchases of most goods and services to 27 percent, one of the highest rates in the world. Parliament also raided private pensions, simply transferring them to the state budget, which could then be used to fund current government spending in exchange for an IOU to future state pensioners. Social benefits, including unemployment, were similarly cut.[34]

Yet, austerity helped depress wages and starve rural and regional communities in Hungary of meaningful economic opportunities. Not surprisingly, the number of talented and ambitious young adults leaving Hungary for better work elsewhere grew at a rate two to three times faster than any other country in Europe.[35] According to the Organisation for Economic Co-operation and Development's International Migration Outlook 2018, between 3 percent and 7 percent of the adult population worked abroad in the middle of the decade—a number that helped explain Hungary's "tight labor market."[36] The exodus helped countries like Germany and the United Kingdom and cities like Budapest to keep wages and prices lower by importing cheap labor, while the flight of labor from distressed peripheral communities lowered unemployment and stabilized wages there.

Hungary's émigré workforce further stabilized the economy through personal remittances, which are the personal transfers of cash from individuals working abroad to their home communities. Apart from Czechia, the balance of remittances was positive across the region, with most of the inflow coming from other EU countries. After Orbán took office in 2010, the rapid growth in workers leaving for jobs elsewhere led to a doubling of remittances to 3.5 percent of GDP by the end of the decade.[37]

Meanwhile, despite Fidesz's often predatory position toward foreign investors in many sectors of the economy, the government doubled down on pleasing its foreign export manufacturing sector. At the height of the crisis, when most businesses in the economy had to pay a crisis tax, the government provided the export-oriented industrial sector with a tax cut.[38] Exports were also assisted by a gradual devaluation of the forint-euro exchange rate from 250 forint per euro at the height of the crisis to about 350 at the end of the decade. Devaluation policy, of course, made Hungarians poorer as international consumers, but it also made everything in Hungary, including labor, cheaper for foreigners to buy.

Labor, therefore, did not improve its position much under Orbán's illiberal democracy. Low wages provided yet another reason for young workers to seek employment elsewhere in the EU. Meanwhile, foreign investors reported that the resulting skilled labor shortages were a barrier to additional investment. This should have given labor greater bargaining power. Yet, in 2012, parliament transferred the right of collective bargaining from industrywide unions to firm-specific workers councils—a move that raised the collective action problems faced by labor in its negotiations with the government and capital. Parliament also sidelined the advocacy of international pro-labor NGOs, like Germany's Friedrich Ebert Stiftung, in redrafting its labor policy, and it demonized the *stiftung* in government rhetoric as anti-Hungarian, mercenary, and socialist. These measures may have likely helped keep wages from rising faster than they did. With little public discussion, the government also lowered the corporate tax and labor tax rates to 9 percent and 19.5 percent, respectively, which were among the lowest rates in Europe.[39]

Beyond providing investment and an outlet for dissatisfied labor, the EU also shaped Hungary's political economy through cohesion funds. Central European member governments annually received between 1 percent and 5.5 percent of GDP from the EU. Hungary generally received between 3 percent and 4 percent of GDP. These transfers were a reprieve from budgetary reality; the injection of EU funds into the economy meant that high-profile projects could be funded without cost to other fiscal priorities.

Yet, with billions of euros in EU-funded government contracts at stake, the public tenders also provided a strong incentive for corruption.[40] Recent work by Laura Jakli and Matthew Stenberg suggests that the quest to control the disbursement of EU-funded projects helped predict where Fidesz put its resources into contesting local municipal elections.[41] More broadly, the fight over lucrative tenders was zero-sum and potentially vicious. In 2015, one of Orbán's favored businessmen and cohesion fund tender recipients—Lajos Simicska—decided to back the ultra-right-wing party Jobbik against Fidesz in elections. The government responded with attacks on Simicska's network of enterprises, and it cut off his access to EU cohesion fund contracts. After Fidesz renewed its constitutional majority in 2018 (with 49 percent of the vote), Simicska sold his holdings to government-tied individuals. Reportedly, he was afraid for his life and carried a radiation detector to protect against polonium poisoning.[42]

Another Hungarian businessman who had been successful in receiving EU-funded tenders alleged that he too was forced to sell his company to a state-owned enterprise. Someone with ties to the government, he reported, simply wanted to secure direct access to the EU contracts that he had been winning. The alternative to selling out was to watch "as the government choked [his company] to death with taxes and regulations." He later emigrated.[43]

Unfortunately, if bringing CEE standards of living up to Western European levels was the goal of EU cohesion funds, they performed poorly. For many years, the value of EU transfers were as much or even greater than the value added to the economy by economic growth. How is this possible? Even after legal reforms improved contract processes in 2016, 28 percent of all EU-funded tenders in Hungary had no more than one bidder. These single-bid tenders, moreover, were disproportionately lucrative and made up 44 percent of the total value of funds dispersed.[44] Usually this was a firm with connection to Fidesz. Prior to 2016, these contracts went disproportionately to *four* Orbán-tied businessmen, including Simicska.[45]

Not surprisingly, Hungarian researchers calculated that cohesion-funded government projects were 15 percent to 24 percent more costly than they needed to be. Over the 2009-16 period, this cost the public between 6.7 billion and 10.6 billion euros.[46]

Much of this siphoned cash seemed unlikely to be reinvested in the economy. As the fate of the two businessmen just discussed above shows, the unraveling of Lockean protections for property likely induced Hungary's wealthiest to secure large portions of their capital in safer havens abroad. Such a drain may explain why, despite millions in EU budgetary transfers, Hungary failed to close the gap in wealth with Western Europe after the financial crisis. Indeed, according to Eurostat data from 2019, Hungary has made the least progress among its neighbors, Baltic states, and Eastern Balkan states in converging with the EU in GDP per capita as a percentage of the EU average. Only Slovenia and Croatia have performed worse. Yet, Croatia did not join the EU until 2013, while Slovenia's income stalled at 85 percent of the EU average. By contrast, Hungarian GDP per capita in 2004 stood at 61 percent of the average. In 2017, it was only 68 percent—a mere 7 percentage points higher. Meanwhile, most Baltic and V4 countries closed the gap by 20 points. Even Czechia, which started from a much higher base than Hungary, succeeded in closing the gap with the EU faster.

In addition to corruption, EU funds incentivize political illiberalism. With billions of euros of EU-funded public contracts on the table, the calculus of power in Central Europe reflects the model of a rent-based economy in which one's path to riches comes from positioning oneself to skim from flows of capital. Possession of this rent-skimming position raises the stakes of holding onto power. One controls it or one does not. Where the stakes are high enough, democratic alternation between parties in power might even become unacceptable to incumbents. Under these conditions, we expect liberal Lockean institutions to come under greater stress. This appears to be what is happening in Hungary and elsewhere in the region. EU largesse is thus incentivizing corruption *and* democratic erosion. It's a vicious circle.

Can the EU do anything about this? As Laurent Pech and Kim Lane Scheppele argue, the answer is more complex than it would appear. The EU is a legitimizing, constraining, *and* enabling entity.[47] They conclude that European investigative mechanisms, like the EU's anti-fraud office OLAF, and treaty-based disciplinary mechanisms, like Article 7 of the Treaty of the European Union (TEU), have had little more than a moderating impact. Article 7 of the TEU allows the EU to suspend the rights of EU membership if a state violates EU values, like democracy, the rule of law, or human rights, as outlined in **Article 2 of the TEU**. Yet, suspension requires the unanimous consent of all EU members. This is unlikely to happen, given the desire of countries like Poland to avoid sanctions themselves. Kelemen adds that the poorly understood European political party system is also serving to protect Hungary. Indeed, the European Parliament's largest party, the **European People's Party (EPP)**, needed its Fidesz deputies to retain its plurality and the European Parliament leadership positions that go with it.[48]

It now seems that only a full turn to repressive authoritarian rule might alter this situation, yet given the importance of EU cohesion funds to Orbán's circle, it also seems unlikely they would put their access to EU funds and markets by doing this. It is also possible that Orbán's supermajority would not withstand the loss of legitimacy that an EU suspension would carry. The EU thus does constrain as well as enable Hungary— albeit, not at a level that protects democracy.

$\wp \propto$

The EU is in a bind in Central Europe. By the end of the decade, the EU had its first nondemocracy, and to an extent, its own policies and institutions were to blame. The difficulty in amending these structures is not good news for liberalism in Central Europe. Yet, there is hope in Hungarian civil society. It was highly active against Prime Minister Gyurcsány when his government raided the public credit to get reelected in 2006, and it is active now as Prime Minister Orbán deprives his people of economic, political, and cultural alternatives to Fidesz rule. Over the past years, tens of thousands and sometimes hundreds of thousands of people have taken to the streets to protest a system designed to corrupt or circumvent their voice. This is not going to go away.

One would expect the Hungarian government to continue to exercise self-restraint in response to its mobilized opponents. Yet, it is also possible that an extended campaign of social and political civil disobedience could force it into an unpalatable dilemma action—the choice between violence and open repression or political liberalization. We should hope for the latter, but it might take the former to force the EU to discipline its illiberal member governments.

Regardless of whether the Hungarian citizens succeed in restoring vitality to their democracy, the EU must work to fix the underlying structural problems that have encouraged voting for illiberal strongmen.

Europeans should consider mechanisms to democratize the EU's financial architecture and develop less corrupting ways to promote solidarity with Europe's many internal peripheries. Above all, however, they must decide whether the EU is to be the democratic assembly of liberal democracies envisioned in Article 2 of the TEU or yet another playground for tyrants and oligarchs.

Liberalism's Fragile Dream

On the evening of that November 1989 day when the Berlin Wall fell, I celebrated with a German beer on a lumpy couch watching CNN. Everything I said to my roommate sounded preposterously optimistic. It was one of the rare times where I could not help thinking, "Everything will be better." I watched on TV as excited East Berliners freely poured through newly undefended checkpoints to mix with West Germans and tourists. Partyers took up sledges and hammers to bore gaping holes in communism's most famous atrocity, the Wall. Everyone who was able eventually climbed up to celebrate.

For Simona's generation, the events of November 1989 indeed changed everything. Over the past 30 years, Simona's small circle of siblings, friends, and cousins—all now in their mid-40s—have found new niches in Europe's single integrated market and beyond. They have built homes and apartments, had families, established new businesses, strengthened their local communities, and demanded and received better roads, schools, and parks. They have voted, by large margins, for European integration and membership, fiscal restraint, and the rule of law. When their elites have been revealed to be venal and corrupt, many have poured into the streets—*repeatedly*—to demand greater accountability. The teenagers of 1989 have evolved, in short, from disaffected cynical subjects of Czechoslovakia's communist state to engaged Slovaks, committed to an EU of liberal market democracies. They form, in short, the backbone of Central Europe's new middle class.

Yet, as I have noted in this book, this is only a keyhole look into the postcommunist experience. It permits us to observe Central Europe's most educated youth, living within the orbit of one of its fastest growing and most dynamic regions. Elsewhere, the liberty to fail—or simply flail—has made as frequent an appearance in people's postcommunist pathways.

Those who have struggled tend to be older, less educated, or living in a rural or postindustrial center on the periphery of Europe's zones of rapid development. Their wages have not grown as fast, and they have been more likely to be underemployed, beset by elite corruption and poor public services, and frustrated by elite inattention to their difficult relations with the Roma. Most tragically, their children have fled in large numbers for a better life elsewhere. It is not surprising that this is where the nationalist imaginary is most appealing. For many, a "better" life has turned out to be a relative term. Since the party in Berlin, it has been one long hangover.[1]

The populist antidote—achieved most fully in Hungary and Poland—is to vest the sovereignty of the "pure people" in an empowered leader who rules with less political constraint. This sort of contract is based on trust in the goodness of the leader and the purity of their vision. Yet, trust is a fallible mechanism. It needs constant renewal through spectacle, polarizing identity politics, and the invocation of real or imagined threats. As a model of governance, it has all the freshness of stale beer and dried blood— the unmistakable scent of last century's dueling totalitarian disasters.

Liberalism in Central Europe has always been fragile, but it remains better than the alternatives. I have always believed that Frances Fukuyama was mostly right. For most things, there really is no better organizing principle available than one that gives political agency to the individual.[2]

Still, liberals must think beyond merely restoring civic control over the political institutions that their politicians have eroded. Central Europe's loss of economic sovereignty preceded and contributed to today's democratic decline. Liberals, therefore, must not only reestablish the Lockean bargain and extend it to everybody; they need to ensure that those who have not done so well can use the bargain to address their economic and social needs. This may mean wresting economic sovereignty back from Europe's core and opening it to the reasonable concerns of the periphery, or it may mean truly democratizing the fiscal choices in the core through more EU federalism.[3] Regardless, a sustainable liberal European future requires sovereign peoples to be in charge of their political elites and to feel safe and hopeful in their economic fortunes. That kind of Europe is also likely to be more generous when confronted with issues of racial or sexual difference and the desperation of refugees.

Colorado Springs, September 15, 2020

Notes

Preface and Acknowledgments

1. Edward W. Said, *Orientalism* (New York: Random House, 1978).
2. Barry R. Weingast, "The Economic Role of Political Institutions," *Journal of Law, Economics, and Organization* 7:1 (April 1995): 1-31.
3. John Locke, *Two Treatises of Government* (Cambridge: Cambridge University Press, 1988).
4. Kevin Deegan-Krause, "Voting for Thugs," *Democracy at Large* 2:3 (2006): 24-27.
5. Quinn Slobodian, *The Globalists: The End of Empire and the Birth of Neoliberalism* (Cambridge, MA: Harvard University Press, 2018).
6. Adam Smith, *An Inquiry into the Nature and Causes of the Wealth of Nations* (Chicago: University of Chicago Press, 1976).

Chapter 1

1. For more historical detail on the uprisings of 1989 in Central Europe, see Gale Stokes, *The Walls Came Tumbling Down: Collapse and Rebirth in Eastern Europe* (Oxford: Oxford University Press, 2011). For fascinating firsthand impressions from across the region, see Timothy Garton Ash, *The Magic Lantern: The Revolution of '89 Witnessed in Warsaw, Budapest, Berlin, and Prague* (New York: Vintage, 1999).
2. Srdja Popović and Sophia A. McClennen, *Pranksters vs. Autocrats: Why Nonviolent Actions Advance Nonviolent Activism* (Ithaca: Cornell Selects, 2020); Majken Jul Sørensen and Brian Martin, "The Dilemma Action: Analysis of an Activist Technique," *Peace & Change* 39:1 (January 2014): 73-100. For an activist's guide, see Srdja Popović, Andrej Milivojević, and Slobodan Đinović, *Nonviolent Struggle: 50 Crucial Points* (Belgrade: CANVAS, 2007).
3. David Hess and Brian Martin, "Repression, Backfire, and the Theory of Transformative Events," *Mobilization* 11:2 (June 2006): 249-67. Kurt Schock, *Unarmed Insurrections: People Power Movements in Nondemocracies* (Minneapolis: University of Minnesota Press, 2005), 156-57.
4. James M. Jasper, "The Emotions of Protest," in Jeff Goodwin and James M.

Jasper, eds, *The Social Movements Reader: Cases and Concepts* (Malden, MA: Wiley-Blackwell, 2014), 175-84.

5. Erica Chenoweth and Maria J. Stephan, *Why Civil Resistance Works: The Strategic Logic of Nonviolent Conflict* (New York: Columbia University Press, 2011). See too, Gene Sharp, *From Dictatorship to Democracy: A Conceptual Framework for Liberation* (Boston: Albert Einstein Institution, 2003); Richard B. Gregg, *The Power of Nonviolence* (New York: Schocken Books, 1966).

6. Gordon Tullock, "The Paradox of Revolution," *Public Choice* 11 (1971): 89-99.

7. For more on the advantages and disadvantages of the game theory approach to social movements, see my work with Edward Moe: John A. Gould and Edward Moe, "Beyond Rational Choice: Ideational Assault and the Use of Delegitimation Frames in Nonviolent Revolutionary Movements," *Research in Social Movements, Conflict, and Change* 34 (2013): 123-51.

8. Bert Klandermans, *The Social Psychology of Protest* (Cambridge, MA: Blackwell, 1997); James M. Jasper, *The Art of Moral Protest: Culture, Biography, and Creativity in Social Movements* (Chicago: University of Chicago Press, 1999); Gould and Moe, "Beyond Rational Choice," 134-37.

9. Roger V. Gould, "Multiple Networks and Mobilization in the Paris Commune, 1871," *American Sociological Review* 56 (1991): 716-29; Douglas McAdam, *Freedom Summer* (New York: Oxford University Press, 1990).

10. Tina Rosenberg, *Join the Club: How Peer Pressure Can Transform the World* (New York: W. W. Norton, 2011).

11. Timur Kuran, "Now or Never: The Element of Surprise in the East European Revolution of 1989," *World Politics* 44:1 (October 1991): 7-48; See, too, Mark R. Beissinger, *Nationalist Mobilization and the Collapse of the Soviet State* (Cambridge: Cambridge University Press, 2002); Sidney Tarrow, *Power in Movement: Social Movements, Collective Action and Politics* (Cambridge: Cambridge University Press, 1994); Peter Ackerman and Christopher Kruegler, *Strategic Nonviolent Conflict: The Dynamics of People Power in the Twentieth Century* (Westport, CT: Praeger, 1994).

12. Stokes, *The Walls Came Tumbling Down*, 139-40; Lee Smithey and Lester R. Kurtz, "We Have Bare Hands: Nonviolent Social Movements in the Soviet Block," in Stephen Zunes, Lester Kurtz, and Sara Beth Asher, eds., *Nonviolent Social Movements: A Geographical Perspective* (Malden, MA: Blackwell, 1999), 113.

13. Please note that in many of these stories, I have changed the names of people who are not public figures.

14. Miroslav Kusý, "The State of Human and Minority Rights," in Soňa Szomolányi and John Gould, eds., *Slovakia: Problems of Democratic Consolidation and the Struggle for the Rules of the Game* (Bratislava: Friedrich Ebert Stiftung, 1997), 169-71.

15. Milan Kundera, *The Unbearable Lightness of Being* (New York: Harper & Row, 1984).

16. Václav Havel, "The Power of the Powerless," in John Keane, ed., *The Power of the Powerless: Citizens against the State in Central Eastern Europe* (New York: Routledge, 2009), 10-59.

17. Stokes, *The Walls Came Tumbling Down*, 148-57; Ash, *The Magic Lantern*, 78-130; John Connelly, *From Peoples into Nations: A History of Eastern Europe* (Princeton: Princeton University Press, 2020), 731-33.

18. Joshua A. Tucker "Enough! Electoral Fraud, Collective Action Problems, and Post-Communist Colored Revolutions," *Perspectives on Politics* 5:3 (2007): 535-51.

19. John K. Glenn, III, *Framing Democracy: Civil Society and Civic Movements in Eastern Europe* (Stanford, CA: Stanford University Press, 2001).

20. Connelly, *From Peoples into Nations*, 732.

Chapter 2

1. Hardy Merriman, "Theory and Dynamics of Nonviolent Action," in Maria J. Stephan, ed., *Civilian Jihad: Nonviolent Struggle, Democratization and Governance in the Middle East* (New York: Palgrave Macmillan, 2009), 18; Douglass C. North, *Structure and Change in Economic History* (New York: W. W. Norton, 1981), 81-109; Reinhard Bendix, *Max Weber: An Intellectual Portrait* (Garden City, NY: Doubleday, 1960).

2. This is explained well by Friedrich Engels, "Socialism: Utopian and Scientific," in Robert C. Tucker, ed., *The Marx-Engels Reader* (New York: W. W. Norton, 1978), 700; Robert Heilbroner, *The Worldly Philosophers: The Lives, Times and Ideas of the Great Economic Thinkers* (New York: Simon & Schuster, 1999), 156-58; Karl Marx, *Capital: Volume 1*, in Tucker, ed., *The Marx-Engels Reader*, 376-78.

3. Karl Marx and Friedrich Engels, *Manifesto of the Communist Party*, in Tucker, ed., *The Marx-Engels Reader*, 469-500.

4. Friedrich Engels, *Socialism: Utopian and Scientific*, in Tucker, ed., *The Marx-Engels Reader*, 713.

5. Vladimir Ilyich Lenin, "What Is to Be Done?" in Robert C. Tucker, ed., *The Lenin Anthology* (New York: W. W. Norton, 1975), 12-114.

6. Vladimir Ilyich Lenin, "The State and Revolution," in Tucker, ed., *The Lenin Anthology*, 311-98.

7. Max Weber, "Politics as a Vocation," in Hans H. Gerth and C. Wright Mills, eds., *From Max Weber: Essays in Sociology* (Oxford: Oxford University Press, 1946), 77.

8. Thomas Hobbes, *Leviathan* (Harmondsworth, UK: Penguin Classics, 1982).

9. Locke, *Second Treatise of Government*, chapters 5-15.

10. For a good introduction to liberal thinking on democracy at the end of the Cold War, see Philip C. Schmitter and Terry Lynne Karl, "What Democracy Is . . . and Is Not," *Journal of Democracy* 3 (1991): 75-88.

11. David Hume, *A Treatise on Human Nature* (Oxford: Oxford University Press, [1739] 2007), 311-36.

12. Robert Bates, *Prosperity and Violence: The Political Economy of Development* (New York: W. W. Norton, 2001).

13. David Harvey, "The 'New' Imperialism: Accumulation by Dispossession," *Socialist Register* 40 (2004): 63-87.

14. Barbara Fields, "Slavery, Race, and Ideology in the United States," in Karen E. Fields and Barbara J. Fields, *Racecraft: The Soul of Inequality in American Life* (London: Verso, 2014), 111-49; James Farr, "Locke, Natural Law, and New World Slavery," *Political Theory* 36:4 (August 2008): 495-522. Farr shows how, even as Locke was imagining new institutional forms to limit European tyranny, he was helping Carolinians develop their legal framework for enslavement.

15. For more on how British colonialism and racism contributed to the docility of the British working class, see W.E. Burghardt Dubois, "The African Roots of War," *Atlantic Monthly*, May 1915; see too, Cedric Robinson, *The Making of the Black Radical Tradition* (Chapel Hill: University of North Carolina Press, 1983); Harold Isaacs, *The New World of Negro Americans*, (New York: Viking Press, 1963); Robin D. G. Kelly, *Freedom Dreams: The Black Radical Imagination* (Boston: Beacon Press, 2002); Ibram X. Kendi, *Stamped from the Beginning: The Definitive History of Racist Ideas in America* (New York: Bold Type Books, 2017).

16. Karl Polanyi, *The Great Transformation: The Political and Economic Origins of Our Time* (Boston: Beacon Press, 1944).

17. The greatest failure of the Lockean state may turn out to be its inability to adequately handle Anthropocene climate change. The world's most advanced democracies continue to respect and protect property rights over the key aspects of Gaia's bodily organs despite clear evidence that this threatens the planet's ability to sustain humanity. It is unclear how property-protecting, representative states can deal with this issue adequately. The simple fact that a small fraction of the globe's politically elite currently have state-validated property rights to over $50 trillion in buried oil reserves puts the problem in perspective. Despite the rise of atmospheric carbon dioxide to levels not seen since the ocean-dominated Pliocene era three million years ago, these private owners show every intention of extracting these resources and releasing their pollutants into our collective atmosphere. Seen in these alarming (and hopefully alarmist!) terms, Lockean institutions that protect the property claims of these people pose an existential threat to contemporary civilization and perhaps even the medium-term survival of humanity.

18. Amartya Sen, "Democracy as a Universal Value," *Journal of Democracy* 10:3 (1999): 3-17.

19. Milovan Djilas, *The New Class: An Analysis of the Communist System* (New York: Frederik A. Praeger, 1957).

20. James C. Scott, *Seeing Like a State: How Certain Schemes to Improve the Human Condition Have Failed* (New Haven: Yale University Press, 1999), 193-222.

21. Anne Appelbaum, *Red Famine: Stalin's War on Ukraine* (New York: Anchor Books, 2017).

22. For more on the communists' ideological success in the Czechlands prior to the coup, see Bradley Abrams, *The Struggle for the Soul of the Nation: Czech Culture and the Rise of Communism* (Lanham, MD: Rowman Littlefield, 2004).

23. James C. Scott, *Weapons of the Weak: Everyday Forms of Peasant Resistance* (New Haven: Yale University Press, 1987).

24. The following section is based on John A. Gould, *The Politics of Privatization: Wealth and Power in Postcommunist Europe* (Boulder: Lynne Rienner, 2011), 14–19.

25. William Easterly and Stanley Fischer, "The Soviet Economic Decline," *World Bank Economic Review* 9:3 (1995): 341–71.

26. Francine du Plessix Gray, *Soviet Women: Walking the Tightrope* (New York: Anchor, 1991). Capitalism has also relied heavily on a gendered labor order; for a small sample, see Diane Elson, "Economic Crises from the 1980s to the 2010s: A Gender Analysis," in Sharin M. Rai and Georgina Waylen, eds., *New Frontiers in Feminist Political Economy* (New York: Routledge, 2014), 189–212; Lourdes Beneria, "Globalization, Gender and the Davos Man," *Feminist Economics* 5:3 (1999): 61–83; Naila Kabeer, "The Rise of the Female Breadwinner: Reconfigurations of Marriage, Motherhood and Masculinity in the Global Economy," in Rai and Waylen, eds., *New Frontiers*, 62–84.

27. See, too, Kristen Ghodsee, *Red Hangover: Legacies of Twentieth-Century Communism* (Durham: Duke University Press, 2017), 101–10.

28. Friedrich A. Hayek, "The Use of Knowledge in Society," *American Economic Review* 35:4 (1945): 519–30.

29. János Kornai, *The Economics of Shortage* (Amsterdam: North Holland, 1981); David Lipton and Jeffrey Sachs, "Creating a Market Economy in Eastern Europe: The Case of Poland," *Brookings Papers on Economic Activity* 1 (1990): 75–147.

30. This story is adopted from an anecdote frequently related by David Stark and others. I retell it here as a generalized, exemplary story using stylized data. It is not a specific case study. For a more thorough discussion of the informal logics that emerged under central planning, see David Stark, "Bending the Bars of the Iron Cage: Bureaucratization and Informalization in Socialism and Capitalism," *Sociological Forum* 4:4 (1989): 648.

31. Stokes, *The Walls Came Tumbling Down*, 57–58.

32. Stark, "Bending the Bars," 648; David Stark, "Rethinking Internal Labor Markets: New Insights from a Comparative Perspective," *American Sociological Review* 51:4 (1986): 492–504.

33. ČTK, "Nedostatok toaletneho papiera odhalil krizu centralneho planovania," *Pravda*, June 17, 2018, https://zurnal.pravda.sk/fenomen/clanok/473651-nedosta tok-toaletneho-papiera-odhalil-krizu-centralneho-planovania/ (accessed September 18, 2020).

34. Stokes, *The Walls Came Tumbling Down*, 10.

35. Stark, "Bending the Bars," 649.

36. János Kornai, *Highways and Byways: Studies on Reform and Postcommunist Transition* (Cambridge, MA: MIT Press, 1994), 13–16.

37. Victor Nee and Peng Lian, "Sleeping with the Enemy: A Dynamic Model of Declining Political Commitment in State Socialism," *Theory and Society* 23:2 (1994): 253–96.

38. Stokes, *The Walls Came Tumbling Down*, 11; Ota Šik, *Plan and Market under Socialism* (Prague: Academia, 1967).

39. Connelly, *From Peoples into Nations*, 622-37.

40. Easterly and Fischer, "The Soviet Economic Decline"; Brenden Beare, "The Soviet Economic Decline Revisited," *Econ Journal Watch* 5 (2008): 135-44; William Easterly and Stanley Fischer, "Reply to Brendan Beare," *Econ Journal Watch* 5 (2008): 145-47.

41. Marie Lavigne, *The Economics of Transition: From Socialist Economy to Market Economy* (New York: St. Martin's Press, 1999), 58-59: Francis Spufford, *Red Plenty* (London: Greywolf Press, 2010), 205-68.

42. Stephen Kotkin, *Armageddon Averted: The Soviet Collapse, 1970-2000* (Oxford: Oxford University Press, 2001), 57; Valerie Bunce, "The Empire Strikes Back: The Evolution of the Eastern Bloc from a Soviet Asset to a Soviet Liability," *International Organization* 39:1 (Winter 1985): 1-46.

43. David E. Spiro, *The Hidden Hand of American Hegemony: Petrodollar Recycling and International Markets* (Ithaca: Cornell University Press, 1999), 74-75.

44. Laura Tyson, "The Debt Crisis and Adjustment Responses in Eastern Europe: A Comparative Perspective," *International Organization* 40:2 (Spring 1986): 247.

45. In 1984, Czechoslovakia owed 46 percent of what it earned in dollar exports, compared to Hungary, 90 percent; East Germany, 95 percent; Yugoslavia, 215 percent; and Poland, 399 percent. Tyson, "The Debt Crisis," 257.

46. Milan Lasica and Július Satinský, "Soirée, 1968 (Stretnutie s obecenstom)," in *Lasica and Satinský a Hostia: Soirée* (STV/Plus Production, 2002).

Chapter 3

1. Hume, *A Treatise on Human Nature*, 311-36.

2. As the government's exploding BMW cover story fell apart, Prime Minister Mečiar's subservient media argued that Kováč Jr. had orchestrated *his own* kidnapping in an effort to frame the Prime Minister. Kevin Deegan-Krause, *Elective Affinities: Democracy, Nationalism and Party Competition in Slovakia and the Czech Republic* (Palo Alto: Stanford University Press, 2006), 49-50. Kieran Williams and Dennis Deletant, *Security Intelligence Services in New Democracies: The Czech Republic, Slovakia and Romania* (New York: Palgrave Macmillan 2001), 130-40.

3. Maxim Boycko, Andrei Shleifer, and Robert W. Vishny, *Privatizing Russia* (Cambridge, MA: MIT Press, 1995), 11.

4. Lipton and Sachs, "Creating a Market Economy," 87-88.

5. Adam Przeworski, *Democracy and the Market: Political and Economic Reforms in Eastern Europe and Latin America* (Cambridge: Cambridge University Press, 1991), 162-87; Leszek Balcerowicz, *Socialism, Capitalism, Transformation* (Budapest: Central European University Press, 1995), 265; Beverly Crawford, "Postcommunist Political Economy," in Beverly Crawford, ed., *Markets, States and Democracy: The Political Economy of Post-Communist Transformation* (Boulder: Westview,

1995), 31-32; John Hall, "After the Vacuum: Postcommunism in the Light of Tocqueville," in Crawford, ed., *Markets, States and Democracy*, 89.

6. John Williamson, "What Washington Means by Policy Reform," in John Williamson, ed., *Latin American Adjustment: How Much Has Happened?* (Washington, DC: Peterson Institute for International Economics, 1989); John Williamson, "The Strange History of the Washington Consensus," *Journal of Post Keynesian Economics* 27:2 (Winter 2004-5): 195-206.

7. Richard A. Easterlin, "Lost in Transition: Life Satisfaction on the Road to Capitalism," *Journal of Economic Behavior and Organization* 71:2 (2009): 130-45.

8. Jeffrey Sachs, *Poland's Jump to the Market Economy* (Cambridge, MA: MIT Press, 1994), 1-34.

9. Balcerowicz, *Socialism, Capitalism, Transformation*, 265; Crawford, "Postcommunist Political Economy," 38.

10. The following discussion of reforms loosely follows a schema offered by Michael Mandelbaum, "Introduction," in Shafiqul Islam and Michael Mandelbaum, eds., *Making Markets: Economic Transformation in Eastern Europe and the Post-Soviet States* (New York: CSFR, 1993), 1-15; but see, too, Sachs and Lipton, "Creating a Market Economy in Eastern Europe"; Sachs, *Poland's Jump to the Market Economy*, 35-78.

11. Sachs, *Poland's Jump to the Market Economy*, table 2.5.

12. Zora Bútorová, ed., *She and He in Slovakia: Gender Issues in Public Opinion* (Bratislava: Friedrich Ebert Stiftung, 1996).

13. Sachs and Lipton, "Creating a Market Economy in Eastern Europe," 125-26.

14. Joseph A Schumpeter, *Capitalism, Socialism, and Democracy* (London: Harper & Brothers, 1942), 83.

15. Andrei Shleifer and Robert Vishny, *The Grabbing Hand of the State: Government Pathologies and Their Cures* (Cambridge, MA: Harvard University Press, 1998).

16. For more on vampire behavior and other scams in Russia, see Paul Klebnikov, *Godfather of the Kremlin: Boris Berezovsky and the Looting of Russia* (New York: Harcourt, 2000); Marshall I. Goldman, *The Privatization of Russia: Russian Reform Goes Awry* (New York: Routledge, 2003); Karen Dawisha, *Putin's Kleptocracy: Who Owns Russia?* (New York: Simon & Schuster, 2014). For a thorough discussion of how these and other Russian players benefited from hyperinflation and how the government finally stabilized prices, see Daniel Treisman, "Fighting Inflation in a Transitional Regime: Russia's Anomalous Stabilization," *World Politics* 50:2 (January 1998): 235-65.

17. Joel S. Hellman, "Winners Take All: The Politics of Partial Reform in Postcommunist Transitions," *World Politics* 50:2 (January 1998): 203-34.

18. Smith, *Wealth of Nations*, 144.

19. For a comparison of the Czechoslovak and Polish reform process, see Mitchell Orenstein, *Out of the Red: Building Capitalism and Democracy in Postcommunist Europe* (Ann Arbor: University of Michigan Press, 2001); for a comparison of the

Russian and Czech cases, see Hilary Appel, *New Capitalist Order: Privatization and Ideology in Russia and Eastern Europe* (Pittsburgh: University of Pittsburgh Press, 2004); for Hungary, see David L. Bartlett, *The Political Economy of Dual Transformations* (Ann Arbor: University of Michigan Press, 1997).

20. Ivan Mikloš, "Economic Transition and the Emergence of Clientalist Structures in Slovakia," in Szomolányi and Gould, eds., *Slovakia: Problems of Democratic Consolidation*, 60-61.

21. We will cover these events in the next chapter.

22. Interview with Ivan Mikloš, MESA10, Bratislava, Slovakia, April 2, 1997.

23. Karla Brom and Mitchell Orenstein, "The Privatised Sector in the Czech Republic: Government and Bank Control in a Transitional Economy," *Europe-Asia Studies* 46:6 (1994): 893-928; Andrew Schwartz, *The Politics of Greed: How Privatization Structured Politics in Central and Eastern Europe* (Lanham: Roman & Littlefield, 2006); Orenstein, *Out of the Red*; Appel, *New Capitalist Order*.

24. Joseph E. Stiglitz, "Comments on 'Czech Republic: Capital Market Review Report,'" speech delivered to the Ministry of Finance, Prague, Czech Republic, May 9, 1997.

25. Interview with Vladimír Rudlovčák, State Secretary, Ministry of Finance, Prague, Czech Republic, July 24, 1997.

26. Stiglitz, "Comments on 'Czech Republic.'"

27. Rudlovčák interview, July 24, 1997.

28. Gould, *The Politics of Privatization*, 103-32; Mikael Olsson, "Ownership Reform and Corporate Governance: The Slovak Privatization Process in 1990-1996," PhD diss., Acta Universitatis Upasalensisi, Uppsala Studies in Economic History, 1999.

29. Soňa Szomolányi, "Identifying Slovakia's Emerging Regime," in Szomolányi and Gould, *Slovakia: Problems of Democratic Consolidation*, 9-34.

30. Steven Levitsky and Lucan A. Way, "Elections without Democracy: The Rise of Competitive Authoritarianism," *Journal of Democracy* 13:2 (2002): 51-65.

31. Ľudovít Hallon, Miroslav Londák, and Adam Hudek, "Economic Developments in Slovakia since 1991," in Mark Stolarik, ed., *The Czech and Slovak Republics: Twenty Years of Independence, 1993-2013* (Budapest: Central European University Press, 2016), 177-96.

32. Anthony Robinson, "Survey of Slovakia," *Financial Times*, December 16, 1994, iv.

33. Hallon, Londák, and Hudek, "Economic Developments in Slovakia since 1991," 189.

34. Mikloš, "Economic Transition," 71-72.

35. Daniel Treisman, "Fighting Inflation"; Andrej Shleifer and Daniel Treisman, *Without a Map: Economic Tactics and Economic Reform in Russia* (Cambridge, MA: MIT Press, 2000), 39-81.

Chapter 4

1. Francis Fukuyama, "The End of History?" *National Interest* 16 (1989): 3-18; Valerie Bunce adds, "With the collapse of the Cold War order in 1989-1990, and the decisive defeat of its 'other,' liberalism came to occupy—for the first time in its life, either in theory or practice—the position of an ideological monopoly." Valerie Bunce, "The Political Economy of Postsocialism," *Slavic Review* 58:4 (Winter 1999): 757.

2. The numbers remain controversial, ranging from over 100,000 to 140,000. The higher number is taken from "Transitional Justice in the Former Yugoslavia," International Center for Transitional Justice, New York, 2009, https://www.ictj .org/sites/default/files/ICTJ-FormerYugoslavia-Justice-Facts-2009-English.pdf (accessed September 18, 2020).

3. Ernest Gellner, *Nations and Nationalism* (Ithaca: Cornell University Press, 1983), 1.

4. Elie Kedourie, *Nationalism* (Oxford: Blackwell, 1993), 91.

5. Gellner, *Nations and Nationalism*, 4.

6. Connelly, *From Peoples into Nations*, 24.

7. Gellner, *Nations and Nationalism*, 6-7.

8. Benedict Anderson, *Imagined Communities: Reflections on the Origin and Spread of Nationalism* (London: Verso, 1991), 5-7.

9. Anthony D. Smith, "Gastronomy or Geology? The Role of Nationalism in the Reconstruction of Nations," *Nations and Nationalism* 1:1 (1994): 18-19.

10. Smith, "Gastronomy or Geology?" 3-23. For an interesting contrast between resonance and charisma, see James C. Scott, *Two Cheers for Anarchy* (Princeton: Princeton University Press, 2012), 25.

11. See, too, Carol Skalnik Leff, *National Conflict in Czechoslovakia: The Making and Remaking of a State, 1918-1987* (Princeton: Princeton University Press, 1988), 19.

12. Connelly, *From Peoples into Nations*, 84.

13. Marcus Tanner, *Croatia: A Nation Forged in War* (New Haven: Yale University Press, 1997), 72-75; Connelly, *From Peoples into Nations*, 86-89.

14. Connelly, *From Peoples into Nations*, 97-99.

15. Connelly, *From Peoples into Nations*, 160.

16. Steven W. Sowards, "Nationalism in Hungary, 1848-1867," *Twenty-five Lectures on Modern Balkan History*, Michigan State University Library, 1996, https://staff.lib.msu.edu/sowards/balkan/lect07.htm (accessed September 18, 2020).

17. Peter A. Toma and Dušan Kováč, *Slovakia: From Samo to Dzurinda* (Stanford: Hoover Institution Press, 2001), 32-35.

18. Tanner, *Croatia*, 87-91.

19. Toma and Kováč, *Slovakia*, 38-40.

20. Connelly, *From Peoples into Nations*, 241-43.

21. By 1910, Hungarian was the language of commerce, administration, and intellectual discourse. Yet, only 54.4 percent of Hungarians listed Magyar as their native tongue. Bennett Kovrig, "Partitioned Nation: Hungarian Minorities in Central Europe," in Michael Mandelbaum, ed., *The New European Diasporas: National Minorities and Conflict in Eastern Europe* (New York: Council of Foreign Relations, 2000), 23.

22. Toma and Kováč, *Slovakia*, 65, 67.

23. Connelly, *From Peoples into Nations*, 336.

24. Toma and Kováč, *Slovakia*, 71-77.

25. Connelly, *From Peoples into Nations*, 353.

26. Joseph Rothschild, *East Central Europe between the Two World Wars* (Seattle: University of Washington Press, 1974), 96.

27. For more on this period, see Leff, *National Conflict in Czechoslovakia*; Rothschild, *East Central Europe between the Two World Wars*.

28. Toma and Kováč, *Slovakia*, 78-16. This territory went to the Soviet Union after the war and is now part of contemporary Ukraine.

29. Rothschild, *East Central Europe between the Two World Wars*, 215-18.

30. Tanner, *Croatia*, 119-40.

31. Simona's grandfather Alexander and great uncles were in the Slovak army at the time and ordered to participate. Her great uncles were quickly captured, however, and survived the remainder of the war in a work camp associated with Buchenwald. Alexander, who joined the Communist Party during the conflict, was wounded in action.

32. In late summer 1946, Simona's grandmother Štefania took a job in a Sudeten village to work in a formerly German-owned glass factory. Around her, Czech police were rounding up remaining ethnic Germans for deportation—producing memories that broke her heart. It was there that she met Alexander, a member of the Communist Party. They married soon after the communist coup.

33. A postcommunist Czechoslovak restitution bill controversially excluded victims of the Beneš decrees from compensation by limiting compensation to expropriations from the beginning of the communist era. Kovrig, "Partitioned Nation," 58.

34. Jelena Subotić, *Yellow Star, Red Star: Holocaust Remembrance after Communism* (Ithaca: Cornell University Press, 2019), 103-5.

35. Connelly, *From Peoples into Nations*, 454; Tanner, *Croatia*, 160.

36. Connelly, *From Peoples into Nations*, 455-57; Tanner, *Croatia*, 160.

37. Interview with Josef Markuš, Director, Matica Slovenská, Bratislava, Slovakia, January 15, 1997; Abby Innes, *Czechoslovakia: The Short Goodbye* (New Haven: Yale University Press, 2001), 99-100. The law that passed permitted administrative use of a minority (Hungarian) language in communities where the minority community made up more than 20 percent of the population. Kovrig, "Partitioned Nation," 58.

38. Jon Elster, "Consenting Adults or the Sorcerer's Apprentice?" *East European Constitutional Review* 4:1 (1995): 36-41.

Chapter 5

1. Tyson, "The Debt Crisis," 270.

2. Susan Buck-Morss, *Dreamworld and Catastrophe: The Passing of Mass Utopia in East and West* (Cambridge, MA: MIT Press, 2000), 11–30.

3. Joane Nagel, "Ethnicity and Sexuality," *Annual Review of Sociology* 26:1 (2000): 107–33.

4. Katja Kahlina, "Nation, State and Queers: Ethnosexual Identities in the Interface between Social and Personal in Contemporary Croatia," in Anna G. Jónasdóttir, Valerie Bryson, and Kathleen B. Jones, eds., *Sexuality, Gender and Power* (New York: Routledge, 2010), 30–44.

5. Zarena Papić, "Nationalism, Patriarchy and War in Ex-Yugoslavia," *Women's History Review* 3:1 (1994): 115–17.

6. Queer theorist Lee Edelman warns that reproductive concerns provide politicians with an ongoing excuse to demand that citizens make present-day sacrifices for future generations. The demand for sacrifice thus deprives the current generation of an adequate present. Moreover, as each generation grows up, it too is asked to sacrifice. The future is thus never realized. Edelman advocates reorienting political horizons to the present, where the needs of citizens can be addressed today and the nonreproductive choices of queer citizens and others will not be considered a threat. Lee Edelman, *No Future: Queer Theory and the Death Drive* (Durham: Duke University Press, 2004).

7. Masha Gessen, "What Is Vladimir Putin Thinking?" William Jovanovich Lecture in Public Affairs, Colorado College, Colorado Springs, April 22, 2014.

8. Wendy Bracewell, "Rape in Kosovo: Masculinity and Serbian Nationalism," *Nations and Nationalism* 6:4 (2000): 563–90.

9. Serbian Academy of Arts and Sciences, "Memorandum 1986," Belgrade, Serbia, September 24, 1986, *Trepca.net*, http://www.trepca.net/english/2006/serbian_memorandum_1986/serbia_memorandum_1986.html (accessed September 18, 2020).

10. Bracewell, "Rape in Kosovo," 563–90.

11. For more on the nationalist media strategy, see Agneza Božić-Roberson, "Words before the War: Milošević's Use of Mass Media and Rhetoric to Provoke Ethnopolitical Conflict in Former Yugoslavia," *East European Quarterly* 28:4 (January 2005): 395–406.

12. Vesna Nikolić-Ristanović, "Sexual Violence," in Vesna Nikolić-Ristanović, ed., *Women, Violence and War: Wartime Victimization of Refugees in the Balkans* (Budapest: Central European University Press, 2000), 41–77; Vesna Kesić, "Muslim Women, Croatian Women, Serbian Women, Albanian Women . . . ," in Dušan Bjelić and Obrad Savić, *Balkan as Metaphor: Between Globalization and Fragmentation* (Cambridge, MA: MIT Press, 2002).

13. Laura Silber and Allan Little, *Yugoslavia: Death of a Nation* (New York: Penguin, 1997), 92–98.

14. Silber and Little, *Yugoslavia*, 180.

15. Silber and Little, *Yugoslavia*, 205-21.

16. Peter Andreas, *Blue Helmets and Black Markets: The Business of Survival in the Siege of Sarajevo* (Ithaca: Cornell University Press, 2008); John Mueller, "The Banality of Ethnic War," *International Security* 25:1 (Summer 2000): 42-70.

17. See, in particular, Mladen Vuksanović, *From Enemy Territory: Pale Diary* (London: SAQI, 2004).

18. Nikolić-Ristanović, "Sexual Violence."

19. Nikolić-Ristanović, "Sexual Violence."

20. V. P. Gagnon, *The Myth of Ethnic War: Serbia and Croatia in the 1990s* (Ithaca: Cornell University Press, 2004).

21. Duca Knezević, "Theatre That Matters: How DAH Came to Be," in Dennis Barnett, ed., *Dah Theatre: A Sourcebook* (London: Lexington Books, 2016), 3-15.

22. Gagnon, *The Myth of Ethnic War*.

23. Peter Andreas, "Clandestine Political Economy of War and Peace in Bosnia," *International Studies Quarterly* 28:1 (Winter 2004): 29-52.

24. Nikolić-Ristanović, "Sexual Violence"; Bracewell, "Rape in Kosovo," 563-90.

25. Kesić, "Muslim Women, Croatian Women," 312.

26. Kesić, "Muslim Women, Croatian Women," 311.

27. Meredith Tax, "Five Women Who Would Not Be Silenced," *The Nation*, May 10, 1993.

28. Samantha Power, *A Problem from Hell: America and the Age of Genocide* (New York: Basic Books, 2002), 247-327, 391-441.

29. For an insider's account of the negotiations leading to Dayton, see Richard Holbrook, *To End a War* (New York: Random House, 1998).

30. For a review of Dayton's political provisions and an assessment of its early political performance, see Gerhard Knaus, "Travails of the European Raj," *Journal of Democracy* 14:3 (July 2003): 60-74.

Chapter 6

1. David Ost, "The Sham, and the Damage, or 'Living in Truth,'" *East European Politics and Societies and Cultures* 3:2 (2018): 301-9.

2. Havel, "The Power of the Powerless," 21.

3. Thank you to Emma Fowkes for making this point.

4. David Stark, "Path Dependence and Privatization Strategies in East Central Europe," *East European Politics and Societies* 6:1 (1992): 17-53; see, too, Ken Jowitt, "The Leninist Legacy," in Ivo Banac, ed., *East Europe in Revolution* (Ithaca: Cornell University Press, 1992), 207-24.

5. Milada Vachudova, *Europe Undivided: Democracy, Leverage, and Integration after Communism* (New York: Oxford University Press, 2005).

6. European Commission, "Agenda 2007—Commission Opinion on Slovakia's

Application for Membership of the European Union," European Commission, Brussels, July 1997; emphasis added.

7. Michael W. Doyle, "Kant, Liberal Legacies, and Foreign Affairs," in R. C. Art and R. Jervis, eds., *International Politics: Enduring Concepts and Contemporary Issues* (New York: HarperCollins, 1996), 95-117.

8. See, for example, William J. Clinton, "Remarks at a Freedom House Breakfast," *Public Papers of the Presidents of the United States: William J. Clinton, 1995,* October 6, 1995, 1544-51, https://www.govinfo.gov/content/pkg/PPP-1995-boo k2/pdf/PPP-1995-book2-doc-pg1544.pdf (accessed September 18, 2020); or Larry Diamond, "Promoting Democracy in the 1990s: Actors and Instruments, Issues and Imperatives," Carnegie Corporation of New York, December 1995, 2.

9. Michael Lind, *The American Way of Strategy* (Oxford: Oxford University Press, 2006), 35-36.

10. Jack Snyder and Karen Ballentine, "Nationalism and the Marketplace of Ideas," *International Security* 21:2 (Fall 1996): 5-40; Jack Snyder, *From Voting to Violence: Democratization and Nationalist Conflict* (New York: W. W. Norton, 2000).

11. Edward D. Mansfield and Jack Snyder, "Democratization and War," *Foreign Affairs* 74:3 (May-June 1995): 79-97; Jack Snyder and Edward Mansfield, *Electing to Fight: Why Emerging Democracies Go to War* (Cambridge: MIT Press, 2005).

12. European Commission, "Agenda 2007."

13. Kevin Foley, "Slovakia: Foreign Minister Seeks Early Admission to NATO," *Radio Free Europe/Radio Liberty*, January 9, 1999, https://www.rferl.org/a/1090409 .html (accessed September 18, 2020).

14. Petr Kopecky and Cas Mudde, eds., *Uncivil Society? Contentious Politics in Post-Communist Europe* (London: Routledge, 2003).

15. Martin Bútora, "OK '98: A Campaign of Slovak NGOs for Free and Fair Elections," in Joerg Forbrig and Pavol Demeš, eds., *Reclaiming Democracy: Civil Society and Electoral Change in Central and Eastern Europe* (Bratislava: German Marshall Fund, 2007), 25.

16. Stella Hanzelová, "Foundations in Slovakia: Introduction to the Independent Funding Community," Donors' Forum, Bratislava, Slovakia, Issue 2, November 1998, 2-3.

17. Bútora, "OK '98," 25-26.

18. Sharon Fisher, *Political Change in Post-Communist Slovakia and Croatia: From Nationalist to Europeanist* (New York: Palgrave, 2006).

19. Demeš represented the SIAA-Service Center for the Third Sector, a major player in the Slovak Donors' Forum and the Third Gremium.

20. Bútora, "OK '98," 31n19.

21. Bútora, "OK '98," 25-26.

22. Interview with Rasto Kužel, MEMO 98, Bratislava, Slovakia, June 1999.

23. Bútora, "OK '98," 25-26.

24. For thorough accounts of the politics of the Mečiar years, see Deegan-Krause, *Elected Affinities*, and Tim Haughton, *Constraints and Opportunities of Leadership in Post-Communist Europe* (London: Ashgate, 2005).

25. Martin Bútora and Zora Bútorová, "Slovakia's Democratic Awakening," *Journal of Democracy* 10:1 (January 1999): 80-95.

26. David Reichardt, "Democracy Promotion in Slovakia: An Import or Export Business?" *Perspectives: Central European Review of International Affairs* 18 (2002): 5-20.

27. Heather Grabbe, *The EU's Transformative Power: Europeanization through Conditionality in Central and Eastern Europe* (Basingstoke, UK: Palgrave, 2006), 3-4.

28. Geoffrey Pridham, "The European Union's Democratic Conditionality and Domestic Politics in Slovakia: The Mečiar and Dzurinda Governments Compared," *Europe-Asia Studies* 54:2 (2002): 203-27.

29. Darina Malová and Tim Haughton, "Challenge from the Pace-Setting Periphery: The Causes and Consequences of Slovakia's Stance on Further European Integration," in Wojciech Sadurski, Jacques Ziller, and Karolina Żurek, eds., *Après Enlargement: Legal and Political Responses in Central and Eastern Europe* (Florence: Robert Schuman Center, 2006), 326-27.

30. Tanja A. Börzel and Diana Panke, "Europeanization," in Michelle Cini and Nieves Pérerez-Solórzano Borragan, eds., *European Union Politics* (Oxford: Oxford University Press, 2013), 115-28.

Chapter 7

1. Sharon Fisher, "Contentious Politics in Croatia: The War Veterans' Movement," in Kopecky and Mudde, eds., *Uncivil Society*; Sharon Fisher and Biljana Bijelić, "Glas 99: Civil Society Preparing the Ground for a Post-Tuđman Croatia," in Forbrig and Demeš, eds., *Reclaiming Democracy*, 56-59.

2. Interview with Ines Krauth, Office of Transition Initiatives, US Agency for Information and Development, Zagreb Croatia, July 20, 2001.

3. Interview with Vladimir Pran, ENEMO/GONG, Zagreb, Croatia, July 18, 2001.

4. Fisher and Bijelić, "Glas 99," 54-63.

5. Pran interview, July 18, 2018; Krauth interview, July 20, 2001.

6. OTI's role appeared, at least to me, more hands-on than I had observed elsewhere, even—as one activist later told Sharon Fisher—to the point of dictating content in flyers. Fisher and Bijelić, "Glas 99," 67.

7. Krauth interview, July 20, 2001.

8. Interview with Karen Gainer, National Democratic Institute, Zagreb, Croatia, November 28, 2001. Gainer points out that the HDZ initially tried to work with NDI to improve its practices, but the party soon dropped out.

9. Krauth interview, July 20, 2001; Pran interview, July 18, 2002.

10. Fisher and Bijelić, "Glas 99," 63.

11. Fisher and Bijelić, "Glas 99," 60-61.

12. Jelena Subotić, "Europe Is a State of Mind: Identity and Europeanization in the Balkans," *International Studies Quarterly* 55:2 (2011): 309-30.

13. Milada Vachudova, "EU Leverage and National Interests in the Balkans: The Puzzles of Enlargement Ten Years On," *Journal of Common Market Studies* 52:1 (2012): 122-38.

14. Jelica Minić and Miljenko Dereta, "IZLAZ 2000: An Exit to Democracy in Serbia," in Forbrig and Demeš, eds., *Reclaiming Democracy*, 79-99.

15. The Federation of Bosnia-Herzegovina is an unwieldy structure of 10 cantons and dozens of municipalities. The federation, the republic, and the autonomous district of Brčko together made up the new federal state of Bosnia. For more on how the structure functioned, see Gerhard Knaus, "Travails of the European Raj," *Journal of Democracy* 14:3 (July 2003): 60-74, and Florian Bieber, *The Rise of Authoritarianism in the Western Balkans* (London: Palgrave, 2020), 63-78.

16. Tim Judah, *Kosovo: What Everyone Needs to Know* (Oxford: Oxford University Press, 2008), 75-83.

17. David N. Gibbs, *First Do No Harm: Humanitarian Intervention and the Destruction of Yugoslavia* (Nashville: Vanderbilt University Press, 2009), 184-87.

18. Powers, *A Problem from Hell*, 443-73.

19. Gibbs, *First Do No Harm*, 187-91; Judah, *Kosovo*, 83-88.

20. Judah, *Kosovo*, 83-88; Power, *A Problem from Hell*, 443-73.

21. Florian Bieber, "The Other Civil Society in Serbia: Non-governmental Nationalism—The Case of the Serbian Resistance Movement," in Kopecky and Mudde, eds., *Uncivil Society*, EPUB.

22. Iain King and Whit Mason, *Peace at Any Price: How the World Failed Kosovo* (Ithaca: Cornell University Press, 2006), 50.

23. Interview with Miljenko Dereta, Belgrade, Serbia, December 4, 2001.

24. Steve York, dir., *Bringing Down a Dictator* (Washington, DC: York Zimmerman, 2002), DVD.

25. Srdja Popović, *Blueprint for a Revolution: How to Use Rice Pudding, Lego Men, and Other Nonviolent Techniques to Galvanize Communities, Overthrow Dictators, or Simply Change the World* (New York: Spiegel & Grau, 2015).

26. Minić and Dereta, "IZLAZ 2000," 87.

27. For more on the Belgrade resistance and the October Revolution, see Matthew Collins, *This Is Serbia Calling: Rock 'n' Roll Radio and Belgrade's Underground Resistance* (London: Serpent's Tail, 2004). For more on authoritarian control in Serbia before the revolution, see Eric Gordy, *The Culture of Power in Serbia: Nationalism and the Destruction of Alternatives* (University Park: Penn State University Press, 1999).

Chapter 8

1. Chenoweth and Stephan, *Why Civil Resistance Works*.

2. NAVCO is in its third version as of this writing. Erica Chenoweth, Jonathan

Pinckney, and Orion A. Lewis, Nonviolent and Violent Campaigns and Outcomes Dataset, v. 3.0, University of Denver, 2017.

3. Chenoweth and Stephan, *Why Civil Resistance Works*, 30-61.

4. Resolution adopted by the General Assembly on September 16, 2005, Resolution 60/1, the General Assembly, United Nations, New York, October 24, 2005, https://www.un.org/en/development/desa/population/migration/generalassembly /docs/globalcompact/A_RES_60_1.pdf (accessed September 18, 2020). For a good critique, see David Hendrickson, *Republic in Peril: American Empire and the Liberal Tradition* (New York: Oxford University Press, 2018), 82-96.

5. John H. Hertz, *Political Realism and Political Idealism* (Cambridge: Cambridge University Press, 1951), 7.

6. Kenneth N. Waltz, *Theory of International Politics* (Reading, MA: Addison-Wesley, 1979). For feminist responses to this gendered conceptualization of the international system, begin with Jane Ann Tickner. "Hans Morgenthau's Principles of Political Realism: A Feminist Reformulation," *Millennium* 17 (1988): 429-40; J. Ann Tickner and Jacqui True, "A Century of International Relations Feminism: From World War I Women's Peace Pragmatism to the Women, Peace and Security Agenda," *International Studies Quarterly* 62 (2018): 221-33; Carol Cohn, "Sex and Death in the Rational World of Defense Intellectuals," *Signs* 12:4 (Summer 1987): 687-718.

7. George F. Kennan, "A Fateful Error," *New York Times*, February 5, 1997.

8. Alexander Cooley and Daniel Nexon, *Exit from Hegemony: The Unravelling of the American Global Order* (New York: Oxford University Press, 2020), 16.

9. Charles Krauthammer, "The Unipolar Moment," *Foreign Affairs* 70:1 (1990): 23-33.

10. Robert Kagan, *Of Paradise and Power: America and Europe in the New World Order* (New York: Knopf, 2003).

11. Charles Krauthammer, "The Unipolar Moment Revisited," *National Interest* (Winter 2002-3.): 5-17.

12. George W. Bush, "Commencement Address at the United States Military Academy at West Point," West Point, New York, June 1, 2002.

13. For a discussion of the full doctrine and how it contributed to the United States' reluctance to intervene in the Bosnian conflict, see Power, *A Problem from Hell*, 261-62.

14. Jason M. Breslow, "Colin Powell Speech 'Was a Great Intelligence Failure.'" *Frontline*, PBS.org, May 17, 2016, https://www.pbs.org/wgbh/frontline/article/col in-powell-u-n-speech-was-a-great-intelligence-failure/ (accessed September 18, 2020).

15. Jan Havránek and Jan Jireš, "Václav Havel and NATO: Lessons of Leadership for the Atlantic Alliance," in Daniel S. Hamilton and Kristina Spohr, eds., *Open Door: NATO and Euro-Atlantic Security after the Cold War* (Washington, DC: Brooking Institution Press, 2019), 173-94.

16. Ian Black, "Furious Chirac Hits Out at 'Infantile' Easterners," *The Guardian*, February 17, 2003, https://www.theguardian.com/world/2003/feb/18/france.iraq (accessed September 18, 2020).

17. The war went well at first, but the US occupation army soon found itself unprepared and ill-equipped for an armed, multiparty uprising and violent inter-communal warfare. For many, the anti-US and intercommunal violence was the direct result of US choices. Many uprising leaders, for example, were former offi-cers from the Iraqi army that the US-led "Coalition Provisional Authority" had just thoughtlessly disbanded. Had we supported a slightly purged and reformed Iraqi army, one argument went, we would have had a much easier time maintaining domestic stability. Instead, Iran emerged as a key power broker in the region, stok-ing intercommunal clashes to keep Iraq unstable and US forces on the defensive. See Hendrickson, *Republic in Peril*.

18. As in the Yugoslav wars, any discussion of causalities is likely to be con-troversial. This is from a cautious and thorough work of the Costs of War project at Brown University. Neta C. Crawford and Catherine Lutz, "Human Cost of Post-9/11 Wars," Watson Institute, Brown University, November 13, 2019, https://wats on.brown.edu/costsofwar/files/cow/imce/papers/2019/Direct%20War%20Deaths %20COW%20Estimate%20November%2013%202019%20FINAL.pdf (accessed September 18, 2020).

19. Vershbow says this was based on paranoia, fed by worst-case assessments in intelligence briefings. Vershbow, "Present at the Transformation," 440. See also Michael McFaul, *From Cold War to Hot Peace: An American Ambassador in Putin's Russia* (Boston: Mariner Books, 2018).

20. See Minić and Dereta, "IZLAZ 2000," 79-100; Giorgi Kandelaki and Giorgi Meladze, "Enough! KMARA and the Rose Revolution in Georgia," 101-26; and Vldyslav Kaskiv, Iryna Chupryna, and Yevhen Zolotariov, "It's Time! Pora and the Orange Revolution in Ukraine," 127-54, in Forbrig and Demeš, eds., *Reclaiming Democracy*.

21. Interview with John Peopsel, International Republican Institute, Kyiv, Ukraine, January 10, 2003.

22. According to Brian Mefford, the government had no intention of irritat-ing the United States by kicking NDI and IRI out of the country. Rather, the delay in reaccreditation was being used by presidential hopeful Viktor Medvedchuk to embarrass his rival, Prime Minister Viktor Yanukovich, before a planned visit to the White House. Interview with Brian Mefford, International Republican Institute, Kyiv, Ukraine, July 18, 2003.

23. Interview with Jeane Kugel, National Democratic Institute, Kyiv, Ukraine, January 8, 2003.

24. Mefford interview, July 18, 2003.

25. Peopsel interview, January 10, 2003.

26. Hendrickson, *Republic in Peril*, 29-30; Mitchell Orenstein, *The Lands In*

Between: Russia vs. the West and the New Politics of Hybrid War (Oxford: Oxford University Press, 2019), 14-16.

27. For a good summary of Russian perceptions of US foreign policy from a US policy maker, see Alexander Vershbow, "Present at the Transformation: An Insider's Reflection on NATO Enlargement, NATO-Russia Relations, and Where We Go from Here," in Hamilton and Spohr, eds., *Open Door*, 425-44.

28. McFaul, *From Cold War to Hot Peace*.

29. Gessen, "What Is Vladimir Putin Thinking?" William Jovanovich Lecture in Public Affairs, Colorado College, Colorado Springs, April 22, 2014.

30. Masha Gessen, *Man Without a Face: The Unlikely Rise of Vladimir Putin* (New York: Riverhead, 2014), 307-16.

31. Ellen Barry, "Former Ukraine Premier Is Jailed for 7 Years," *New York Times*, October 11, 2011.

32. For critiques of US foreign policy up to and including the Ukraine crisis, see John Mearsheimer, "Why the Ukraine Crisis Is the West's Fault: The Liberal Delusions That Provoked Putin," *Foreign Affairs* (October-November 2014); Hendrickson, *Republic in Peril*; David Hendrickson, "The New Interventionism," *National Interest* (September-October 2014): 53-58. For the US administration's view, see McFaul, *From Cold War to Hot Peace*.

33. Yuri Teper, "Official Russian Identity Discourse in Light of the Annexation of Crimea: National or Imperial?" *Post-Soviet Affairs* 32:4 (2016): 378-96.

34. Cooley and Nexon, *Exit from Hegemony*, 52.

35. John Gould and Carl Sickner, "Making Market Democracies? The Contingent Loyalties of Post-Privatization Elites in Azerbaijan, Georgia and Serbia," *Review of International Political Economy* 15:5 (Fall 2008): 740-69.

Chapter 9

1. The Serbian sections of this chapter are drawn from Gould and Moe, "Nationalism and the Struggle for LGBTQ Rights." In this chapter, I follow the practices of local umbrella advocacy groups in using the LGBTQ+ acronym to describe a dynamic, multifaceted community with many activist voices and efforts.

2. Viera Lorencová, "Becoming Visible: Queer in Post-socialist Slovakia" (PhD diss., University of Massachusetts, Amherst, 2006); Viera Wallace-Lorencová, "Queering Civil Society in Postsocialist Slovakia," *Anthropology of East Europe Review* 21:2 (2003): 103-12; Viera Lorencová, "Taking Off a Cloak of Invisibility: The Clash of Discourses about Sexual Difference in Slovakia," in Fejes Nàrcisz and Andrea P. Balogh, eds., *Queer Visibility in Post-Socialist Cultures* (Bristol: Intellect, 2013), 83-104.

3. Věra Sokolová, "State Approaches to Homosexuality and Non-heterosexual Lives in Czechoslovakia during State Socialism," in Hana Havelková and Libora Oates-Indruchová, eds., *The Politics of Gender Culture under State Socialism: An Expropriated Voice* (New York Routledge, 2014), 85-87.

4. Lorencová, "Becoming Visible," 128.

5. Lorencová, "Becoming Visible," 127-28, 162-63.

6. Serbian activists at the Queer Beograd Festival introduced the Serbian word for "malfunction," *Kvar*, as a loose replacement for the word "queer." It refers to anyone who through action or performance throws a wrench into the machinery of heteronormative politics. Nevertheless, the Western acronyms have stuck and remain the dominant identifiers for activists. Interview with Zoe Gudović, Public Relations Manager, Reconstruction Women's Fund, Belgrade, Serbia, April 11, 2014. See Queer Beograd Collective (QBC), "Preparing a Space: Documentation of Party and Politics Festival," Queer Beograd, Belgrade, Serbia, 2006; QBC, "The Malfunction," Ksenija Forca, Belgrade, Serbia, 2007; QBC, "Anti-Fascism and Direct Action," Queer Beograd, Belgrade, Serbia, 2011; Bojan Bilić and Irene Dioli, "Queer Beograd Collective: Beyond Single-Issue Activism in Serbia and the Post-Yugoslav Space" in Bojan Bilić and Sanja Kajnić, eds., *Intersectionality and LGBT Activist Politics: Multiple Others in Croatia and Serbia* (London: Palgrave, 2016), 107-12.

7. Lepa Mladjenović, "Notes of a Feminist Lesbian during Wartime," *European Journal of Women's Studies* 8:3 (2001): 382-85. Meanwhile, according to Saša Gavrić of the Sarajevo Open Center, the 1992-95 wars drove gay men into hiding or emigration to avoid conscription. The LGBTQ+ community across the former Yugoslavia lost many of its potential activists early in the postcommunist period. Interview with Saša Gavrić, Sarajevo Open Center, Sarajevo, Bosnia-Herzegovina, May 26, 2014.

8. Bojan Bilić and Irene Dioli, "Queer Beograd Collective: Beyond Single-Issue Activism in Serbia," 106n3.

9. Interview with Daša Duhaček and Katarina Lončarević, Center for Women's Studies, Faculty of Political Science, Belgrade University, Belgrade, Serbia, March 6, 2013; Karen Louise Boothe, "Enemies of the State: Gays and Lesbians in Serbia," *Lavender*, February 11-24, 2000, 123; Karen Louise Boothe, "Gays in Belgrade Struggle to Find a Sense of Self," *The Advocate*, October 12, 1999.

10. Shirley Mahaley Malcom, Paula Quick Hall, and Janet Welsh Brown, "The Double Bind: The Price of Being a Minority Woman in Science: Report of a Conference of Minority Women Scientists Airlie House, Warrenton, Virginia," American Association for the Advancement of Science, no. 76-R-3, April 1976.

11. Serbian homophobia made being openly out extraordinarily difficult at the time. A man who queered hetero-normative public space risked becoming the victim of sudden, random homophobic violence. Interview with Milan Pantelić, Gay-Straight Alliance representative on the Council for Gender Equality of the Serbian Government, Belgrade, Serbia, June 23, 2013; interview with Igor Vojdović, Gay-Straight Alliance, Belgrade, Serbia, January 30, 2013.

12. "Milošević's removal from office may best be described as a negotiated transition [in which] many of his entourage and supporters switched allegiances in order to maintain their personal prerogatives." Mark Downes and Rory Keane, "Police Reform Amid Transition: The Organization for Security and Cooperation in Serbia," *Civil Wars* 8:2 (2006): n3; see also Timothy Edmunds, "Intelligence

Agencies and Democratization: Continuity and Change in Serbia after Milosevic," *Europe-Asia Studies* 60:1 (2008): 25-48.

13. Gould, *Politics of Privatization*, 178-80.

14. See also Svetlana Slapšak, "The After-War War of Genders: Misogyny. Feminist Ghettoization and the Discourse of Responsibility in Post-Yugoslav Societies," in Sanja Bahun-Radunović and Julie Rajan, eds., *Violence and Gender in the Globalized World: The Intimate and the Extreme* (New York: Ashgate, 1988), 91-106.

15. Timothy Edmunds, "Illiberal Resilience in Serbia," *Journal of Democracy* 20:1 (2009): 135-36.

16. Eric Gordy, *Guilt, Responsibility, and Denial* (Philadelphia: University of Pennsylvania Press, 2014), 69-86.

17. Jessica Greenberg, "Nationalism, Masculinity and Multicultural Citizenship in Serbia," *Nationalities Papers* 34:3 (July 2006): 324; Marek Mikuš, "'State Pride' Politics of LGBTQ Rights and Democratization in 'European Serbia,'" *East European Politics & Societies* 25:4 (2011): 834-51; Ana Simo, "Violence Stops Yugoslavia Gay Pride." *TheGully.com*, May 7, 2001, http://www.thegully.com/ess ays/gaymundo/010705gay_yugoslavia.html (accessed September 18, 2020).

18. For a firsthand account, see Greenberg, "Nationalism, Masculinity," 324; Mikuš, "State Pride," 834-51; Ana Simo, "Violence," May 7, 2001. Interview with Lepa Mladjenović, Belgrade, Serbia, February 6, 2013.

19. See, too, Edmunds, "Illiberal Resilience in Serbia," 128-42.

20. Daša Duhaček, "Engendering Political Responsibility: Transitional Justice in Serbia," in Ola Listhaug, Sabrina P. Ramet, and Dragana Dulić, eds., *Civic and Uncivic Values: Serbia in the Post-Milošević Era* (Budapest: CEU Press, 2011), 252-60.

21. Duhaček, "Engendering Political Responsibility," 252-60.

22. Christian Axboe Nielsen, "Stronger Than the State? Football Hooliganism, Political Extremism and the Gay Pride Parades in Serbia," *Sport in Society: Cultures, Commerce, Media, Politics* 16:8 (2013): 1038-53.

23. Interview with Hana Fábry, Bratislava, Slovakia, July 14, 2014.

24. Fábry interview, July 14, 2014. Slovakia's leading civil society think tank, the Institute of Public Affairs (IVO), published its first article concerning sexual minorities in 2001; Vladimír Pirošik, "Marginalized Groups: Gays and Lesbians," in Grigorij Mesežnikov, Miroslav Kollár, and Tom Nicholson, eds., *Slovakia 2000: A Global Report on the State of Society* (Bratislava: IVO, 2001), 557-65. Prior to that, most reporting was in feminist magazines, e.g., Zora Bútorová, "Homosexualita vo svetle verejnej mienky," *Aspekt* (Lesbická existencia), 1/1996. After 2004, IVO stopped reporting on LGBTQ+ rights in its annual report.

25. Lorencová, *Becoming Visible*, 193.

26. Lorencová, *Becoming Visible*, 369-71.

27. "Slovak Gays Say Minister's Critical Stand on Gay Partnership 'Discriminatory,'" *SITA News Agency*, August 17, 2000, http://infoweb.newsbank.com/resourc es/doc/nb/news/1034B75EA7CE4B9B?p=AWNB (accessed July 21, 2015).

28. Fábry interview, July 14, 2014; Martina Pisárová, "Peter Králik: Making an Issue of Homosexuality in Slovakia—2000 Man of the Year," *Slovak Spectator*, December 25, 2000, http://infoweb.newsbank.com/resources/doc/nb/news/14C2D B754F17AD90?p=AWNB (accessed July 21, 2015).

29. Lorencová, *Becoming Visible*, 369-71. See also Conor O'Dwyer, *Coming Out: The Emergence of LGBT Activism in Eastern Europe* (New York: New York University Press, 2018), 196-97.

30. O'Dwyer, *Coming Out*, 197.

31. "Council Directive 2000/78/EC of 27 November 2000 Establishing a General Framework for Equal Treatment in Employment and Occupation," *Official Journal* L 303 (December 12, 2000), 16-22, http://eur-lex.europa.eu/LexUriServ/LexUriServ .do?uri=CELEX:32000L0078:en:HTML (accessed September 18, 2020).

32. Fábry interview, July 14, 2014.

33. "Slovak Christian Democrats' Declaration on Relations with EU Criticized," *TASR News Agency*, Bratislava, Slovakia, July 27, 2001, http://infoweb.newsbank .com/resources/doc/nb/news/1034BA3442605416?p=AWNB (accessed July 23, 2015).

34. Marianne Schulze, "Slovakia," in Gerda Falner, Oliver Treib, and Elisabeth Holzleithner, eds., *Compliance in the Enlarged European Union: Living Rights or Dead Letters?* (Aldershot, UK: Ashgate, 2008), 108; Martina Pisárová, "Homosexuals Denied Labour Code Umbrella," *Slovak Spectator*, July 16, 2001, http://infoweb.ne wsbank.com/resources/doc/nb/news/14C2DB7C0A40A628?p=AWNB (accessed July 21, 2015).

35. Viera Wallace-Lorencová, "Queering Civil Society in Postsocialist Slovakia," *Anthropology of East Europe Review* 21:2 (2003); Viera Lorencová, "Taking Off a Cloak of Invisibility: The Clash of Discourses about Sexual Difference in Slovakia," in Fejes Nàrcisz and Andrea P. Balogh, eds., *Queer Visibility in Post-Socialist Cultures* (Bristol: Intellect, 2013), 83-104.

36. Vachudova, "EU Leverage and National Interests," 122-38.

37. The United States quickly recognized the move, followed by most EU members. Slovakia, fearing its Hungarian minority might eventually follow suit and try to succeed, did not recognize the action.

38. "Serbian Parliament Speaker Calls for Closer Russia Ties," *RFE/RL*, May 9, 2007, http://www.rferl.org/content/article/1076353.html (accessed September 18, 2020).

39. Interview with Boris Milićević, Socialist Party of Serbia, Belgrade, Serbia, June 14, 2013.

40. Nielsen, "Stronger Than the State?" 12; The Catholic Church, the Islamic Community of Serbia, and evangelical groups similarly lobbied against the measure. Jelisaveta Blagojević, "Between Walls: Provincialisms, Human Rights, Sexualities and Serbian Public Discourses on EU Integration," in Joanna Mizielińska and Robert Kulpa, eds., *De-Centering Western Sexualities: Central and Eastern European Perspectives* (Burlington, VT: Ashgate, 2011), 32.

41. Dana N. Johnson, "We Are Waiting for You: The Discursive (De)construction of Belgrade Pride 2009," *Sextures* 2:2 (2012): 6-31; Aleksandra Djordjevic, "Has the International Human Rights Paradigm Failed Lesbian, Gay, Bisexual and Transgender People? If So, What Can Be Done to Fix It?" (master's thesis, University of British Columbia, April 2013).

42. Blagojević, "Between Walls," 32.

Chapter 10

1. Mark Blyth, *Austerity: The History of a Dangerous Idea* (Oxford: Oxford University Press, 2013).

2. Sheri Berman, "Populism Is a Symptom Rather Than a Cause: Democratic Disconnect, the Decline of the Center-Left, and the Rise of Populism in Western Europe," *Polity* 51:4 (October 2019): 657; Jonathan Hopkin and Mark Blyth, "The Global Economics of European Populism: Growth Regimes and Party System Change in Europe," *Government and Opposition* 54 (2019): 193-225; Abby Innes, "Draining the Swamp: Understanding the Crisis in Mainstream Politics as a Crisis of the State," *Slavic Review* 76 (2017); Eric Lonergan and Mark Blyth, *Angrynomics* (New York: Columbia University Press, 2020); Julia Lynch, "Populism, Partisan Convergence, and Mobilization in Western Europe," *Polity* 54:1 (October 2019): 669-77.

3. Cas Mudde, "The Populist Zeitgeist," *Government and Opposition* 39 (2004): 542-63.

4. Anna Grzymala-Busse, "Conclusion: The Global Forces of Populism," *Polity* 51:4 (2019): 718; Kevin Deegan-Krause and Tim Haughton, "Towards a More Useful Conceptualization of Populism," *Politics and Policy* 37 (2009): 821-41.

5. Milada Anna Vachudova, "From Competition to Polarization in Central Europe: How Populists Change Party Systems and the European Union," *Polity* 51:4 (October 2019): 689-706; Ben Stanley and Mikołaj Cześnik, "Populism in Poland," in Daniel Steockemer, ed., *Populism around the World: A Comparative Perspective* (Cham, Switzerland: Springer, 2019), 67-88; Anna Grzymala-Busse, "How Populists Rule: The Consequences for Democratic Governance," *Polity* 51:4 (October 2019): 707-17.

6. Tim Haughton and Kevin Deegan-Krause, *The New Party Challenge: Changing Cycles of Party Birth and Death in Central Europe and Beyond* (Oxford: Oxford University Press, 2020), draft copy of chapter 1.

7. The first section is based on John A. Gould and Darina Malová, "Toxic Neoliberalism on the EU's Periphery: Slovakia, the Euro and the Migrant Crisis," in Jozef Bátora and John Erik Fossum, eds., *Towards a Segmented European Political Order: The European Union's Post-Crisis Conundrum* (London: Routledge, 2020), 112-31; see also Darina Malová and Branislav Dolný, "Economy and Democracy in Slovakia during the Crisis: From a Laggard to the EU Core," *Problems of Post-Communism*, 63:5-6 (2016): 300-312.

8. Appel and Orenstein, *From Triumph to Crisis*, 4.

9. In Slovakia, neoliberals in the Dzurinda government failed in their efforts to introduce fees for university and only partially succeeded in health care. Sharon Fisher, John A. Gould, and Tim Haughton, "Slovakia's Neoliberal Turn," *Europe-Asia Studies* 59:3 (September 2007): 977-98.

10. Abby Innes, "Party Competition in Postcommunist Europe: The Great Electoral Lottery," *Comparative Politics* 35:1 (2002): 85-104; Herbert Kitschelt, Zdenka Mansfeldova, Radoslaw Markowski, and Gabor Toka, *Post-Communist Party Systems* (Cambridge: Cambridge University Press, 1999), 137.

11. Appel and Orenstein, *From Triumph to Crisis*, 90-115.

12. Fisher, Gould, and Haughton, "Slovakia's Neoliberal Turn."

13. Gabriel Machlia, Branislav Zudel, and Slavomir Hidas, "Unemployment in Slovakia." Institute for Financial Policy, 2014; Unless indicated otherwise, all data in this chapter are drawn from the EU's official statistical office, Eurostat, European Commission, Brussels, Belgium, 2020, https://ec.europa.eu/eurostat/ (accessed September 18, 2020).

14. Stephen Holmes and Ivan Krastev, *The Light That Failed: Why the West Is Losing the Fight for Democracy* (New York: Pegasus, 2020).

15. Machlia, Zudel, and Hidas, "Unemployment in Slovakia."

16. Marek Rybář and Kevin Deegan-Krause, "Slovakia's Successor Parties in Comparative Perspective," *Communist and Post-Communist Studies* 41:1 (2008): 497-519.

17. Jameel Ahmad, *Floating Exchange Rates and World Inflation* (London: Palgrave Macmillan, 1984), 143-44.

18. Malová and Dolný, "Economy and Democracy in Slovakia," 300-312.

19. See "Slovak Republic," The World Bank, Washington, DC, 2020, https://data.worldbank.org/country/SK (accessed September 18, 2020).

20. Machlia, Zudel, and Hidas, "Unemployment in Slovakia."

21. See "Slovak Republic," World Bank, Washington, DC, 2020.

22. Joseph Stiglitz, *The Euro: How a Common Currency Threatens the Future of Europe* (New York: W. W. Norton, 2016); Blyth, *Austerity*.

23. Nicolas Jabko, "The Elusive Economic Government and the Forgotten Fiscal Union," in Matthias Matthijs and Mark Blyth, eds., *The Future of the Euro* (Oxford: Oxford University Press, 2015), 70-89.

24. Independent Evaluation Office, "The IMF and the Crisis in Greece, Ireland and Portugal," International Monetary Fund, Washington, DC, 2016; Ambrose Evans-Prichard, "IMF Admits Disastrous Love-Affair with the Euro and Apologizes for the Immolation of Greece," *The Telegraph*, July 29, 2016, https://www.telegraph.co.uk/business/2016/07/28/imf-admits-disastrous-love-affair-with-euro-apologises-for-the-i/?WT.mc_id=tmg_share_fb&fbclid=IwAR1HKaOCJ1qfcAa-hI21gG5z4ruuTu1xssWIs-8W_kmm3l1vR_9mg8QaydQ (accessed September 18, 2020); Graham Bird, "The Eurozone: What Now?" *World Economics*, 113 (2010): 41-59.

25. Abraham Newman, "The Reluctant Leader: Germany's Euro Experience and the Long Shadow of Reunification," in Matthias Matthijs and Mark Blyth, eds., *The Future of the Euro* (Oxford: Oxford University Press, 2015), 117–35.

26. Malová and Dolný, "Economy and Democracy in Slovakia," 300–312.

27. Martina Jurinová, "Gays and Lesbians Seek Recognition—Political Scene Is Unsympathetic to Homosexual Cause," *Slovak Spectator*, March 5, 2007, http:// infoweb.newsbank.com/resources/doc/nb/news/14C2D75BA30A17C0?p=AWNB (accessed September 18, 2020).

28. "Human Rights and Democratization in Slovakia," Commission on Security and Cooperation in Europe, Washington, DC, September 1997, 23.

29. As I write, I look out onto my college's beautiful Tava Quad—named for the Ute people's word for the 14,000-foot peak just to the west of campus. A plaque on the lawn reminds me that I am on "unceded land," a nice word for property rights over land that the state took by force, in this case from the Ute, Apache, Arapaho, Comanche, and Cheyenne peoples who once made use of it. If you are an American or Australian, the land you are sitting on right now probably acquired its legal property title through a similar process of acquisition. For more, see Roxanne Dunbar-Ortiz, *An Indigenous People's History of the United States* (Boston: Beacon Press, 2014).

30. Holmes and Krastev, *The Light That Failed*.

31. For the English version, published five years later, see Gabriele Kuby, *The Global Sexual Revolution: Destruction of Freedom in the Name of Freedom* (Kettering, OH: LifeSite/Angelico Press, 2015).

32. Petra Ďurinová, "Slovakia," in Eszter Kováts and Maari Põim, eds., *Gender as Symbolic Glue: The Position and Role of Conservative and Far Right Parties in the Anti-Gender Mobilizations in Europe* (Budapest: Foundations for European Progressive Societies, 2015), 104–25.

33. Benjamin Vail, "Interview: The Global Sexual Revolution and the Assault on Freedom and Family," *Catholic World Report* (September 9, 2014), http://www.cat holicworldreport.com/Item/3357/The_Global_Sexual_Revolution_and_the_Assau lt_on_Freedom_and_Family.aspx (accessed September 18, 2020).

34. For more on Russian disinformation efforts in Slovakia, see Veronika Golianová and Aliaksei Kazharski, "'The Unsolid' Pro-Kremlin Narratives in Slovak Cultural and Educational Institutions," *RUSI Journal*, August 14, 2020; Orenstein, *The Lands In Between*, 116–20; Cooley and Nexon, *Exit from Hegemony*, 137–58. For more on French, US, and Russian ties to the KDH and Slovak social conserva-tives, see Ján Kozubik, "Slovenské referendum o „ochraně rodiny"—příčiny, průběh a výsledek v kontextu proti-LGBT vlny ve východní Evropě" (master's thesis, Pol-itics Department, Faculty of Social Studies, Marsaryk University, 2015).

35. Interview with Dagmar Horná, Bratislava, Slovakia, July 9, 2014; phone interview with Olga Pietruchová, Bratislava, Slovakia, July 2014; interview with Dagmar Kusá, Bratislava, Slovakia, July 9, 2014; Alliance for the Family pamphlet, distributed in Bratislava, Slovakia, July 12, 2014.

36. "Pastiersky list Konferencie biskupov Slovenska na prvú nedeľu adventnú," Slovak Bishops' Conference, December 1, 2013.

37. "Pastiersky list biskupov Slovenska k Národnému pochudu za život," Slovak Bishops' Conference, September 1, 2013.

38. "Homophobe of the Year Is Anton Chromík," *Slovak Spectator*, July 15, 2015, http://infoweb.newsbank.com/resources/doc/nb/news/1569E534A216B710?p=AWNB (accessed September 18, 2020).

39. For a thorough history of LGBTQ+ struggles in Slovakia through 2012, see Lorencová, "Taking Off a Cloak of Invisibility," 83-104.

40. Kozubik, "Slovenské referendum o 'ochraně rodiny.'" 31-32.

41. Siobahn O'Grady, "Slovakia to EU: We'll Take Migrants—If They're Christians," *Foreign Policy*, August 19, 2015, https://foreignpolicy.com/2015/08/19/slovakia-to-eu-well-take-migrants-if-theyre-christians/ (accessed September 18, 2020).

42. Aliaksei Kazharski, "Frontiers of Hatred? A Study of Right-Wing Populist Strategies in Slovakia," *European Politics and Society* (January 16, 2019): 1-13.

43. Holmes and Krastev, *The Light That Failed*, 152.

44. "Protest against Migrant Quotas Paralyses Downtown Bratislava," *Slovak Spectator*, June 22, 2015, https://spectator.sme.sk/c/20058267/protest-against-migrant-quotas-paralyses-downtown-bratislava.html?ref=av-center (accessed September 18, 2020); Roman Cuprik, "Anti-Immigrant Protest Organisers Seek to Unite Extremists," *Slovak Spectator*, June 23, 2015, https://spectator.sme.sk/c/20058361/anti-immigrant-protest-organisers-seek-to-unite-extremists.html (accessed September 18, 2020).

45. Daniel Vražda, "Odkrývame nové bašty Kotlebovej ĽSNS. Ako vyrástla tam, kde bol roky dominantný Smer," *Denník N*, April 6, 2016, https://dennikn.sk/427550/kotleba-vyrastol-tam-bol-roky-dominantny-smer (accessed September 18, 2020).

46. European Commission, "Public Opinion in the European Union," Eurobarometer, European Union, Brussels, 2016, 86.

47. Marek Hlavac, "Performance of Political Parties in the 2016 Parliamentary Election in Slovakia: Regional Comparisons and District-Level Determinants," *Regional & Federal Studies* 26 (2016): 433-43.

48. Olga Gyárfášová, "The Rise of Radicalism among Young People in Slovakia: Causes and Consequences," *Aspen Review* 2 (2017), https://www.aspen.review/article/2017/the-rise-of-radicalism-among-young-people-in-slovakia-causes-and-consequences (accessed September 18, 2020).

49. Innes, "Party Competition in Postcommunist Europe," 85-104; Haughton and Deegan-Krause, *The New Party Challenge*, draft chapter 1.

50. Michael Bernhard, "What Do We Know about Civil Society and Regime Change Thirty Years After 1989?" *East European Politics* 26:3 (2020): 341-62.

51. Matúš Kostolný, "Fico je Gorila. Počúvajte," *Denník N*, October 16, 2019, https://dennikn.sk/1619822/fico-je-gorila-pocuvajte/ (accessed September 18, 2020).

52. Haščák held his meetings in the flat of a security guard who looked like one

of the muscular, bald bouncers Slovaks liked to refer to as "gorillas," hence the code name of the surveillance operation.

53. Radičová is a former colleague from my brief period at Comenius University in 1996. As prime minister of the SKDÚ-led coalition government, she was rumored to have been incorruptible and to have clashed repeatedly with Dzurinda, whose party colleague appeared in the Gorilla transcripts.

54. Ján Kuciak, "Talianska mafia na Slovensku," *Akutality.sk,* February 28, 2018, https://www.aktuality.sk/clanok/568007/talianska-mafia-na-slovensku -jej-chapadla-siahaju-aj-do-politiky/ (accessed September 18, 2020).

55. Martin Turček and Ján Kuciak, "Ďalšie zvláštne prevody okolo Kočnera," *Aktuality.sk,* February 9, 2018, https://www.aktuality.sk/clanok/562609/dalsie-po dozrive-prevody-kocnerovej-firmy-vo-five-star-residence-sud-ju-chce-zrusit/ (accessed September 18, 2020).

56. "Vražda Novinara a jeho priateľky," *TA3,* February 26, 2018, https://www .ta3.com/clanok/1122756/vrazda-novinara-a-jeho-priatelky-nevycerpane-eurofon dy.html (accessed September 18, 2020).

57. Monika Tódová, "U Kočnera v trezore našli nahrávky Gorily," *Dennik N,* December 4, 2018, https://dennikn.sk/1315464/policajti-nasli-u-kocnera-v-trezo re-nahravky-gorily/?ref=in (accessed September 18, 2020).

58. Monika Tódová, "Ďalší nahratý je Počiatek. Na Kočnerovom videu žiada od Trnku krytie v kauze Tipos (video)," *Dennik N,* November 29, 2018, https://denni kn.sk/1668678/dalsi-nahraty-je-pociatek-na-kocnerovom-videu-ziada-od-trnku -krytie-v-kauze-tipos-video/ (accessed September 18, 2020).

59. Kočner, in one recording, alleges that after Slovak Information Service agent Holúbek was fired and the Gorilla investigation was squashed, Penta Group CEO Haščák paid him a million euros to acquire and destroy the recordings. Yet, Kočner claimed to have secretly kept a recording that he stashed in a safe in Attorney General Trnka's office, the safest place he could think of. In 2010, Kočner alleges, he and Haščák did all they could, including bribery, to ensure that Trnka's mandate as attorney general would be renewed by parliament. Yet, despite allegedly paying large sums to parliamentarians, Trnka still failed to win by a single vote. Kočner then accused Trnka and two others of using the Gorilla recording to bribe Haščák anew. Kočner was furious and threatened the life of Trnka and his son, at which point Trkna admitted the deed to Kočner. Afterward, Kočner sounded hurt; if Trnka needed money, why didn't he ask him for the sizable funds he held for him in trust? Monika Tódová, "Kočner: Zabijú ťa. Trnka: Viem, že ma zabijú. Nahrávka o násilí, kupovaní poslancov a vydieraní (+podcast)," *DenníkN,* October 14, 2019, https:// dennikn.sk/1616396/kocner-zabiju-ta-trnka-viem-ze-ma-zabiju-nahravka-o-n asili-kupovani-poslancov-a-vydierani-podcast/?ref=in (accessed September 18, 2020).

60. Attila Molnár, "Sulík: Radičová o stretnutiach s Kočnerom vedela - „Ja som ich rozoštval," tvrdí Kočner!" Hlavný Denník, November 19, 2019, https://www.

hlavnydennik.sk/2019/11/19/sulik-radicova-o-stretnutiach-s-kocnerom-vede-la-ja-som-ich-rozostval-tvrdi-podnikatel/ (accessed September 18, 2020). As I turn this manuscript over to the publisher, the gunmen have been convicted for their murder, but the judge acquitted Kočner. His defense established a lack of clear evidence that he ordered it. The prosecution is expected to appeal the decision. Kočner remains in custody on other charges.

61. When given a clear choice between liberalism and its alternatives in presidential elections, Slovaks have twice chosen pro-EU liberals over the less liberal candidates. After 2013, President Andrej Kiska and especially President Zuzana Čaputová impressed liberals everywhere by using the office to defend human rights, the rule of law, and Slovakia's place in the EU's democratic order.

Chapter 11

1. Bálint Madlovics and Bálint Magyar, "Post-Communist Predation: Modeling *Reiderstvo* Practices in Contemporary States," *Public Choice*, January 29, 2020, https://doi.org/10.1007/s11127-019-00772-7; see also Timothy Frye, *Property Rights and Property Wrongs: How Power, Institutions, and Norms Shape Economic Conflict in Russia* (Cambridge: Cambridge University Press, 2017). Vadim Volkov, *Violent Entrepreneurs: The Use of Force in the Making of Russian Capitalism* (Ithaca: Cornell University Press, 2002).

2. R. Daniel Kelemen, "The European Union's Authoritarian Equilibrium," *Journal of European Public Policy*, 27:3 (2020): EPUB.

3. Kelemen, "The European Union's Authoritarian Equilibrium."

4. Kim Lane Scheppele, "Europe's Largest Party Suspends Its Resident Autocrat—For Now," *Foreign Affairs*, March 28, 2019, https://www.foreignaffairs.com/articles/hungary/2019-03-28/europes-largest-party-suspends-its-resident-autocrat-now (accessed September 18, 2020).

5. Zsolt Enyedi, "Plebeians, Citoyens and Aristocrats or Where Is the Bottom of Bottom-up? The Case of Hungary," in Hanspeter Kriesi and Takis Pappas, eds., *European Populism in the Shadow of the Great Recession* (Colchester, UK: ECPR Press, 2015), 235.

6. Enyedi, "Plebeians, Citoyens and Aristocrats," 231.

7. Unless indicated otherwise, all economic data in this chapter are drawn from the EU's official statistical office, Eurostat, European Commission, Brussels, Belgium, 2020, https://ec.europa.eu/eurostat/ (accessed September 18, 2020).

8. Bernhard, "What Do We Know about Civil Society and Regime Change," 351.

9. Reintje Maasdam, "Hungary: Country Report," *Rabobank*, Utrecht, the Netherlands, February 2010.

10. Maasdam, "Hungary: Country Report."

11. Grzymala-Busse, "How Populists Rule," 709.

12. Enyedi, "Plebeians, Citoyens and Aristocrats," 234.

13. Dorottya Sallai and Gerhard Schnyder, "The Transformation of Post-socialist Capitalism—From Developmental State to Clans State?" Greenwich Political Economy Research Centre, Greenwich, UK, GPERC57, 2018, 11-12.

14. Enyedi, "Plebeians, Citoyens and Aristocrats," 239.

15. Kevin Deegan Krause, "Donald Trump and the Lessons of East-Central European Populism," in Kurt Weyland and Raúl L. Madrid, eds., *When Democracy Trumps Populism: European and Latin American Lessons for the United States* (Cambridge: Cambridge University Press, 2019), 71.

16. Grzymala-Busse, "How Populists Rule."

17. Kim Lane Schepple, "Understanding Hungary's Constitutional Revolution," in Armin von Bogdandy and Pál Sonnevend, eds., *Constitutional Crisis in the European Constitutional Area: Theory, Law and Politics in Hungary and Romania* (Oxford: Hart, 2015), 111-24.

18. Smaller populations of Ethnic Hungarians live in Croatia, Austria, and Slovenia.

19. Grzymala-Busse, "How Populists Rule," 710.

20. Kelemen, "The European Union's Authoritarian Equilibrium."

21. Deegan-Krause, "Donald Trump and the Lessons," 70-72.

22. Zsolt Enyedi, "Democratic Backsliding and Academic Freedom in Hungary," *Perspectives on Politics* 16:4 (December 2018): 1067-74.

23. András Bozóki and Dániel Hegedűs, "An Externally Constrained Hybrid Regime: Hungary in the European Union," *Democratization* 25:7 (2018): 1173-89; Deegan-Krause, "Donald Trump and the Lessons," 71.

24. "Viktor Orbán's Speech at the XXV. Bálványos Free Summer University and Youth Camp, July 26, 2014, Băile Tuşnad (Tusnádfürdő)," Romania, *Budapest Beacon*, July 29, 2014, https://budapestbeacon.com/full-text-of-viktor-orbans-speech-at-baile-tusnad-tusnadfurdo-of-26-july-2014/ (accessed September 18, 2020).

25. Andrea Petö, "Hungary's Attack on Gender Studies," *Public Seminar*, November 29, 2018, http://www.publicseminar.org/2018/11/hungarys-attack-on-gender-studies/ (accessed September 18, 2020); Patrick Kingsley, "Orban Encourages Mothers in Hungary to Have 4 or More Babies," *New York Times*, February 11, 2019.

26. Grzymala-Busse, "How Populists Rule," 713.

27. Deegan-Krause, "Donald Trump and the Lessons," 71; Grzymala-Busse, "How Populists Rule," 709-12.

28. Anouk Ruhaak, "Country Report: Hungary," *Rabobank*, Utrech, the Netherlands, September 2012, 3.

29. Éva Várhegyi, "The Banks of the Mafia State," in Bálint Magyar and Júlia Vásárhelyi, eds., *Twenty-five Sides of a Post-Communist Mafia State* (Budapest: CEU Press, 2017), 304, as cited in Magyar and Madlovics, "Post-Communist Predation," 20-21.

30. Sallai and Schnyder, "The Transformation of Post-Socialist Capitalism," 11-19.

31. Magyar and Madlovics, "Post-Communist Predation," 17-18.

32. Reporters without Borders, "Hungary, 2019," Paris, France, August 31, 2020, https://rsf.org/en/hungary (accessed September 18, 2020).

33. Kelemen, "The European Union's Authoritarian Equilibrium"; See also András Bozóki and Dániel Hegedűs, "Constraining or Enabling? Democratic Backsliding in Hungary and the Role of the EU," paper presented to the European Studies Association Convention, Denver, May 10, 2019.

34. Marton Dunai, "Hungarian Savers Say Government Is Stealing Their Pensions," *Reuters*, November 26, 2014, https://www.reuters.com/article/hungary-pensions/hungarian-savers-say-government-is-stealing-their-pensions-idUSL6N0TG2MP20141127 (accessed September 18, 2020).

35. Kelemen, "The European Union's Authoritarian Equilibrium."

36. Eva S. Balogh, "Leaving in Hordes: Emigration from Hungary," *Hungarian Spectrum*, June 22, 2018, http://hungarianspectrum.org/2018/06/22/leaving-in-hordes-emigration-from-hungary (accessed September 18, 2020).

37. Kelemen, "The European Union's Authoritarian Equilibrium."

38. Ruhaak, "Country Report: Hungary," 3.

39. Bureau of Economic and Business Affairs, "Hungary," 2018 Investment Climate Statements Report, US Department of State, July 19, 2018, http://www.state.gov/e/eb/rls/othr/ics/investmentclimatestatements/index.htm?year=2018&dlid=281591

40. István János Tóth and Miklós Hajdu, "Intensity of Competition, Corruption Risks and Price Distortion in the Hungarian Public Procurement—2009-2016," Corruption Research Center, Budapest, Hungary, CRCB-WP/2017:2, December 2017, 143, http://www.crcb.eu/wp-content/uploads/2017/12/eu_hpp_2016_report_170616_.pdf (accessed September 18, 2020).

41. Matthew Stenberg, "Subnational Consolidation in Single-Party Dominant Regimes: Evidence from Hungarian Mayoral Elections," University of California, Berkeley, September 7, 2019; see also Laura Jakli and Matthew Stenberg, "Everyday Illiberalism: How Hungarian Subnational Politics Propel Single-Party Dominance," *Governance*, March 28, 2020.

42. András Pethő, "Inside the Fall of the Oligarch Who Turned against Viktor Orbán," *Direkt36*, January 14, 2019, https://www.direkt36.hu/en/feltarul-simicska-bukasanak-titkos-tortenete/ (accessed September 18, 2020).

43. Zack Beauchamp, "It Happened There: How Democracy Died in Hungary," *Vox*, September 13, 2018, https://www.vox.com/policy-and-politics/2018/9/13/17823488/hungary-democracy-authoritarianism-trump (accessed September 18, 2020).

44. Tóth and Hajdu, "Intensity of Competition," 6.

45. Jennifer Rankin, "How Hungarian PM's Supporters Profit from EU-Backed Projects," *The Guardian*, February 12, 2018, https://www.theguardian.com/world

/2018/feb/12/how-hungarian-pms-supporters-profit-from-eu-backed-projects (accessed September 18, 2020).

46. Tóth and Hajdu, "Intensity of Competition," 6.

47. Laurent Pech and Kim Lane Scheppele, "Illiberalism Within: Rule of Law Backsliding in the EU," *Cambridge Yearbook of European Legal Studies* 19 (2017): 3–47.

48. Kelemen, "The European Union's Authoritarian Equilibrium."

Liberalism's Fragile Dream

1. For a pessimistic view of the accomplishments and failings of liberalism, see Ghodsee, *Red Hangover*.

2. Fukuyama, "The End of History?"

3. Jurgen Habermas, *The Crisis of the European Union: A Response* (Cambridge: Polity Press, 2012).

Index